BOX! What Box?

Musings on a New Approach

Eric Dowsett

Copyright © 2018 by Eric Dowsett.

All rights reserved.

No portion of this book may be reproduced—mechanically, electronically, or by any other means, including photocopying—without the express written permission of the author.

ISBN: 978-0-646-98418-6 (paperback)
ISBN: 978-0-6482706-0-7 (ebook)

First Printing

Typeset and designed by Patricia Wallenburg

First published in Eric's monthly newsletters over several years, this is not a book that you read sequentially—rather one that you pick up, open to a random page, read a piece or two, put the book down and let the words work their magic. Come back another day and try again.

Musings

THIS IS THE FIRST

I have been giving a few private, one on one consults here in Mexico City, and, as many of the people coming to see me don't speak very much English. My Spanish falls very short of trying to explain this work, or anything else, so I have been reduced to pictures and simple examples to help people understand.

A big issue for many people is anxiety, surprise, surprise. It is a feeling that has presented many times in both workshops and one on one consults. It is also a feeling that I have some first hand knowledge of.

I believe that, like an air born virus, anxiety (in common with all other feelings) is contagious. It doesn't matter where you are, how well insulted or protected you are you are susceptible to this feeling. We have seen, at residential workshops, how a group of people can 'pick-up' on a feeling from one single person.

We have also seen how each individual that picks up on the feeling of another interprets that information/feeling often in their own unique way. Many times the groups reaction to the feeling of another is similar, if not identical to the feeling of the individual. We have noticed, as we sit quietly, observing our own thoughts and feelings how our feelings change as we 'tune into' someone else.

Through this process it becomes increasingly obvious that many (if not all) of the feelings that we experience are stimulated by an external source (include anxiety in this). The individual cells in our bodies, all trillions of them, have thousands of antenna, each tuned into a specific frequency.

I am not sure of the technical order or the correct terminology but I believe it goes something like this. The antenna pick up environmental information (external to the body or internal) the brain, connecting various neural pathways as a result of these various stimuli, creates chemicals, neuropeptides, which flood the body. The antenna (receptor sites) on the cells will be activated, assuming there is some resonance between the individual antenna's and the specific frequency of the chemical.

We experience intense emotions because we have an excess of receptor sites (antenna) for that particular feeling/chemical. The more receptor sites for any chemical (read emotion) the more we feel that emotion, the more we are a victim to it. So we are very much prisoners of our past conditioning.

I think it is important for us to recognise that we are not the emotion. As I mentioned recently, like the radio receiver which picks up information, seemingly from nowhere and translates the signals into sounds, music, talk etc. We are like the radio itself, picking up information from our environment. The radio itself is not the music, or the chat show, the radio is just the receiver, interpreting and passing on information. The information that we pick up is not ours, but our conditioning strongly associates with the emotion that arises as a result of the chemicals released into the body. The more we associate with that chemical/feeling the more we become that emotion.

SO MUCH FOR THE MECHANICS

Back to anxiety/fear. The difficulty in developing greater objectivity around strong emotions has its roots in our past. We have, inadvertently, unwillingly and unconsciously, given energy to particular feelings. The more energy we have given a feeling in the past (or the more we have denied a feeling) the harder it is to simply let it go.

The 'clearing' work is very much about noticing, and while you are still able, acknowledging the feeling and then simply letting it go. No grasping, no attachment, just observing. If you sit quietly, it a stress free situation and then once you are still, bring to mind a situation, event or person that you feel less than comfortable with and notice the feelings that present. They may be quite subtle, certainly less intense than if the situation were truly presenting. Now remember the radio, and as simple as changing the radio station, change your mind. At first you may need a little trick to help you, shift your focus, become aware of traffic noise, bird song, the sun, the clouds, the wind in the trees.

The more you practice the less you will need to practice, this easily becomes a way of life after you get over the initial challenges of non attachment to feelings.

Anxiety is a strong feeling and has been cultivated, knowingly or otherwise, but we must accept responsibility for the part we play in spreading this 'dis-ease.'

If we simplify the concept of Yin and Yang, the eternal opposites, the conflict they create produces the world we live in. (Perhaps not the physical earth, but certainly the emotional and mental climate). Whilst we remain polarised in our personal judgements, likes and dislikes, while we continue to identify with the chemicals and the emotions arising in the body we are a part of the system that propagates anxiety, and all other emotions.

Ponder This

> There's someone in my head but it's not me.
> Pink Floyd, Brain Damage,
> The Dark Side of the Moon, 1973

That's good to know, now we need not take ourself quite so seriously. But if it is not 'me' in 'my' head, then who is it? And how did they get there?

Good questions. But that pre-suppose that the above lyric from 'Brain Damage' is true. Have you ever wondered where 'your' thoughts come from? Where do they originate. For many years I have been talking about not taking the emotions that arise personally, but this also applies to the thoughts.

The difficulty is in being able to step back a little and observe the thoughts./ How can the observer separate themselves from the thoughts that arise! We are convinced that thoughts that we have our indeed ours, how can they belong to anyone else, they are 'happening' inside 'my' head after all.

A fundamental error in calculating whose, what, why, when is the sense separation that we grow into. New born babies don't have this sense of separation to the same degree, it sort of grows with them, as they develop and age, their brain wave state changes and they start to see themselves as separate, they start to question and to judge phenomena. Prior to the questioning mind there was a state of oneness.

For those who have been practising this way of being for a while, many of the emotions that arise can be seen as coming from some external source, see the previous mini news sheet article on anxiety… With close observance it can be understood that all emotions are the result of some external stimuli. An emotion is how the body reacts, physically to environmental conditions. Having said that, for many of us, being caught in the emotional energies that present is a common and currently accepted way of dealing with emotions. We trigger off somehow a response/reaction to certain environmental conditions (for example, another person upsetting us), the response/reaction is turned into chemicals which the body then interprets as an emotion. The more chemical associated with the response/reaction, the more intense the emotion, the more likely we are to take it personally, which in turn adds to the chemicals in the body, increasing the intensity of the emotion.

PHEW!!!

Yet the conditioning to personalise the emotion is so strong we continually fall back into the old habitual way of relating to emotions.

And so it is with thoughts, perhaps even more so than emotions. A thought arises in our awareness, no sooner has it presented itself than we assume it is ours and act accordingly. We respond or react to the thought, we give it energy by subscribing to it (or rejecting it) and co-create a reality based upon the thought. As we energise particular thoughts, so that gives rise to a subsequent thought following on from the previous one. Unless we take a moment to question the origin of the thought we can build castles in the air which have no relevance to what is really happening. If we need to examine possibilities associated with a project we may build daisy-chains of thoughts, all strung together leading us to some conclusion. Providing the original assumption was correct, in so far as the goal we have in mind, and the subsequent thoughts are rational, then we may well reach a logical conclusion.

But these are not really the thought patterns that I am referring to here. Day to day thoughts, images that present themselves that we assume to be our own, these are the thoughts whose origin I would question.

Having you ever had a thought and wondered where the heck it came from, so out of the box, so 'not you' was it that there was no choice but to question it? I have, often. We get used to certain thoughts and ways of thinking, certain processes are so familiar we never question them. But now and again, in comes a thought from left field and we are left wondering. This often happens when we are working, clearing the space for someone. We put ourselves in a very different environment, someone else's home, and tune into the energy of the space.

Happened to me just the other day. Working away, yawning and processing a lot of 'stuck' information in the house. Then, all of a sudden, I had thoughts of serious racial intolerance, I was working in the home of African Americans. Wow, where did that come from, wasn't mine, I just don't think like that. But it was so strong, so overwhelming for a moment I wondered if I had not developed into a racist overnight. But then, associated with that thought, a great shiver and a shudder of energy passing through my 'body' and the thought disappeared. I settled back into some amazement that I could have ever had such a thought, when whammo, it happened again. Pretty explicit, followed by another shiver as the charge was released through my awareness. And a third time, each time the intensity of the thought reducing.

I shared all this with the owner of the house, and she knew exactly what I was talking about. The charge was to some degree released and a calmness came upon the house which had not been there before. How much this is going to affect the occupants remains to be seen. The point of this 'story' through was to illustrate how a thought can come into your 'mind' wherever that may be, and take root, causing you to respond or react. The moment you take a thought personally you give it energy, when you give a thought energy you may well create an internal, chemical, environment based upon that thought, and then find yourself dealing with the results of that thought turned emotion.

If this can happen once, it can happen often. Simply because we are familiar with a certain thought process doesn't mean that process is ours, or that we have to entertain those particular thoughts. This is not to say that we simply disregard all thoughts, but that we become aware that some, possibly many, of them are nothing to do with us at all and best left on the shelf. Out of our thoughts arises our reality.... Do you really want to have to deal with that reality?

Just a thought.

And This!

AND WHAT A MONTH MARCH WAS

THE MORE ANYONE PRACTICES THIS WAY OF BEING, THE more they become the way. The more they become 'the way' the less conflict arises. It is easy to forget sometimes, for me at least, that which I have become (as opposed to that which I was!!!)

I still use the word 'me' though even the meaning of that has changed. Who is this 'me' that I refer to? Labels are good as markers along the way, when they are no longer required they fall away, but like everything else, they are not to be taken too seriously, not too literally.

'I' was at a meeting the other day. Lots of opinions needing to be expressed, concerns to be addressed, points of view arising. The usual stuff you find at meetings all over the world, at least I suspect it was, I do not attend many meeting these days. I was the 'guest speaker' at the meeting, so sat patiently, I hope, waiting for 'my' turn. While I was observing the meeting unfold, the main feeling that I was aware of in my body, was anxiety. I suspected, at the time, that perhaps it was my anxiety, I was going to be speaking to a few doctors in the audience to share with them the benefits, as I perceive them, of this path.

Yet I have spoken to professionals many times in the past, and anxiety is not something 'I' feel prior to any public speaking engagement. I used to certainly, in days long gone, but again, one of the products of this journey is to let go of the tight hold we may have had on any sense of the self, so 'self' consciousness falls away. (For one who had been very self conscious for most of his life this is a welcome change) So, I felt that the anxiety was not mine, but a part of the collective energy in the room, an underlying energetic 'charge' that people carry wherever they go, the meeting was in New York, maybe that was an influencing factor!

ENERGETIC CHAOS ... KNOW WHAT I MEAN?

The general sense of the meeting was one of some energetic chaos, perhaps that is standard at meetings, what even should be expected at meetings, but to me this was not the best way to achieve goals. Certainly opinions needed to be expressed, concerns shared and worked through but my sense was that it was the underlying energetic reasons that each of us carry that created the 'anxiety' that I felt in the room.

This is not something that most people would be aware of, so caught up are we in the busy-ness of the day that we often fail to recognise what is happening in the moment. Our past dictates how our present unfolds and as such pretty much lays out what our future will be.

As I said, I am not familiar with meetings, but I have spoken to large groups of people all over the world for many years now and can read the energy of a group quite quickly. There was considerable dis-order in that room, never (not quite never, perhaps once in Mexico) have I experienced something similar! People were moving around during the talk, speaking on their cell phones, standing up, sitting down, moving across the room to talk with other people in the room, crossing in front of others to 'sign in', all a reflection of the dis-order, chaos even, of the energy in the room.

I did notice though, that the more I talked, the more the energy settled. People became present, attentive, interested, not that they were not interested before, but the interest was in a fragmented, nervous way. Slowly the energy in the room became calm, focused, much more harmonious. All this can be a judgement, and if you know me that is one things I try to be conscious of not doing, but in this case it wasn't judgement, just observations, again words as labels can be helpful along the way, just as long as we don't take them too seriously.

Many people have commented on the calm-ness that I present/offer to those around me. This was very obvious at that meeting and is a delightful product of the practice, because out of the calmness dialogue can arise that is not so polarised, not so 'self' oriented, with much less charge, and, from my perspective, this leads to a more constructive talk. Perhaps I should have been 'clearing' the energy of the room before the meeting got too advanced, but it is interesting to let things unfold and observe, in that way we can become more aware of the change that is possible.

So, for those who need to attend meetings, practice finding, and maintaining that place of inner peace, and see how it/you can affect meetings and outcome, effortlessly.

Something to Think About!

THE SOURCE OF ALL THAT IS

For a long time now I have felt that 'healing' on whatever level it may be required is available in the space between thoughts. A quiet place of no time, no space. A place of infinite possibilities.

A place the Buddhists call the 'True Nature of Mind', referred to at times as 'The Field', 'The Ether' and my own contribution, 'The Cosmic Soup'. The place from which all arises, all is made manifest. Sounds like a special place. Special in its nature but not in some far and distant place or future.

For those not so familiar with this place which we will refer to as the Cosmic Soup which may avoid possible conflict with other interpretations. I would like to share my understanding, gained along the path of 'clearing' of what this place means to all of us and how we can possibly access it to bring about a different world.

This place is sometimes called the formless void, a place where, when an impulse is expressed, form is made manifest, and, depending upon the intensity of the impulse, which could be a thought an emotion or an action, adds to the manifesting world that we perceive to be real. 'As within—so without'. Our conditioned expectations are charges, or impulses that we, for the most part without any awareness, express into the cosmic soup, those impulses contribute to the manifesting reality. We identify with the manifesting world and respond or react to the manifestations. By taking this seriously we work hard at controlling or manipulating the world to suit our individual, personalities, needs. So, if this is indeed the case, then we are adding fuel to a fire by trying to bring order to what began as a figment of the imagination.

From memory the Buddhist claim that recognising and remaining in this place equates to deliverance from the cycle of birth, death and rebirth and the best chance most of us have of seeing this place is at the moment of death. When the physical and all associated phenomena falls away we are left with the rue nature of mind. Yet I suspect this is not so easy to see, and remain in. Any 'charge' that we still carry at the moment of death, (for charge read physical, mental and emotional desires, obvious or hidden and any addictions to certain ways of being, requirements un-met etc.) may well take over and express itself in the cosmic soup. Whilst we associate strongly with any of the deeply held points of view and related charge, while we have expectations still unmet, desires unfulfilled, anger unexpressed, then this diminishes our chances of recognising, and remaining in the true nature of mind.

THE QUESTION ARISES

Why would I want to remain in this cosmic soup place when there is so much still to be gained by living on earth in the physical body. Good question, but, if, for no other reason, to recognise how the world we perceive is created, the part we play and how we can, by acting with awareness, make a more positive contribution to the world of form. The Buddhists may have said that the best chance of our recognising the True Nature of Mind is at the moment of death, but it is not our only chance. Why wait till you die to understand your true nature?

The more I have walked the path of 'clearing' the more obvious this has become. A side effect of clearing is to gradually let go of our hold on points of view, to slowly work through and release sub-conscious addictive patterns, and with this, move out of time and space as it is commonly thought to exist. This is a natural state to move towards, not something unpleasant or lacking in 'life'. As this develops so it becomes the obvious, accepted answer to all situations that manifest. The more energy given to a thought or a belief pattern the more likely it is to manifest. The more energy, the more powerful the manifestation. If this is all too esoteric, bring it down to earth, the media, and the influence the media has over the majority of the population of the planet. This is the same concept but put rather more obviously.

ONE FOOT HERE, ONE FOOT THERE!

As we practice the clearing so we naturally spend more 'time' in a more peaceful inner state. This state is almost like having a foot in two worlds at the same time. The manifesting world and the un-manifest, formless world. The more familiar this becomes the easier it is to remain in this place. The more comfortable we become the more obvious it is that any thought or emotion that arises is being fed, directly, into the cosmic soup. With awareness comes the ability to notice what you are feeding into the soup, and why life presents to you the way it does.

With clearing comes a release from old, conscious and sub-conscious patterns, this in turn releases charge, or preferably, doesn't allow charge to build up in the first place. When there is no sub-conscious charge then there is no adding impulse to the soup without awareness. Hey Presto—'conscious co-creation'.

We may see how the external world is created by understanding the above, but what about our internal world, is that created any differently? Personally I don't think so. Assuming the formless void, the cosmic soup contains the blueprint of who you are, what impulses are you putting into the soup (with our without awareness) that are creating your inner world?

Would you continue to supply those impulses if they are creating a less than happy, healthy life?

I believe that a part of the gift I have to share is this knowledge, and also, the ability to step into the formless state, insert a more 'beneficial' impulse on your behalf, and add to total health and happiness, and to teach this to others. For we are all in both these worlds, but as long as we remain unaware, then our impulses are reactive, the manifesting reality a product of those impulses. We spend our lives putting out the fires of our own creation rather than realising we lit the fire in the first place. Know that you are doing this, right now, with every breath you take, with every thought you have, with every emotion expressed, with every desire, known or not, with every word and every action.

And then try to choose what you are adding to the soup of the day.

A Piece to Finish the Day

LIFE ON THE ROAD

One of the benefits of being on the road so much is that I get to spend time with different people around the world. Each culture has its unique ways of being and doing, none necessarily better or worse than any other. Just different.

I suspect this is one reason the Buddha had his followers travel during the dry season, spending no more than three nights under any one roof. This way they developed no attachment to the people or the place, a part of their training. They got to ease up during the rainy season when they would remain in one temple where they could use the library, repair their robes, sweep the place, whatever was required.

If you don't have the need to be surrounded by the familiar, then this type of lifestyle is not such a challenge as you might think. We are most often challenged when things change simply because we have gotten used to 'things' being a certain way. We are creatures of habit, and, without realising it we get lost in those habits, they sort of creep up on us, and, before we know it, that is who we think we are. We tend to identify ourselves through the people and things around us, our partners, our children, our job, or lack of job! The clothes we wear, the food we like, and so it goes.

We fall into routine because that is what is demanded of us, particularly when we have families, responsibilities, a job, we play a part, often so well that we forget that it is a part that we are playing ('all the worlds a stage'—William Shakespeare). Our circumstances require us to adapt in order to survive, sometimes those adaptations are pleasant sometimes not, but we manage. If we have the luxury of certain freedoms, we may move to an environment that is more in harmony with who we believe ourselves to be, this can, and does change however. For many that is not an option. For others and change may be very stressful.

For some the routine is never questioned, the need to question never even arises. For others the idea of this routine is something they struggle against, invariably though the dominant social conditioning wins out and they succumb, with dreams unfulfilled. My father was like that, his passions were art and travel, the global and social conditions of the time did not allow him to explore either. In some ways I lived that life for him.

PAST LIVES?

Without getting into 'past lives' it is often hard to understand why some people turn out as they do, given similar backgrounds, education, opportunities. And so it was with me, I have often wondered why my life is so different from my peers. I have been a wanderer from an early age. It is something within that has to be expressed and I have been fortunate enough to be able to follow those inner demands. Though I have resisted often, surrender is eventually the easiest path to follow.

Moving from place to place, from country to country not only opens ones mind to the lives of other people and cultures, but prevents one becoming too comfortable (familiar) with any one place. It has helped me notice attachments to particular ways of being, and to see how they prevent me from being in the moment with those who hold other ideals/expectations to those I had, through my own upbringing, associated myself with.

This lifestyle is no better or worse than any other, but it is me expressing some desire, or charge held within. I believe we all do this, express those inner desires, whether it means remaining in one place for ones entire life, or traveling the world, or working or not working, of living in peace or not, have becoming addicted to various emotions or substances, or not. This is called 'karma' in some cultures. Energy, or charge that we hold within, expressing itself. Until that charge is exhausted there is always still something else to do. Because we associate and identify with the charge, we think that is who we are, it is hard to be objective about the reality we are enveloped by. It doesn't matter whether your lifestyle is rooted in one place, with commitments, or lost on the road, a wanderer, while this inner charge exists and there is any identification with it, there appears to be a path, a journey, and there is someone (you?) on the road. While we associate with the thoughts and emotions that are expressed as a result of this 'charge' we take ourselves seriously, the more seriously we take ourselves, the more lost in the drama we become. The more lost we become, the more we take the situations that arise as a result of our taking ourselves seriously in the first place, seriously!!!

NO, SERIOUSLY

And then we have to fix the situation so that we will feel better. We try to fix things based upon the same model (without being aware of this of course) that created the situation in the first place. We end up spending much of our time putting out fires, in damage control mode, all because we identified with the emotions that arose in the past. So instead of releasing any inner charge, we maintain it, by taking ourselves so seriously. Yet even this is a result of any in built charge we may have. It does mean that we get caught in the drama and being caught in it, perpetuate it.

Life on the road has helped me let go of attachments and see where I add energy to the manifesting reality, it has also shown me the value of clearing in community. To sit and notice, without buying into what you notice, for a few minutes every day, supported by friends, is a powerful way to change the charge that you believe your self to be. Changing the charge allows different points of view to surface, it also helps to notice those points of view and to release them, before they start to create yet another reality.

'Clearing' after all is about releasing charge, emotional or physical, which in turn allows a different perspective to manifest, and, with enough clearing, attachment to particular ways of being falls away, opening doors previously unimagined.

LIFE, WHAT A JOURNEY

I suspect that some charge that remains within 'me' would be to create a physical space where people could come and hang out, a place where clearing was a regular and frequent occurrence, a place to release stress and remember what inner peace feels like. A base camp for the climbers. Any people out there who think they have the place to do this, I look forward to hearing from you. Maybe I will do less traveling then!

And This!

CHANGE

WHAT DOES IT MEAN ... AND ARE WE READY FOR IT? Whatever it may be.

Last month I wrote about my perceptions of who and what we become, and why. Living a rather nomadic life I have been able to see situations a little more objectively than many who are caught up in the day to day hustle and bustle of life. But in itself this lifestyle can become routine, we get used to most things given time, and I am well used to a life on the road. How much can I change, is there any real need to change at all?

For whatever reason we develop certain ways of being, certain expectations, we hold certain values and judgments, often on a very deep, sub-conscious level. I have often spoken at workshops about how, because of these deeply rooted perceptions we expect life to be a certain way. This 'way' has nothing to do with good or bad, right or wrong, healthy or not. We have seen, through the various images of blood cells, how the body is not discriminating. It will produce balance and harmony or chaos and ill health without seemingly a choice. Something must be instructing the blood cells to continue to reproduce in particular ways.

If the system reproduces itself in a chaotic state it often manifests in ill health, given time the chaos becomes more and more physical until it reaches a point where the body starts yelling out, loudly, for help. The difficulty is recognising the chaos before it manifests as dis-ease. From my very limited experience it appears that the majority of us are all in some degree of chaos, which the body continues to reproduce. How crazy is that?

Again the difficulty is recognising that we are in chaos, this can be hard, at least until the body lets us know in no uncertain manner, that it needs help. Over the years I have been teaching and consulting it has become apparent that any system in chaos seeks other systems in a similar state of disorder, whether it actively seeks them out or is simply drawn to them through an internal resonance is a point for later discussion. If a distressed system (a body) remains in an environment it will affect that environment, this is true for healthy bodies as well those in distress. These 'external' effects can be quite subtle, at least to the person living in the space, as they creep up gradually, and after all, are only reflections of the internal chaos of the individual or group of individuals. As such they represent a part of the individual or group, a part of which the individual or group are unaware. The challenge being to observe oneself with total objectivity and honesty. Not an easy task, to step outside of the self and take a good hard look.

AS WITHIN—SO WITHOUT

Over time then, the environment adjusts to harmonise with those living in it. This may appear to be quite uncomfortable, since very few are comfortable with their shadow (assuming they are even aware of it to begin with). It is when we notice discord that we call in the Feng Shui expert, or the space clearer. Someone to help us bring balance back into our environment, for as long as we externalise our problems we fail to see the part we play in creating the world we live in.

Because of conditioning, and we are all conditioned in some way or another, we get used to being a certain way. This 'way' may not be healthy, it may not bring abundance, it may impose many limitations on what we believe we can and cannot do, it also reproduces conflict internally. We adjust to or create an environment that reflects our internal expectations and feel comfortable within that model. All goes well until the model is challenged, as it invariably will be, because others live by different models, have different values and expectations. There are few choices open to us when this happens, because we have lived a life according to certain perceptions, our choices are limited to something within those perceptions.

So our dependance upon the values of our past deepens and it is harder still for us to break free and learn to respond to situations and not react to them.

When for whatever reason, our external world changes dramatically there arises even greater conflict internally. We struggle with 'new' ways, different ways, we either run way from or fight the changes. Whichever path we choose our internal system is thrown into greater chaos because our external world no longer matches the safe, comfortable reality that we have spent much time in.

This may well lead to dis-ease made manifest, a system already in a delicate state of balance, but having gotten accustomed to the stress has little opportunity to realise just how stressed it is. It, the stress, having crept up on us over many years, very subtle, not at all obvious. Now our internal system has to cope with a new reality but it rarely has the experience, or the mechanism for new ways, so established has the body become on old 'familiar' ways that change is truly challenging.

We may think we can handle the change, because, after all, how many of us are so in touch with the body that we know at any given moment in time what it is feeling and how it is responding/reacting to various stimuli. Over the years I have been teaching this one thing among many has become obvious, most people do not know their body is stressed until it breaks down.

We may state that we are ready for change, but, if we were truly ready, then we would be the change, not just talk about it and claim our readiness. Change itself is not so easy to accept because change is so alien to an energetic system (our body) that has established itself in certain patterns. Patterns that have become so routine as to have become addictive. Without our conscious knowing we follow certain ways of being, present to the world certain expectations, which, if not met, create an agitated state internally. If the agitation persists the body goes into greater chaos and discomfort, adding to an already tense situation. This is not the path to change, this is the path to internal, and external conflict. A path we have all been down many times.

COMING—READY OR NOT

Change is often challenging to certain points of view we hold about the world and our place in it. All the time we say we are ready for change but at the same time hold on tight to our points of view, whatever they may be, we are resisting change.

Letting go of old patterns does not imply that chaos will follow. Quite the opposite, but until we have direct experience of that, we live in fear of change. This fear not only keeps us from change but it slows down change in the world around us.

| And This! |

Notice your points of view. Ask your self, is this point of view truly valid, is it really better than someone else's point of view, simply because it is yours? Simply because it is shared by your friends? Understand how addiction to points of view causes war, hatred, distrust, abuse. Then decide, are you really ready for change.

Something to Think About!

TO DO—OR NOT TO DO

THAT IS, AS THEY SAY, THE QUESTION. THE CLEARING work requires that we be available, that we do nothing, seemingly, to or for any other. The work for the clearer is, simply, to become clearer themselves. Less shadow issues, less attachment to outcome, less judgement and less personalising with thoughts and emotions.

By developing this personal practice it appears the clearer is able to provide a 'safe' place for the person being cleared, which in turn allows stress stored to release. So, the clearers goal is to become a vehicle through which stress, stored as charge, in the person being cleared can express itself safely and gently. Nothing to do. The work, essentially work on the self, has already been done by the time the clearer meets the clearee. Meaning the do-ing part is work on the self, and there is nothing to be done at the time the client shows up, other than be available.

Clearing someone who has a lot of stress in their system may give the impression that the clearer is doing something, as the clearers body reacts to the large amount of information it is being asked to process in a short space of time, but still the clearer is not doing anything to the client.

It is possible to extend the state of be-ing into all aspects of our lives but there always comes a time when we need to 'do' something. The state of be-ing though is only half the story, the 'first' half, the half we practice because we have forgotten how to simply be. To notice what is happening inside and around us without personalising the thoughts and feelings.

If we were not to practice how to be more available then we would continue to move through life much the same as we have in the past, continually identifying with the phenomena that arises in our awareness. All the time thinking that the thoughts and emotions are ours. Establishing very set patterns of behaviour/response which we then apply to issues, situations and to people who present in our lives. We 'do' an awful lot, but we 'do' based on our past, and hence react out of habit.

MORE OF THE SAME?

If we are not content with the world we live in we try and change it, but again, coming from a place of conditioned reactivity. So all we end up doing is creating more of the same.

If you have a social conscience, you will become involved in schemes to create a better world. Often those schemes are in opposition to other schemes seen as valuable by other people. This conflict forces us to do more and more to remain 'in the game'. So we continue to ride the round-a-bout without realising there could be another way to bring about change. So conditioned are we to work toward a 'better' world based on currently held points of view about what is real and what is not that we miss the obvious, namely, there are other ways.

That is the dilemma. In a world that takes itself so seriously we believe that we have to take things equally seriously to get change to happen. This inevitably evolves into conflict, the more energy one side puts in, the more energy required by the opposing group. In this model there seems then to be always a place for action, for people to do things to bring about change.

What this perhaps comes down to is the clarity of the persons involved. If both 'sides' are coming from places of deep personal convictions and a personal history of reaction rather than response then conflict will arise. In a Western legal system the team with the most money often wins this game. In some cultures those willing to use violence will win. And so it goes.

If we can accept the old maxim, "As within—so without" then even the thought that we have choices only arises because of internal conflict. Although many of us may not accept internal conflict exists in most of us, the manifestation of external conflict are everywhere, we still hold onto the belief that they are the product of an others actions rather than a manifestation of our own internal conflict. (We have photographs of blood samples to demonstrate this internal conflict and its prevalence)

And still we want to 'do' something about it, change the world, make it a better place. I repeat something I have quoted before in my news-sheets: "The world is neither good nor bad nor defective, nor is it in need of help or modification because its appearance is only a projection of one's own mind. No such world exists."—David Hawkins, *The Eye of the I*.

But, you may say, "I have to live in this world, albeit an illusory one". Or do you?

TAKING THE WORLD APART

A part of Buddhist training is to de-construct the reality you have built and unconsciously support. Zen tries to rip the carpet out from under your feet, leaving nothing. There are other ways. Not everyone is drawn to Zen or any other aspect of Buddhism's non-identification but there are many paths, some less obvious than others.

While we are hanging out, waiting for enlightenment, or the tax refund cheque, whichever comes first, we do indeed have to live in the illusion. So, why not make some effort to changing it to something that supports the whole instead of select parts. Well, if you belong to the select parts I can imagine why you would not want to change things, in fact a lot of your energy will be spent in maintaining the status quo.

While we may like to consider ourselves as being able to love unconditionally, the truth is in the manifesting world around us. As we see through the illusion, which can often mean letting go of our attachment to certain aspects of it, the energy that we previously used to support the illusion falls away, this allows other illusions to take its place!!! Hence the analogy of the layer of the onion, peeling away, one at a time. This is not the Zen way! Quicker by far to realise there is no onion, and no one to observe it.

But most of us like our comforts and securities, even though they are only illusory (the Blue Pill or the Red Pill?), so, back to the onion. When you take a stand for any issue, just see if you can see who is taking the stand, and why…

Meanwhile, we wait.

A Piece to Start the Day

IS THERE ANYONE HOME?

I WAS ASKED RECENTLY, WHETHER, IN THE DEPTH OF MY BEING do I believe that, there is any choice we can make anywhere at all? That there is anything/anyone that can choose whatever happens or not, that there is any possibility on any level at all?

Some question.

Which reminded me of another question, asked several years ago. If the 'goal' is to become enlightened, to see through the illusory nature of the world we live in, why bother with clearing, which just creates a different illusion.

Very good question.

Add to that the concept that enlightenment is random. As there is no one to whom all the associated feelings belong, there is no one to become enlightened, therefore there is no one who can do anything to get closer to the goal. This may mean that there is no goal after all a goal is a place aimed at, with the hope/expectation of someone arriving there one day. But who is traveling the road toward the goal? It is the concept only of the 'I' that is the traveler, taking the 'I' seriously, the 'I' assumes it is on a path, to learn something, to get somewhere, to achieve something, whatever.

The more energy the 'I' gives to the journey, the goal, the more real the journey/goal becomes. When collective 'I's' add more energy we have manifesting reality. Nothing real about it of course, numbers don't add up to reality.

Yet the little 'i's' lost in the illusion of the reality they have supported, albeit unknowingly, take the manifestation so seriously, they add more charge, and so it goes.

CLEARING—A BIT LIKE A SWISS ARMY KNIFE

The clearing is a multi-level tool, or way of being, designed to support the release of the identification with phenomena. It may or may not assist the awakening of the 'i' but it does help deflate the manifesting reality by not adding further charge to it.

Awakening has been assumed by many to mean awakening to the true nature of self. Bit of a joke really, when at any given moment, we are completely, without confusion, manifestations of the true nature of the self. How can it be otherwise?

Acceptance is the key, and the stumbling block. Accepting that this is it, there is nothing else, no where to go, nothing to do. Yet it is hard to step back, take time out and observe because the manifesting true nature is one of busy-ness for the majority of 'i's'. This is not wrong, nor is it right, it just is. The sense of 'I' through which 'i' have seen life appears to be quite different from anyone elses 'i', but who can say, perhaps everyone's 'i' has that same sense, at least for a while. My ' i' held out, refusing to go along with the collective belief, neither good nor bad, right or wrong, just so different as to not fit in comfortably with what all the other 'i's' around my 'i' took seriously.

"This is how things are—so fit it", what rubbish, perhaps it would be better said, "this is how I believe things to be, and if you want to be my friend/join my club you'd better believe it to." The 'clearing' appears to allow things to be as they are, even though we may approach it with an intention, perhaps of do-ing something, ultimately it is simply about be-ing available for whatever shows up.

Being can be hard, it means we accept, unconditionally, what arises or presents. The 'i's' are conditioned to always be doing something to make a better world (?). If we have had no training in be-ing, we resort to default, which is do-ing, even with training the default setting is ever ready to step in and take over.

THE LESS WE DO!!!!

Yet, seemingly paradoxically, the less we do, the less there is to do. It becomes obvious. Still, when all the 'i's' around are taking something seriously it is hard to remain apart and not do anything to change the circumstances.

So hard to sit and simply be, accepting that which arises, no judgement, no attachment, no identification.

Harder still when we first begin to sit and notice. Without training the default is roaring, out of control and heading to who knows where. To sit and observe this unfold without do-ing anything, which is to stop feeding the manifestation energy, which, eventually will cause it to run out of steam and come to a gently halt (and then what???).

But even to get lost, once again, in the default setting is to express the true nature of the self. We may say that any awakening opens the door to a different perception, but attachment to any 'new' perception leads us back into the idea that there is a separate 'i' that is perceiving.

While 'we' have any addiction to particular ways of being, while any charge remains to be expressed, 'we' will express it, when there is no more charge, nothing to seek, no further desire, then our reality may change. Into what? Well that is the 64 million dollar question isn't it.

BUT IT WORKS

One thing 'I' am noticing, as any charge 'i' clung to falls away the power of being is so much more supportive for all those 'i's' around who still carry a lot of stress on their shoulders. Ever have flash-backs?

You know, times when the mind regurgitates a memory, a fond memory? Or, more to the point here, a not-so-fond one? Or is it just me? Don't think so, but you never can tell, especially when there is no one else out there.

I get moments of recall, something I am not normally prone to, of past events and feelings, mostly where I consider I have been a bit silly, immature, embarrassing or just plain clumsy. Learning to love those parts of the self can be a challenge.

It is often, at moments like these, the Buddha's words return, better in hindsight, but can be applied to the here and now, "Never do or say anything that will create remorse." Easily said. Yet these flashbacks can also be a great form of clearing. Why they happen, I don't know, and no particular desire to find out either, but happen they do, and when they do, I do my best to notice any reaction, any judgement, of self or others involved. Really I am noticing the amount of charge I still hold, and then, to the best of my ability, let go of the charge. Rarely will the same memory return.

Sleep on This One

LOST IN LA LA LAND

WHEN WE FIND OURSELVES EMBROILED IN A DRAMA, in economic crisis, secular conflict, battles carried over from the past, the pressure of survival is so strong that it takes all of our energy and all of our thoughts. We need to deal with life's situations, it's emergencies, it's needs. This state gives us little time or energy to reflect upon any possible root cause for the condition we are caught coping with. This has been a 'truth' throughout time, it is often only those with a comfortable lifestyle (one where each day is not spent searching for food, carrying water, protecting one's interests) who can afford the luxury of self reflection.

In the West we appear to have gone down a very material road. When science plays such a large part in the development of a culture, answers are sought in science, religion takes a back seat as it relies on its traditional past more and more, yet society moves on, not necessarily ahead, but it does move.

Material and spiritual are, when seen as incompatible, simply a reflection of an inner division, a compartmentalisation of the self. The inner dialogue that arises as a result of this conflict is a nonstop inner conversation for many people, people who feel they will be content when. When they have more, or less, when they have new car, a new partner, a new job, a new outlook are symptomatic of the internal conflict that rages in us all. It is a result of this inner conflict that people seek answers/resolution outside of the self, by blaming others, by enlisting support, by joining organisations, safety in numbers.

When we are absorbed in whatever it is we happen to be doing at any given time, we are at peace, no internal dialogue arises to disturb that peace. Loosing ourselves then in a task is a good way to still that inner voice. Yet this is not always an easy thing to do, the very nature of who we believe ourselves to be, who we have become through the life long process of identifying with thoughts and emotions is often at odds with a peaceful state of mind.

While there is any internal conflict, whether we are conscious of it or not, life appears to be a constant struggle, we are caught dealing with the situations that arise, spend our time putting out the fires, in damage control mode almost. This is so 'real' to us that we are always looking for ways to help put out the fires, little realising that however much we try to control the situations around us (or avoid them) we are simply adding fuel to the fire. It is as though, on an unconscious level, we are addicted to the drama.

SOME BAD HABITS!

Whilst we remain lost in the drama, feeding the addiction we are simply guaranteeing more of the same tomorrow. It is hard to step outside of that perception, particularly when we are not even aware we are in a drama. Add to that the sub-conscious addiction to the drama and we do everything we can to remain in the unfolding experience, denying even that we are caught, lost in a manifesting reality that we, on some level, are responsible for creating, or at the very least, supporting.

I am often asked, if indeed this is the case, and those who are asking are accepting to some degree the role they are playing and are at a stage where they would like to 'play a different game' what can they 'do' to change things.

There is no one answer I have, no stock sentence that applies to all people, rather, the words must arise in the moment, and be attuned to the person you are in dialogue with. Mostly though, it goes something like this. CLEAR, yourself, your friends, your relatives as often as you remember to do it. No more, no less. Remember, every time you make a conscious effort to tune in to thoughts and feelings, including those you associate with another person you are making internal adjustments to your reaction to those thoughts and feelings. By working on the self at this level, the cellular memory changes and becomes less reactive, more responsive. With practice this allows you, on an internal level, to be more available and accepting of all thoughts and feelings that arise, which also means that you attract less of the shadow aspects of self, so you have less to deal with, less fires to put out, this frees you up to begin to notice things in a very different way.

ONE STEP AT A TIME

An everyday practice is also to see that all situations, and I mean *all* situations, are karmic. The good old cause and effect. Now, we might argue that, as per last months newssheet, there is ultimately no one home, no 'I' to be creating or consequently affected by 'karma' and that may well be true. It has been my experience though that the addiction to a sense of self is a part of the journey into this 3rd dimensional reality, otherwise what would be the point? Recognising that simply who we have become, through the process of identifying with phenomena is, like a magnet, attracting experiences to us and that it is a natural human condition to want to improve our life. If there is no-one home, then there is no need to improve anything, but while we take the body, the thoughts and the emotions as belonging to 'us' then 'we' have to do something, it is a very deep part of our conditioning.

Back to karma. Even if we only pretend that all situations are karmic, we can see how, by adding energy (thoughts, emotions, physical expressions) we are charging up the karmic cash register. The more energy we put into any thought, feeling, emotion the more seemingly real it becomes. The more real it becomes the more energy it takes to manipulate, control, deny the manifesting reality. Like a physical disease, imagine any state of dis-ease must have been lurking in the background for a while before it is manifest. Once it manifests, we can continue to deny it or do something about it. But while it is hiding away in some dark, unseen corner, there is nothing we can do about it, other than wait for it to become obvious. If we were to become aware of the imbalance early enough then surely it is easier to deal with energetically than once the manifestation has taken on strong physical aspects.

So, treating all manifesting situations as karmic, when we are able, we can make a choice, able here means there is a moment of choice, a short time before we go into conditioned reaction. The choice that reduces the charge is simply to accept, don't judge, don't identify with, don't deny, don't blame. Hard to do at first, so full of charge are we that the time between stimulus and reaction is very small. So, again, step by step, we start to notice, awareness, as usual, being the key. With practice it becomes easier to notice and easier to accept. The more we can accept, the less energy we give to the situation, the more likely it is that charge falls away, soon to be truly a thing of the past. This allows us to be more fully in the moment, to notice, respond instead of react, and enjoy the benefits of a freedom from the past.

These benefits are immediate, no hanging around till you die and then hoping for the best.

Another Day, Another Thought

IF IT IS NOT MINE—THEN WHOSE IS IT?

A NEW YEARS RESOLUTION, FOR THOSE OF YOU WHO practice that rather desperate attempt to bring about change.

I received an email from a friend in Canada recently which I am going to quote later, and then add my comments. You may find this useful (when you remember it) to help get you through times that may appear uncomfortable. Clearing, for the practitioner, is all about accepting, by increasing degrees, discomfort, among all other feelings, as a means of setting the self free. Through the practice of non-identification the practitioner is able to move through various feelings with greater ease, each time they do not take the feeling personally, they reduce the energy stored in the body that had previously judged the feeling and created an intense physical/emotional reaction. The less energy stored in the body, the less intense the feeling, the easier it is to let it go.

With practice this gets easier and easier. For those who have not been introduced to 'clearing' this is not so easy to do. Most people tend to take themselves very seriously. What does it mean, to take oneself seriously? It means, from my current perspective, to associate and identify with the thoughts, feelings, emotions, in general with body consciousness. As we energise emotions, for example, we reinforce a belief in those emotions as being ours. This in turn creates the pathology of those emotions, which support the concept that they are 'ours'. Were we able to put the brakes on, giving ourselves a moment of reflection, we would see that an emotion is an internal chemical reaction, triggered by external phenomena. Most of us do not have a choice when this happens, the body becomes the emotion, we believe it is ours and we add energy to that emotion, thereby losing ourself in the rush of chemicals.

All basic stuff for the practitioner I would hope!, but for those with no experience in this way of being I could well be speaking an unintelligible language.

THE EMAIL

You've requested anecdotes. The one that pops into mind is the time I was walking with my sister. She is a very athletic person and in top-notch shape. I am not. We were on a 'way too serious for me' power walk along a couple of kilometers of pathway. My left hip (which I had never had issues with) was bothering me, and the discomfort grew more and more intense as we continued along. But there was no point in resting and we had to continue. Finally the discomfort was so great I reached my thresh-hold of pain tolerance (I had felt it growing and growing ... had tried to just 'notice' and let it go, but it was just taking me over.)

Just as I was about to confess my 'unfit dilemma' and beg for a mercy halt, my sister abruptly stopped in the middle of nowhere, plopped down and said ' I'm in agony. This hip is just killing me and I can't tune it out any longer. We have to stop'. You could have blown me over with a feather. Though I try to keep a balanced awareness I had totally owned the discomfort because of my insecurity about poor physical condition and not being able to keep up. As I realized 'this is not my hip issue nor is it my pain' it was completely gone.

In a nano second I was pain free. I remember this scenario constantly when feelings and stuff arise that 'just doesn't seem to make sense'. Thank you for bringing this awareness of how inter-connected we are into better focus. I continue to practice.

MY RESPONSE

I did think, on reading this again, that the 'hip' could have been yours after all. Just imagine, for a moment, that your sister picked it up from you, always difficult to know which/who came first, the old chicken or the egg thing.

So, anyway, she has a sore hip, or so she believes, did she pick on in it because you had a sore hip? Or does she physically have problems with her hip? Will we ever know the answer? She identifies with it, you are both identifying with it, perhaps this even amplifies the feeling. You kept quiet longer than she did, perhaps she is less used to this sort of discomfort and spoke up first. You then felt great relief, thought, hey, this isn't mine, and let it go. And it went. She still had it!

But, and here is the interesting point, had your sister picked it up from you, was it 'yours' but you were able to let it go anyway. So, either way, you were able to move beyond the pain into peace by simply believing that the pain originated in your sisters hip! Cool.

This same type of thing has happened, in obvious ways, to me many times. A story I often tell at workshops goes something like this; I was riding an elevator in the US, two other people in the elevator, one complaining about a sprained ankle, damaged while skiing. The elevator arrives, we depart, they one way, me the other. Within three paces my ankle gave way with a lot of pain. I was limping to the exit, in a lot of discomfort, before I realised the sprained ankle was not mine, it belonged to the guy in the elevator. With that realisation that pain left.

CONCLUSION

We live in a world where pain (physical, mental, emotional) can be transmitted, like a radio signal, and picked up by others. Where did it begin, is what I think I am truly who I am, or is it the result of my having identified with some transmission in the past. I'll leave you to think on that one for a while.

And This!

THE HORNS OF THE DILEMMA

WHEN TIMES GET TOUGH, WHEN PEOPLE FACE WHAT appear to be very personal dilemmas, they seek help. Nothing unusual about this. There are many avenues that help can come from. I believe that most people asking for help are asking within the system, out of which their 'issues' arose.

As an example, you find yourself in conflict with a neighbour, if dialogue with the neighbour fails, you speak to the local authorities, trying to resolve the problem through the intervention of someone in authority. Most of us look to the outside for help.

For those practicing the clearing (and some other methods of course) the request for help still goes out to others, but, hopefully, there is a growing recognition of the part the individual plays in the creation of the drama that is their life. Clearing after all is simply the act of being available in a non-judgmental way for self and others. This being available allows stress build up to release in a relatively safe and gentle manner. But still the person is asking for help.

There remains a sense that the individual is not good/strong/experienced enough to handle the situation for themselves. And this is often the case, the circumstances leading up to whatever it is that caused help to be asked for is seemingly, an inherent part of the individual, albeit one hidden deep in their psyche. These 'hidden' aspects of the self (Jung's 'shadow') have become a part of who we are, often unrecognised, working away in the background if not actually creating our manifesting reality, certainly colouring the glasses through which we observe that reality. When pressure in any system reaches a certain point, that pressure is expressed either internally as sickness/dis-ease or externally as conflict with others. Having failed to recognise the cause for the imbalance, we continue to follow societal patterns and seek help 'outside'.

For the clearer, and others on similar paths, we are caught in a dilemma. The manifesting reality is not going to change while we continue to energise it, which we do, often without awareness. It is hard to step outside of the self and be objective enough to do this.

THE MICROSCOPE LOOKING AT ITSELF!

As a part of the training in clearing, developing the ability to become more objective, we take the stand that any emotion or thought that arises in our awareness is not ours, simply how the body has conditioned itself to respond/react to external stimuli. Which I suspect is true. This 'not mine' clause is a hard one to work through, in part because we are using a microscope to examine the same microscope, and partly because the collective is strongly attached to concepts of mine/yours. Often I hear "well—if it is not mine, whose is it?" Or: "What is mine and what isn't?" The concept of mine yours is a part of the problem. Essentially no 'one' is having the experience, the experience is simply happening, it is the association with the thoughts/feelings, over time, together with societal conditioning that leaves us thinking the thoughts are our thoughts, the feelings out feelings, the emotions our emotions.

The dilemma is, for the 'clearer', the idea that the feelings are not theirs, yet they, perhaps, are caught in great financial distress. Not something they can run away from, not something they can divorce themselves from, as globally, concepts of financial security, sustainability, fall away. As individuals we have invested time, energy, and money into a system, that system has its faults, as do all human made systems, when the faults affect out lives in negative ways, we blame the system.

We are caught between two worlds, one where the feelings are not ours and the other, where they are very much ours, because they impact upon us so severely. It is hard, when lost in such a dilemma, to see beyond the immediate needs. Imagine a person just beginning the path of 'clearing' and then financial disaster strikes, the little training they have had falls away as seemingly greater issues present. The unanswered question is, would the person practiced in the clearing have experienced the financial collapse at all? And if so, to what degree would they have suffered.

Like a child's playground see-saw, the closer the end of the balanced bar you sit, the more violent the action, the higher you go, the lower you go. Imagine the cause of your distress sitting at one end and you at the other. Totally out of control. What happens if you move closer to the centre point? You stay up, the other stays down, to maintain equilibrium, they must move closer as well. Keep this up and before you know it conflict falls away (internal or external). Still we are left with our past, deeds and actions that are entrenched on a cellular level, these will continue to express, all we can do (?) is having the experience is choose how we deal with each as it arises.

Karma and obscuration—two 'things' that prevent us from seeing our true nature.... Karma, energetic charge, build up and release. Obscuration, smokescreens maintained by the collective (of which we are a part) which leads us to add charge and not see though it—thereby maintaining the status quo.

Just another angle on last months news-sheet. Take it or leave it, run with it or dance with it, it is your choice, but remember—who is doing the choosing?

THE DILEMMA REMAINS

And yet the dilemma remains, for those caught in devastation and loss, these things are real, they happen and there is little or no escape. The pain of loss is great and real. Whether the cause is financial or earthquake, sickness or ignorance, this is the world we live in.

It is easy to misunderstand the clearing, individual preferences and personal histories all cloud the vision. For those of us working on polishing our glasses, then practice is all we can do, daily take a moment, or two, and embrace all thoughts and feelings that arise with equanimity. Make a small difference in your daily life, and while you are at it, support others lost in pain and suffering.

DISAPPEARING DAYS (? DAZE)
AN OBSERVATION

Anyone else noticing days aren't what they used to be? I mean, I understand that beauty is in the eyes of the beholder, a day is interminable if you are waiting on something, yet flies if you are content, a watched pot never boils etc. But what about in general. I am content, yes, but no more nor less than usual, not so busy, but for me, at this time of year, that is not unusual.

Is it my perception of time, or is times perception of me the real issue? The little clock in my computer will marches off the hours, minutes, seconds, at the same rate as it has in the past, at least I don't think the clock has sped up to further convince me all is as it was. Yet still, something seems different, less 'time' in the day for what I once-upon-a-time, accomplished.

I have certainly noticed this in workshops, particularly space clearing workshop, not so long ago I was able to cover a lot of information and still have plenty of time for the participants to get in lots of practice. No longer the case. My biggest worry is that I am talking a lot more, but about what? I try and stick to the areas needing coverage, but that doesn't explain why, out of workshops time flies, when I am not talking at all! I would be interested to hear about your perceptions of time, any interesting anomalies you may have noticed.

I do recall various explanations, how true they may be is always debatable, only in hindsight will we be able to say, "Ah yes, that was what was going on!!!" But then who is going to observe the changes? And will the observer remain unchanged by the changes, or will the symbiotic relationship humans have with planet Earth mean that as situations (external) change, so does the observer, in which case how will anyone know there have been any changes?

I have maintained, rightly or wrongly, for many years that only through resistance to change can we notice change, and, let's face it, most of us are in some degree of resistance, the more resistance the more dramatic the change. But, what happens when there is no resistance? I'd like to hear your views on that as well.

Musings

IS REAL CHANGE POSSIBLE? IS IT DESIRABLE?

Still between the horns of a dilemma, only this time it is change. We may want to change our lives but can be frustrated beyond all measure by the slow pace at which this occurs or more likely, by the complete lack of change. Whether we want a change in our financial state, our love life perhaps, our health or lifestyle, change can be hard to come by.

We see our health as a problem when it manifests as dis-ease or sickness, it is then that we try and 'do' something about it, change our circumstances. When relationships hit a wall, when finances dry up, when life just gets too hard we try and do something about it. Work harder, work longer, work smarter. It is a condition of our upbringing to seek help outside of ourselves when the going gets tough. Often outside help can be very valuable and necessary but it is not necessarily going to bring about long term change, it depends upon the nature of the help and the inner workings of the person seeking help.

We see just the tip of the iceberg, the pointed bit that sticks up above the surface, this is the obvious sign that all is not well at the inn. If we fail to recognise that the tip of the iceberg is simply the product of belief patterns which have been given power, albeit subconsciously, over many years, we think we should be able to bring about change instantly, by medication, surgery, diet, a workshop or two!

Often, when we use medication to control or stimulate change we are just dealing with the manifesting symptoms, those uncomfortable feelings that tell us something is not quite right in the state of our being. This is not just applicable to physical dis-ease or sickness—psychological or emotional turmoil will have their roots in a long, forgotten, oftentimes subconscious past. Even our financial state, our relationships, our life-style, all arise from our past.

BEWARE THE ICEBERG!

We may be able to improve our health through medical intervention, great, go for it if it is available, we may be able to improve our finances by a windfall, 'lucky' you. We may be able to change out relationships by joining an online dating service! We may change our lifestyle when confronted by some dramatic event, forcing us to live life differently. But all these things are still only, for the most part, surface or cosmetic fixes. Like blowing the tip of the iceberg out of the water, what happens then? More of the iceberg surfaces, giving us something else to aim our attention at.

It has taken us years to reach this state of imbalance, how can we truly expect to restore balance in a couple of weeks.

It does not matter who we are, where we live or what our circumstances are, the conditions that hold us to our current life's patterns are all rooted in our past. I personally do not believe that we need to understand our history to know who we are or where we are going. History is the past, while we focus on the past we fail to live in the moment. And whose version of history are we focusing on? Is our version any more correct than any other version? This is a part of the dilemma, we see history through eyes that have already been taught to see things, certain belief patterns, it certain ways. Rose, or purple, or blue, or green coloured glasses limit our view of reality.

From my perspective, while we refuse to see that who we are now, where we are now, what we are now, is a manifestation of who, where, what we have been in the past, we will continue to face the same old challenges, the same health issues, the same relationships, the same lifestyle issues. If we continue to deal with those issues in the same old way, we are really guaranteeing more of the same tomorrow.

It may just not be possible to effect quick, dramatic change 'just because we want to' or, as I have heard so many times 'I am ready for change' as if that implies change should be happening. What a load of hooooey. No one is truly ready for change while they live in the past, and, to some degree or other, we all live in the past. The present is quite alien to most of us, never having had the direct experience of being in the moment free from the past. That is completely understandable, the ideas of what it means to be human are for the most part very self-centred and encourage us to live for tomorrow. Established cultural organisations tell us that if we behave according to certain rules, we will be much happier in the 'next' life.

LOST IN SELF IMPORTANCE

We tend to take a very short sighted view of our lives, job security at the expense of the health of the planet, leaving a rather uncertain future for the generations to follow; abuse of those around us to satisfy our own insecurities, the list is endless. This, to me, is again a product of failure to recognise that our lives are the end point of a long series of events, as is the manifesting reality on the planet. If we were to see that we are the product of our past, as is everyone else, then we understand that if we continue to enforce old patterns, we are in essence, digging a deeper hole, out of which we will want to climb one day, but the deeper the hole the harder it appears to get out. A friend once said, "If you find yourself in a hole, stop digging."

To seek change, when a country has been pretty much living in the past, by choice or otherwise, overnight is naive, and by overnight I mean several generations, to think that money is the answer to all problems is just as naive.

It seems that few people really do want change, many pay lip service to the need for change, but real change, that is something else. Change, lets face it, means letting go of the past and moving into a different reality. For many an unknown reality! Who wants that! Most people are willing to change as long as they are in control of the change, have a sense of direction, manipulating to achieve a goal, an end result that is often at odds with other's perceptions of what and where change should be heading.

It is hard to follow the example laid out in the Tao Te Ching "Practice not-doing—and everything will fall into place." But therein lie the answers to change. Having no investment in the future, having learnt that, no matter where you run, no matter how much money you have your past follows you around—and shows up when you least expect, or want it to. What to do? Nothing, of course. Through developing non-attachment to that which arises, that which manifests, we begin to see through the veils of the self made illusions, the so called 'reality'. And insight gives us reason to continue the practice, but for those who never take the first step, no reasons appear to make such change.

The first step is not so difficult, even if you are only after a taster, put your toe in the water, check it out. Changing the

| Musings |

external has, in the past, been very much a matter of do-ing something, it is not easy to set aside old conditioning, especially when it is reinforced on a daily basis by those around you. Some appear more ready for change than others, a delusion of cellular biology.

Sleep on This One

THE 'WHO' AND THE 'WHY"

Last month I spoke about change and the challenges we met when we went looking for it. This month we can take a look at the other side of that coin, a way to achieve goals with much less struggle and conflict. Acceptance.

Acceptance is so much harder than the usual struggle and strife for most of us because we have been raised in a world where conflict and overcoming by doing is as natural as breathing. A big issue might be, 'who' is wanting change? And why?

The 'who' is a product of the past and the past has been one of do-ing to achieve. As a result of this journey the 'who' has become more defined on a cellular level. The physical body, responding to some desire or aversion to various ideas and concepts, has changed and now supports the reality that is reflected in the physical body. The physical body in this case primarily referring to the 'chemistry' of the body. When we become, on a physical level, our thoughts, then we lose ourselves, more and more in the world that we have created. The more lost we become, through a process of taking the manifesting reality seriously the harder we try to change things.

A possible problem arises here because the 'who' that is seeking to control or manipulate the external world is not coming from a place of great clarity or wisdom. Instead they are caught within a world that is reflecting back to them their own inner beings which, if we are indeed a product of our past, and that past has been manufactured to a large degree on a sub-conscious level, then what we see around us is a mixture of our conscious desire but also, and likely to a greater degree, our unconscious conditioning. The unconscious conditioning more often than not is made up of aspects of our past that we have denied, shut away, experiences we try to forget, feelings that dis-empower us, aspects that we would prefer not to have. All this bundles up into what Jung called 'the shadow'.

When we accept that there are parts of us of which we are not conscious that are supporting our view of the world, then the 'who' would be represented by a person with a large paper bag on their head! Imagine a condition of entry into this world being that you had to put a paper bag over your head, to keep you in the dark, to maintain a level playing field. You would not see too much of what was going on, it would be all guess work. And then having someone, who also has a paper bag over their head, claiming to know the path to a better future. If that person is persuasive enough, or if their personal history, their paper bag, matches our own, then we might believe them for a time and follow, just as blindly— our own paper bag?—up to the point where their goals begin to differ to widely from our own. Or, when something else happens to poke a hole in our own paper bag, letting in some light, after a long period of darkness. Now we might claim to see more than, better than, clearer than another, and people might follow us. And so it goes.

'WHO' IS BENEATH THE PAPER BAG?

Yet still whoever claims to 'know' is still suffering from the paper bag syndrome. What really can they know other than how to make life more, or less comfortable from within the limitations of the paper bag. So the 'who' and their ability to effect change is essentially someone, lost in their own drama, trying to affect the manifesting drama, imposing perceptions already confused, onto others and the world.

The 'why' is obvious. Because the 'who' is not content. I don't believe the 'who' can be content while they suffer the, probably illusional, effects of 'the shadow'. This is because of what has been created on an inner level. Inside most of us exists a strongly polarised world which is in eternal conflict with itself. This conflict reflects in those around us, in world conditions. This leads the person, with the paper bag on their head, to do even more to try and fix things which only adds to the chaos and confusion, which leads to a greater need to 'fix' things as more and more the world reflects back the state of inner turmoil. And so it goes.

I imagine the individual, the community, a country, the population of the world, to be on a great steam train, thundering through time. Getting faster and faster, along tracks that are determined by the collective will, each and everyone of us adds some energy, some emotion, some thought to the process so we are all contributing to direction and speed.

If the train, traveling at great speed, tries to change tracks to abruptly there could be a serious derailment, ouch! If individuals jump off the train they are going to have a hard landing, but, still driven by their own energy, needs and desires, will form little steam engines or their own, till they attract other like minded people, making a bigger train, which may, or may not end up in conflict with the 'original' train. ("I have lost my train of thought!")

STOP ADDING FUEL TO THE FIRE

To me, a solution to the runaway train might be for those riding the train to stop feeding the engine that needs thought, emotion, desire, to keep it running. Let the thing run down on steam, perhaps when it gets a little slower it will make for a more comfortable transition. More likely it will also present new opportunities, ones that were not visible before because the single minded train was moving too fast for people to take a moment to reflect. Perhaps, the slowing of the train would mean that some paper bags began to fall apart, the changing many 'who's' may offer vastly different perceptions.

One way that I know of to stop feeding the collective engine is to accept—simply accept—what is happening. Acceptance is just a way to stop energising old thoughts, old ways of being, to take a breather from your personal history, stick your head up, paper bag free, from the sand and take a fresh look around.

Acceptance stops feeding, on a cellular level the 'you' you have become. Breaking old patterns can be hard, the old keeps pulling back, the more we struggle, the harder the pull becomes, acceptance is not about struggle, it is not about judgement, it is just an acknowledgement of what is happening right now.

This is of course, the basis of the Clearing work, learning to accept a feeling, emotion, thought in the moment, by not identifying with the phenomena we gradually step free from any hold over us it might have had.

Acceptance is not an easy way out, it is not running away. Quite the opposite, it is facing up to yourself, but from a new place, a different way of viewing the self which makes embracing the shadow something that we can all achieve.

This is, after practice, an effortless process. Just have to get that train off those same old tracks.

Try it and see for your self. Maybe it will need some practice, but that steam engine has been running along the same old track for a long time now and any divergence is a challenge, but well worth the effort.

To sum up, most desire for change is a product of discontent. Discontent exists on an inner cellular level and is the result of how we have identified with the experiences in our past. If we continue to try and deal with the world and all it presents based upon our past, then we will get more of the same, requiring more time, money, and energy to deal with it. Acceptance is a means by which we can release some of the head of steam that has built up opening the door to different ways of being.

PERSONAL CHANGE/TRANSITION

Last month I mentioned change that I was going through, perhaps transition is a better word. Still early days but the plan is to combine my energy and experience with another and develop a new business aimed at promoting clearing to a much bigger audience. We will be offering a host of resources, both hands on and online to support people all around the world to 'get clearer'. I shall be heading over to England after my workshop coming up in Switzerland to develop this idea even more.

I will keep in touch on progress, and certainly let you know when we are launching the new web site. Stay tuned for an exciting breath of fresh air into the clearing world.

And This!

A WINDOW OF OPPORTUNITY

I HAVE BEEN WRITING ABOUT CHANGE, HOW WE ARE LIMITED in our choices by our personal history. Who we have become, on an energetic level, has reduced our choices so that we now follow a rather narrow path and the choices that are available to us are contained within that pathway. So, freedom to choose is correct up to a point, but the choices are already limited so we are not quite as free as we might have hoped we were. If you think you would like to see some change in your life, then this article may be helpful.

I was interested, when I watched *What the Bleep*, in the scene on the basketball court where there were literally hundreds of basketballs bouncing around at the same time, each representing a possible reality. I got to wondering, how can this be, when we, for the most part, only see the one basketball, (thank goodness!) But of course each basketball is representative of a future, a manifesting reality, you just have to take your pick, and once you have chosen that is the ball you see, not the many, they just exist as possibilities, the potential for different futures.

As far as I am aware, our moment of choice happens so fast we don't even register the moment of choice, we just go along with what presents as though there had been no point when we could have made an alternative decision.

| And This! |

Simplistically put, I think that our world view, our beliefs about what is real and what is not, our personal judgements, have all conspired to expect the world to be a certain way. That expectation we might say is based upon past experience or current collective values, what we see is what we get but because the majority of basketball opportunities are outside of our current expectations we fail to see them.

We have become fixated upon a certain reality and see nothing that doesn't fit into that rule book. We have convinced ourselves that our perceptions are real and are therefore caught in a position where we have to operate within that paradigm. The more we work within the established rules, the more seriously we take them the more energy we give them. This process can be likened to entering a large funnel. At the mouth of the funnel, the wide part, there is plenty of room to move, lots of choices, but each time we make a choice, we move further into the funnel, the nature of the funnel as we move into it is to get smaller, so, less room to move, less choices to make, until we are in the very narrow part of the funnel and there appears to be no room to move and no real choices to make. This is because of our identification with one particular picture we took personally at some stage of our journey.

Of course we would not want to be in the situation where we had to choose from multiple possibilities at each moment of the day. Imagine even simple choices like breakfast, if the choices were unlimited, how long would that take? To turn right, left ahead, or around at every step! We would go nowhere, except perhaps a little mad. Even just picturing all the possibilities would overwhelm us. It is a good thing that the brain processes the information so quickly that life seems like a seamless journey, not a mad patch together of mini scenes with time out in between.

WHAT CHOICE DO WE HAVE?

It seems then that the choices are made for us, the world is as it is and we have had little or no say in that. When we consider, though, that our expectations may have created the world we might just stop and think for a moment and try to imagine what it would be like to have more conscious choice. To move out of being victim to our past into a realm where conscious co-creation was not only a possibility, but a reality. I often think that we have convinced ourselves that we are victims to circumstances and that life has to follow a particular path and we discount that path as being something that we have created. Yet every moment is one of co-creation, the fact that we create one thing as opposed to another doesn't lessen its value. I think recognising this takes us a big step towards the awareness that, perhaps, just perhaps, we could create something quite different.

Increasingly, scientific knowledge comes to our awareness about how, on a fundamental level, thoughts are controlling the world we see and live in. Because of the path I have been traveling, this has been obvious to me for some time, nice to see 'science' delivering the proof! Common answers to changing our reality are based on changing our mind, by identifying 'negative' thoughts and emotions we take the first step towards changing ourselves. Although this may well have benefits, I think if it were so easy we would have done it long ago (change our minds).

Perhaps we are/have been 'changing our minds' slowly over many ages. We may see a revolution, a change of government, new laws as being indicative of change, but all of those changes are only made within the current paradigm, trying to make life easier for particular groups of individuals, often at the expense of other groups of individuals.

The difficulty is being able to even begin to visualise another way, outside of the currently accepted belief patterns that regulate the world we live in because the personality that has arisen is based upon limited perceptions. Easy to say 'change your mind'—hard to do. This is where 'clearing' demonstrates the potential it has for freeing us from our past enters the scene. When an attempt to force change is made it is met with an equal and opposite reaction, further deepening the gulf between balance and chaos. 'Clearing' allows any potential charge to release in a safe and gentle manner, from a relatively stress free place (post 'clearing') it is more possible that choices can be made that will enable, step by step, a move from past limitations into a different way of being.

A Piece to Finish the Day

SHARE-ABILITY

I STARTED THIS ARTICLE WRITING ABOUT PERSONAL PRIVACY ON the web. Not the keep your passwords secret sort of privacy, but the personal sharing stuff. This reminded me of how, in my youth, I was a very private person, holding onto all the parts of me, not sharing much, particularly my shadow side.

From that memory came the knowledge that I am still, perhaps to a lesser degree, quite private. Though I have come a long way in a few short years there is still a part of me that holds back, which would explain why 'I' and the clearing work are still relative unknowns in the world of alternative approaches.

I have long recognised the need to be open, for whatever it is we hide from the public is that which keeps us separate, maintains a senses of private/personal self. All the time we hold back parts of ourselves we are maintaining an internal polarised state. This internal 'conflict' for that is what it amounts to on a cellular level, keeps us a prisoner to our past and isolated from a greater sense of community.

For many of us there is little or no recognition that we keep parts of our self hidden, we have become so used to being a certain way that objectivity about that state of being is not something that we can readily access. So we carry on trying to deal with life's situations based on conditioned reaction rather than considered response.

I have often opened up in workshops and spoken of 'personal' issues, much to the amazement of some of the people present. The purpose behind this sharing is the recognition that what we fail to share keeps us a prisoner. I have seen through many workshops where we look at the shadow, that each and everyone present has the same issues, the same shadow. If I am not prepared to share then I cannot expect the workshop attendees to share.

If we understand better just what the 'shadow' is then it becomes easier to share those parts of ourselves. The benefit of sharing is that once 'downloaded' the information has less impact upon us on a daily basis. There is a difference between downloading and wallowing, which we all tend to do at some time or another. To 'wallow' is to take ones troubles personally which continually energises those troubles, to download is to let them go which leads us towards a greater sense of freedom.

DEAL WITH YOUR PAST AND THE FUTURE WILL TAKE CARE OF ITSELF

A friend recently commented on a video she had seen where a polar bear was tracked across the ice floes by a helicopter as a part of a research program. The goal was to sedate the polar bear and fix a transmitter (I think this was the plan) to the bear and track its movements. The polar bear tried all known methods to escape the helicopter, but in the end gave up, there was nothing it could do, nowhere to run.

The polar bear was duly sedated. The researchers noticed an interesting phenomena as the polar bear slowly recovered from the tranquilliser, its body ran and jerked and shuddered as it came back to full consciousness. Their opinion was that the bear was re-writing the script, to one where it was not trapped but escaped. So once it was conscious it did not carry the memory of the chase and capture as trauma into its tomorrow.

This is a classic example of clearing, letting go of the charge of an experience before it can become established internally and thereby affect each moment of subsequent life. We, unlike the polar bear (and I suspect, many other animals), fail to process the experience in a healthy way, we do this by identifying strongly with the feelings and emotions that arises as a result of the experience. We take things personally and hold grudges, complaints, hurts, we hold others to blame for our experience. Often we do this sub-consciously, we are not aware this is happening because it is such an entrenched part of the human conditioning, so the collective supports our perceptions and we have no role model to suggest any other way of dealing with the situation.

The stronger we identify with the emotions and feelings associated with experiences, the more we establish a reactive state when those 'buttons' are pushed in the future. Each time a button is pushed and we react, we fall into the old way of being and react, by taking the feelings personally once again, we are adding energy to those feelings, creating an even deeper, stronger bond which guarantees next time that button is pushed, we are going to experience a strong reaction. And so it goes. All because, unlike the polar bear, we failed to move through the experience, rewrite the script and leave the past trauma behind.

This is what is meant by failing to share our shadow. But the shadow if ignored or empowered, grows into an unmanageable beast the more energy we give it, it gets so strong, so intense that we become total victims to it. Because of its intensity, we try to keep it hidden, to run away, to continue to deny its existence. This suppression of aspects of our self leads to huge imbalance on an inner level which may well result in serious illness. At the very least we have created a monster, a personal demon, that follows us every where we go and colours the world we see, creates a reality where the demon keeps arising. Past patterning is to run away, to blame others, to seek solace in various substances, all of which deny the existence of the monster and guarantee its continued presence.

PRACTICE MAKES PERFECT, OR SO I HAVE HEARD!

Clearing is a safe and gentle way to de-energise the monster, to gradually re-write the script. For those of you familiar with clearing, every time you yawn, every time to shudder, every time you feel an emotion or experience a physical feeling, while 'clearing' you are, in effect, changing the past, letting go of tension and association with trauma. Whether you are 'clearing' yourself or another, you are supporting the release of a stressful memory stored in the body which opens the door to a more responsive approach in place of conditioned reaction.

Through developing this ability for oneself several things become possible. To begin with you start to rewrite your own script, consciously or not, you are revisiting traumatic memories and letting go of the charge you held around that experience. This of course then changes how you deal with such situations in the future, more than that, it reduces the likelihood of your having to face that situation again, because when there is little or no charge around any particular memory, there is less chance of you meeting it on the road. (The Lestrygonians and the Cyclops, the angry Poseidon—do not fear them: You will never find such as these on your path, if your thoughts remain lofty, if a fine emotion touches your spirit and your body. The Lestrygonians and the Cyclops, the fierce Poseidon you will never encounter, if you do not carry them within your soul, if your soul does not set them up before you.—Constantine Cavafy, *Ithaca*).

THE WORLD IS AS IT IS BECAUSE YOU MADE IT THAT WAY

As you are more able to do this for your self, you are better able to 'hold the space' for others. As old charge falls away new opportunities open up, it is only through the application of this understanding and frequent practice that the benefits become obvious, that a new life can present itself. Our past reactivity maintains a certain state of expectation. We have come to believe that the world is a certain way and our behaviour supports that way keeping us a prisoner to our own past, our own beliefs about how things are, and will be. This, to me, is what it means to share, not sitting in some circle and spilling the beans, opening up closets, airing dirty laundry or shaking out the skeletons. When we can share who we are without guilt, without fear, without shame, then those parts of us that we had previously denied, as Carl Jung once said:

> The shadow is that part of the unconscious psyche that is nearest to consciousness even though not completely accepted by it. Because it is contrary to our chosen conscious attitude, the shadow personality is denied expression in life and coalesces into a relatively separate splinter personality in the unconscious, where it is isolated from exposure and discovery.
>
> When you bring your shadow personality to awareness and assimilate it, it reduces its inhibiting or destructive potentials, releasing trapped positive life energy.

Ponder This

THE LINE IN THE SAND

For those who have embraced 'clearing' as a part of their journey life can never be quite the same as it was pre-clearing. For the few who might read this who have not been introduced to clearing, the information is still relevant, though you might have different ways of dealing with life's experiences.

For most of us, operating in auto pilot mode, we deal with events, people and feelings as they arise, often from the same model we operated from yesterday (and the day before …) We have become accustomed to the collection of thoughts, feelings and emotions that we call our personality. We have become accustomed to the world presenting itself in certain ways. As long as our 'world' remains within certain parameters we can manage, we may not like some of the people, some of the emotions, some of the events, but as they were pretty much expected we have learnt ways of handling such people, emotions and events. (Auto pilot!).

For the 'clearers' amongst us, hopefully we have begun to see how many of the challenges that present in our live arise from the more hidden aspects of ourselves, the 'shadow' the unloved, whatever you want to call it. For those still into blaming others for their own predicaments, then the concept of the shadow is not even on the radar. Even 'clearers' can have trouble seeing the part they play in the creation of the world they 'see' on a daily basis. As long as we are 'clearing' others we are okay, and, while others 'clear' us, we are fine. This is a comfortable, simple and effective way to move through issues.

Yet these 'issues' are, for the most part, low level patterns, with little charge, the 'easy' ones. These are on the fringe of our comfort zone, the penumbra between shadow and light, not too challenging because they don't hold so much tension or generate intense reactions. They are on the right side of the line we have drawn in the sand, the line beyond which we are not yet prepared to step, for on the other side of this, imaginary, line lies our deeper fears, our shame, the private parts of us that even we are not particularly conscious of.

Most of those reading this will recognise those moments, when the deep dark depths of the shadow are exposed, how we immediately go into an old pattern of reaction. When these parts of ourselves are challenged how old defences immediately kick in. When this happens clearing is thrown out of the window. So quickly do we identify with the emotions and thoughts that there is not even a brief moment in time where we can even remember the word 'clearing.'

FAIR WEATHER SAILORS

During my blue water sailing days, there was an oft heard expression, 'a clear weather sailor'—a person who would sail only when the weather was fine. Much like a lot of people practicing clearing today. Only venture out when it is safe to do so. I admit to preferring fair weather myself, but when you are out at sea, no sight of land, the weather does what the weather does. A few storms are good now and then, they break up the patterns and complacency. Fair is good, time to do some maintenance on the boat, work on your tan, read, take you time preparing a special meal. Sitting on a sail boat out of sight of land is a good place to practice being in the moment, for the clearer, on dry land, roof and electricity taken for granted complacency sets in very quickly. For the sailor the storm clouds can appear at any time and demand action, you can't just close the windows and go back to sleep.

For the sailor, the preparation of self and boat is so important, to be as ready as you can to face whatever the journey throws at you. For the person on the journey of life good preparation is equally important (see my latest book, *First Aid: A Guide to Greater Health and Happiness*, for some clues on how to prepare). Yet how many remember reading the instruction manual before landing in the body they now inhabit? Or did you just blank out and pick things up from your parents, siblings, social environment and begin the long journey of taking your 'self' seriously.

How many of us are, on the surface, happy to continue in auto pilot? Don't rock the boat (back to boats!), don't do this or say that. Clear as long as it is safe to do so! Well, clearing can certainly be seen as an energetic approach to all issues, and clearing can help relieve the pressure from many, if not all situations. Yet clearing is also something more, a lot more. Clearing is a training—training the body, on a mental, emotional and cellular level to respond to information and not react.

We are all 'clear weather sailors' while there is still energy hidden in the shadow that is pretty much ruling our day to day affairs, the more we have denied our past, the more pressure it exerts on our present—and future. No one wants to open that Pandora's Box and release the demons that we have been running from since we lost ourselves in the human form. See clearing then as a training for a journey, a way to come to terms with ones demons in a safe and gentle manner. The more you clear others, the more your own balance shifts the less likely you are to take a lot of emotional energy so personally.

THE PENNY DROPS

With continued practice there may well come a time when the penny drops, the light goes on and you realise the true emptiness of the shadow, the impersonal past that has kept you in denial for so long. You may experience the squalls, the storms, the approaching rocky shore, no longer a fair weather sailor but one who appreciates all that life has to offer with absolute equanimity. Life in a sail boat is very much about being in the moment, life on dry land is not so different, to be in the moment, to accept whatever, whoever shows up (another good book to read, *Loving Who Shows Up*!!!) without personalising presents a very different world. The world you had come to expect, and as such co-created, is only a figment of your imagination, ruled as much by your shadow as any integrated aspects of the self. Love the shadow, change the world. How to love the shadow? Practice clearing on a daily basis.

Remember, breathe and smile, try to not grasp at thoughts or emotions, allow all to pass without energising any of it, and enjoy the beauty of the moment.

WHOOPS!

Have you ever noticed, when an exciting opportunity presents, whether it is a person you 'fall' for, a business opportunity, a house or a holiday, how your energy can go out in a great rush? How easy it is to lose oneself in another, in a dream, in a fantasy. For those who can recall such feelings, can you also remember what happened when 'reality' hit? Not 'reality' in what is truly real, but your own reality, your expectations, your hopes, your fears, your shadow. When you came back to earth! Ouch! Not that we can do much about the situation, we are truly victims to desire, hope, a better future.

But then there is always 'clearing'.

And This!

THE IMPORTANCE OF A SPIRITUAL PRACTICE

What if all of the points of view you hold about life, your self and others is based upon stories that have nothing to do with your true nature, many of them designed to keep you from discovering the true nature of mind?

Waking up from the story is possibly one of the most difficult tasks we face today while we continue to hold onto the belief that we are our thoughts, feelings and emotions. We are continually reminded of the story every time we turn on the TV, open a newspaper, access the 'news' online, go to work, meet socially with friends. When all around you sleep, how can you possibly wake up? When everything around you holds you in the story, the dream, do you even realise you are dreaming?

When there is no role model for you to focus on, and many of those who set themselves up as role models are equally lost in the dream what chance is there of even realising the need to wake up?

Life beyond the story. Is there such a place? Lots of questions and few answers. I don't claim to be wide awake, hence you should not believe a word I say.

When I started 'clearing' I was already well down the path of the teachings of the Buddha, though not a Buddhist, I took a lot from their teachings, along with other more gnostic teachings. As I became more involved in 'clearing' and read various books that were recommended by trusted friends I began to combine the old teachings with the new insights of modern psychology and science. It has not been possible to travel this path, particularly the later part where teaching and sharing this information (essentially called 'clearing'), without a lot of internal change taking place.

Along with internal change comes a broader view of life. My 'story' began to change, to open up. I began to see the world—the reality that I create on a daily basis—as simply a result of my own past. I had been conditioned, or conditioned myself, either way it is ultimately immaterial to the way out of the dream, to expect the world to be a certain way. We all have, although groups and individual perceptions may vary according to personal history, there is a common thread running through the lives of just about everyone on the planet. That perception is that the dream is real. That error in thinking is, according to my current perceptions, the basis for all suffering, struggle, violence, greed and abuse, both personal and environmental that the peoples of the world experience today.

THE DANGER OF HOLDING ONTO A POINT OF VIEW

Clearing is, essentially, the letting go of attachment to points of view. The more attached we are to a point of view, even the point of view of 'clearing', the less open or available we are. Any point of view anchors us in time and space, the moment we identify with a point of view conflict is bound to arise as we meet others with different points of view. Letting go of points of view, from one point of view, could be seen as 'giving in' to the opposition and allowing them a victory. This is still a point of view. The perception is that safety, abundance, health and wealth are all obtainable if a particular point of view is held and enforced. But these points of view are still only possible within the dream, arise as a result of the dream. Personal liberation is not about creating more wealth within the dream. Although a lot of people would disagree, that is just their point of view.

We are all held prisoner to our own perceptions and values by our habitual acceptance of who we believe ourselves to be. This manifests on a cellular level, becomes a sub-conscious addiction which we then feed by repeating old patterns. All the time we identify with our past there is no room, on a cellular level, for change. We mistakenly believe that by developing greater powers to manipulate the illusion we will find peace and happiness.

Through regular and frequent 'clearing' attachment to belief patterns fall away, there is a sense of an expansion of the self. When limitations that were held as truths are seen in a different light, from a different angle, they cease to have the same power. I began to get a picture of how we, collectively, create the 'reality' we live in. Still a belief perhaps, not any final truth, for that, to the personality, is unknowable. However, recognising how the world we live in is created and maintained offered an opportunity to create a different world, consciously, or rather more consciously than I have been doing in the past.

THE FLAVOUR OF THE MONTH, OR, THE LATEST KIDS ON THE BLOCK

There have been many books written on the subject of personal empowerment, the creation of wealth and abundance, movies made, followers gathered. Is all this stuff, the creation of abundance, representative of the collective? Are we all getting caught in another dream, one where we can manufacture, out of thin air, everything our heart desires? The challenge, as I see it, is the dreamer, we have moved from total victim consciousness, to partial victim consciousness (one where we still have to do something in order to get what we want.) But, who is it who wants? The personality. Still aspects of personality who feel they know best, or at least, feel they know of a better way. This, the voice of personality, is driven by its desire to create a world in which it feels safe, comfortable, abundant, happy, at peace. This is the voice of judgement, judgement that arises from the needs of the personality. This is the voice of desire, wanting change, always wanting something.

Because of my involvement in the 'clearing' and the constant practice, hearing the voice of desire gets easier, letting it pass easier still. Who lies beyond the desire? Letting go consciously of desire that is driven by personality is not easy, meditation is a good practice, for those able and willing, clearing for those who are not.

Every time you 'tune in' to be for someone ('clear') you enter a state of meditation. A place where all is noticed (to whatever degree you are able at that point in time) and nothing is personalised. Where feelings arise, are acknowledged, and released (accepted), where emotions present, are noticed and accepted, where thoughts are observed, and released. All this without any part of the observer reaching out, grabbing a hold of the thought, feeling, emotion.

This practice allows a more peaceful state of being to exist, the more peace one experiences internally, the more peace arises externally. Particularly valuable in a world caught in polarity. A world where people have stopped thinking before they speak or act, acting—or reacting—to stimuli in the same old way, time and time again. In the simple act of acceptance, energy, your energy, that would previously have gone into the maintenance of the illusion, is withdrawn. Attempts to recreate the world in your image become meaningless, for until you are without personality, without desire, your creation will simply be more of the same, perhaps a different shade of the original colour, but ultimately no different at all.

SOME QUESTIONS TO ASK

Does having a different view of how reality is created, and the part the individual plays in maintaining that reality, necessarily mean a better future? Does it mean the liberation from the dream? Is it important to awaken from the dream while we inhabit the human form? Will we awaken after death of the physical? Who is it who awakens? Or is it just another game we have made up to entertain ourselves? And does it really matter? Will your view of a future be a total win win situation for all mankind? Or are you so lost in keeping your current reality afloat none of this is important to you?

CHANGE

I have spoken recently about some changes in the way I work that are on the horizon. Well, they are still on the horizon, how they are going to manifest is open to speculation, something I am not much given to. Big question marks that I do see now are whether or not to continue teaching this, especially in the manner I have in the past—or not.

In the fascinating journey that has evolved during my days sharing this information, the global travel, meeting so many wonderful people along the way, I was supported,

| And This! |

very much, by others. Different people have stepped up and taken over the promotion and organisation of workshops, for all those who have been so supportive, I offer my heartfelt thanks, without you 'clearing' would still be unknown by many around the world.

More recently that support has fallen away, for good reason I am sure, but without it the responsibility for getting people to workshops has fallen back on my shoulders. This is not something I am particularly good at, so numbers slowly fade. There are still people in several countries who are excited by the work and do all they can to ensure a successful workshop, but this energy is scattered. A sign of the times? Quite likely. So, a period of uncertainty to some, a period of deep R and R for me. Out of which something will arise, it always has in the past, and even with the times changing as they are, will in the future. Meanwhile all is good. Acceptance, that word again, the key to a peaceful heart and mind.

A Piece to Start the Day

AS WITHIN

I have often written about the world that we see/manifest being a reflection of our inner world, an interpretation of information picked up and passed through the filter system of the personality. This month I'd like to spend some time on the manifesting physical reality, the energy of our homes and the planet.

With awareness increasing many people are looking outside the old boxes for answers to whatever problems they face, this has led, or driven, a great range of 'modalities' which have presented in the recent past, and continue to do so today. Some people turn towards other people—there's a water leak, call the plumber!—Many of us have become dependant upon others to fix our lives, as we have moved into a more technological society, as transport developed, the need to care for ourselves was replaced by 'experts'. Now don't get me wrong here, I don't have time to go back to school to study plumbing, or become an electrician, a nurse, an engineer etc. I think that we all have something to offer society and let those with the skills deal with the problems.

Many problems in our live exist because somewhere back down the line the job was not done properly, stop thinking of plumbers and electricians, builders and engineers, doctors and lawyers, although poor workmanship does exist especially where the motivation is purely profit, and look at a broader picture. Bring it all back to something more personal, your feelings. In particular those feelings that tend to dominate your reality. The big ones; fear, anxiety, anger, depression, manic swings, greed (a non-stop need for more), issues of self worth. Think of anything that runs your life from the back seat, not always something obvious, we are, for the most part, all driven by sub-conscious conditioning. Is there anything 'missing' from your life right now?

HERE'S A THOUGHT

Problems can only arise out of problems.

According to quantum physics we are either a series of waves of energy or a whole lot of particles bound together. Let's imagine we are the wave forms, as is everything else. Picture a stone dropped into a pond, the ripples spread outward in growing circles until the energy has been dissipated. Imagine everything as stones dropped into a pond, waves crashing into each other creating ever more complex patterns. When we encounter a problem, the immediate reaction is to drop a stone, an attempt at solving the problem, into the pond. All this does is create more ripples, which go on to interact with the ripples still left over from all the other stones. Imagine this approach to problem solving going back, way back into the past. Then we see that what we are doing today is a continuation of what has been done in the past. Essentially we are in damage control mode, trying to fix the problems of the past manifesting today.

A problem arises, we try and fix it based on methods used over and over again in the past, our inherited, if you like, way of dealing with life. Yet if throwing another stone in the pond solved the problem, then how can problems still arise?

This way never worked and it is not going to start working now just because we have bigger stones, or more people throwing in identical stones. This approach simply creates more problems, problems that we have to deal with in the future, and guess how we are going to deal with them! More stones.... This must make you think, is there another way to solve my problems. Well, there is, all problems have solutions.

So, how is my environment reflecting back to me my inner being? If 'all' is simply wave forms, energy changing from one form to another, including us, then all wave forms are connected, interacting with each other, responding to the same inputs. We might say that the environment, the earth upon which we 'live' is constantly responding/reacting to information. When we throw a stone in the pond (try to fix our lives by inherited methods) we send out a signal, the signal can be likened to a radio transmission, expanding waves of information, that affect everything they touch.

The energy or wave forms of our home environment are all the time responding to the information that we send out and create some sort of balance between the energy of the home and us, the people who live in that environment. So we live in harmony with our world. All is well, until the balance shifts, which simply means that the internal reality is no longer in harmony with the external reality. This happens because we are not the only person throwing stones in to the pond, someone rocks the boat and our immediate response is to throw more stones in to try and fix things, and so it goes.

IS ANOTHER BAND-AID GOING TO FIX IT?

It should be pretty obvious now that a different way is required. If you have a problem do you look for someone who will 'fix' your problem, or have you discovered that the problem is of your own creation, and as such, you have the answers. Look around your home, what degree of chaos are you living in, most people live in some chaos! Are you content within the chaos, is your life cluttered? Is it empty? Are you in peace or in pieces?

It is not so easy to stop throwing stones, many times we react to situations so quickly that there is no time to think "would life be better if I did not throw this stone"? So our sub-conscious, already conditioned to throw stones controls our life, not giving us a moments respite, does not allow us to take a step back and see things for what they are.

If we perceive problems in our personal environment, or the greater environment, then surely the first step to harmony is to stop throwing stones. At least become aware of the stones you are throwing.

Stopping this process requires great personal awareness, it requires that we become more mindful of our thoughts our words and our actions.

But first, we must see the part we are each playing in the ongoing manifestation that is our world. Only then will we stop looking outside of the self for answers and play a more conscious part in co-creating the world we live in coming from a place of understanding rather than conditioning.

WAITING—WAITING—WAITING

How many of you feel as though you are in some undefined, limbo state? As though you are waiting for something but are not quite sure what it is! As though the past year has been slowly dismantling whatever it was you thought was 'real'? Leaving you where?

One great explanation offered in the interpretations of the Mayan Calendar is that the rate of change is speeding up.

| A Piece to Start the Day |

What once took 30 years to change in our parents and grand parents lifetimes is taking only a year or so to change now. We no longer seem to have the luxury of getting comfortable in a situation before circumstances change.

And what about projects that keep running into dead ends, you start something up, lots of energy and excitement, and before very long it all falls into a heap. Do you recognise this? Or are you hanging onto familiar ways as tightly as you can, is life still rolling along in the same old way? Our conditioning has been to do something about this hole in space time, fill it up, throw in more stones (???), but the stones aren't fixing things as they appeared to do in the past.

Perhaps there is a new dance coming to town, and we are being asked to learn the steps in advance. The new steps aren't going to resemble the old in any way, so what to do, how to learn new steps when the teacher hasn't arrived yet. There are plenty of people who think they know the steps, but who told them? My approach has been, and still is, to let go of the past dance, become aware of the steps, and let go, allowing space within for the new to enter. If we continue along as before there is no room, on a cellular level, for change to manifest.

We may not know what the change is, we may buy into the flavour of the month, hang our hats on something that we feel safe with, would like to happen, but is that just wishful thinking?

Let go, and let in. Nothing else to do. Be at peace in the moment, observe the thoughts and feelings and do your best not to follow up with stones that may have their origin in fear.

Sleep on This One

THE SPOTLIGHT OF OUR ATTENTION

Upon what do we focus our energies? Do we have a choice where that focus is? We all want to believe we have a choice but I suspect any choice is limited by our past conditioning, which has in many ways, been where we have focused our attention, albeit subconsciously, from a very early age.

I imagine this journey to be like entering a funnel. Starting at the wide end, we have a broad range of movement, a lot of choices. Each choice we make takes us deeper into the mouth of the funnel, restricting our range of movement and limiting out choices. As each choice is made we limit our future options. Much of this decision making process is not really under our control, it is the past which is in control, a past handed down to us through ancestral lineage or a past experienced in very early childhood on a subconscious level.

Many still think they have freedom to choose but even this thought is a product of the past. Maybe, within certain limitations we do have a choice but the basic structure within which we think we have a choice is already established, like the funnel, the deeper in you go the less choice you have, (until you come out the other end!—that could be likened to the process of being born, now there's a thought!)

'Lateral thinking' was a popular phrase a few years, ago, 'thinking outside of the box', same thing described from a different perspective. If we operate from within the box of our own understanding then any choices that present must also exist within the box. We either remain unaware of choices existing outside of the box of our perceptions, or we deny them as 'unrealistic', attempt to manipulate anything that doesn't fit into our box comfortably or condemn those who think in different ways.

The point of this though is not who, if anyone, makes a choice nor which 'choice' they make but that 'choices' arise from the past conditioning and are not really choices at all. In some ways we are like wind-up toys, that run for a certain time and follow certain behaviour patterns. This is the karmic perception, work through the charge, or line up and keep getting your batteries recharged, the 'choice' is yours. But of course it isn't. You are following the process of energetic conditioning and it is within this process that you 'think' you have a 'choice'.

Choice is an illusion that we cling to, for to imagine life, from the point of view of an established personality, to have no choice seems defeatist, and rather pointless. I suspect it is only the personality that requires a choice, and even then, it chooses realities that support its fundamental perceptions. (Even though those perceptions may be killing the body or creating havoc for the personality). As the attachment to the personality falls away, so does the need to choose, indeed, even the concept of choice takes on a new meaning when the personality is taken out of the equation.

Cellular biologist Dr. Bruce Lipton believes that we do have some choice, not very much, but some, from a cellular biologists point of view! The non-duality people, if there are any? believe there is no choice, for there is no one to make the choice.

'IT' IS HAPPENING ANYWAY!

I currently believe that the nature of the 'world' we 'live' in arises out of the stones thrown in the pond, see last months news-sheet. Whether there is anyone to throw stones in to the pond or not, whether it is a conscious act or not is not important. The energy of the human form is itself a transmission of information. The information generated by the human body are the stones constantly being tossed into the pond. The thoughts that arise, the emotions that present are all products of the bodies perceptions of itself, this happens whether we think there is anyone responsible or not. This constant input of energy/information continues creating a 'reality' that the personality then has to deal with. So you, whoever you may be, create a reality by simply being who you are, no need to make any choices, it is happening anyway.

If we follow this point of view, then we are all dealing with phenomena that arose as a result of our simply being. We spend our time on this delightful planet in damage control mode, putting out fires, manipulating reality in an attempt to feel in control, to satisfy the needs of the personality. While the information that is transmitted remains the same, so the same manifesting reality continues to unfold, and we continue to put out the fires! We have no choice because either there is ultimately no one to choose, or, because all choices have been made already. We are just experiencing the results of those choices. This would lead us deeper into the funnel, a place where there is less and less obvious choice.

I heard Deepak Chopra say once, that only 5% of those who came to his workshops followed through, the rest went off looking for something else. Did either group have a choice? To go or to stay? Whilst we (the personality) remain addicted to certain ways of being, created out of the past, there is little room for change, 'we' become lost in the drama unfolding around us and react, rather than respond to conditions. Our reaction (or response) is a product of how the personality has dealt with information previously.

When we stop taking ourselves so seriously—a result of a previous moment in time when the personality stopped taking itself seriously?—when we stop personalising with everything that happens to 'us' we create more space, room to breathe, but we also create a path upon which the human form stops transmitting so much confused energy and starts to respond in different ways to that which arises on its path.

This doesn't mean that we have more choice but it may well mean that we spend less time in damage control mode and more time in a peaceful state. If the energy of the human form becomes more at peace then less stones of chaos are thrown into the pond and less chaos arises to be 'dealt' with by the personality. This arises naturally, bringing with it the growing realisation that there are less choices to be made.

Just about everyone I know puts the spotlight of their awareness on 'their' thoughts, emotions and feelings that arise out of 'their' past conditioning, what else can they do? Well one possibility would be for them to stop for a moment and observe what they are doing and move that spotlight, stop giving energy to the old conditioning, for when this is practiced enough, the past will stop reappearing and constantly demanding attention.

The more people giving their attention to a particular path, the more energy that path gets. The more energy the path gets, the more 'real' it becomes. The more real it becomes the better it works. Everything works. It is the nature of the world we live in, where energy is focused reality is made manifest.

And this is true on a more personal level as well. If we focus on troubles, troubles arise. If we focus on happiness,

happiness arises. Remember though, while we are lost in the drama, while we take any aspect of the drama personally, whilst we remain unconscious of the part we play in creating that reality, then we will continue to try to 'fix' the world and give our attention to the past, which is a guarantee that the past will continue to control our lives.

The choice then, of the personality, is to stop taking itself so seriously, to become conscious co-creators instead of automatons producing the same old reality every day.

Breathe, and smile, works every time.

ALL ABOARD!

A friend often gets caught in anxiety and depression—does she have a choice? I doubt it, who would choose anxiety and depression on purpose? I suggested she imagine herself on a train. Was the train heading into the darkness, taking her deeper into her shadow, or was the train full of fun and light? The moment of choice comes when the personality realises it is on a train.

Stop the train, I want to get off!

This practice implies that one train is better than another, and for someone lost in anxiety and depression, one train is certainly much better than another. Though with practice the energy given to anxiety and depression reduces, so the manifestation reduces, the point of view of the 'passenger' changes and all trains are just trains. No one better or worse than another. Until that realisation arises though, choose your train carefully.

And This!

A SIGN OF THE TIMES

Last month I shared my understanding of how and why we create the world that we live in. From a personal 'point of view' which means of course, the seemingly personal world. Our conditioned response/reaction maintains the particular illusion that we accept as reality.

This month I would like to offer a different perspective. Part of which is the collective force that co-creates the world we live in. By our collectively subscribing to various beliefs in what is real and what is not, the world continues to unfold as it did yesterday. There is something else at work though that is constantly putting pressure on the system. Any system that fails to change and adapt is doomed to failure. 'Civilisations' and I use the word loosely, that failed to change with the times collapsed, species that are either unable or unwilling (and this includes humanity as the species capable of making more conscious decisions) die out.

We see signs of this everyday, man made institutions that fail to 'move with the times' collapse, societies that adhere to old established ways of being are constantly challenged, both from within and without and either change or suffer the consequences.

We could say that without a solid foundation houses will fall, people will get sick, civilisations will collapse. I suspect though that there is no such thing as a solid foundation, it is just not possible within the collective illusion we subscribe to.

I have mentioned in workshops that the moment we become attached to a point of view we anchor ourselves in time and space. If we picture the 'big bang' as the start of this cosmic age then we could well imagine that the universe is still expanding. It is this expansion that shows up areas of resistance. If the universe is expanding but we, as individuals remain fixed because we hold on to particular points of view, we will experience pressure build up, the more we resist the more discomfort we experience.

Collectively we subscribe to various points of view, beliefs about what is good, bad, real, not real yet the true nature of who we are is not fixed it is expansive. Being a herd animal, we have always felt there was safety in numbers. Groups form rules, develop systems, hold onto certain ways of being. They become clumsy, top heavy, too many rules, not enough flexibility, and they die out. Survival of the species then could come down to adaptability—the ability to 'receive' information and act upon that information. If the individuals access to information is limited by 'rules' then their ability to survive is also limited.

If you have noticed a feeling that could be described as the heat being turned up then you are experiencing the pressure build up that is demanding change. While you resist this pressure you will experience discomfort, the more resistance, the more discomfort. Imagine a pot of water on the stove top heating up, the source of heat either constant or increasing very slowly. There is a lid on the pot, and, on top of the lid a brick. Slowly pressure in the pot builds, the lid starts to move, so what do we do? Put another brick on the lid. This applies to institutions as well as individuals. We need to find ways to release the pressure, not contain it. To release the stress associated with that pressure and to release the idea that the belief pattern, or point of view, that allowed the pressure to build up in the past is just that, a belief pattern.

Remember, change is only problematic when it encounters resistance. Notice where you have resistance, physical symptoms, build up of heat/energy, manifestation of imbalance, problems in health or relationships, with finances with inner peace. Many don't notice they have resistance until it manifests.

Some symptoms associated with clearing—running nose, watering eyes yawning, belching, tired-ness. These are all signs that the body is de-toxing, don't deny it enjoy it. It means that resistance, on whatever level it is being held in the body is being released. And you don't have to know what it is.

AMAR LO SE QUE DÉ

I am delighted to announce that my second book, *Loving Who Shows Up*, is now available in Spanish. This will be available from my web site or Amazon.com. I am working on spreading the word through the Spanish speaking world and this is a major step along that road.

At the moment all books are only available in paperback but we are working on creating e-books, which include *The Moment That Matters* and its German translation *Indras Netz*, *Loving Who Shows Up* and its Spanish version *Amar lo se que Dé* and *First Aid*.

Many thanks to Alicia Arnold Martin in Mexico City for her wonderful translation of *Loving Who Shows Up* and Patricia Wallenburg, currently of Atlanta, GA, for her incredible support designing the new books.

GOING GLOBAL

I have just heard that the print on demand company I use to print *First Aid*, and now *Amar lo se que Dé…* is opening shop in Australia. Good news for the Australians as it will cut down on the cost of the postage to you. And soon all books will be available as print on demand as well as e-books, so more accessibility globally.

COMMUNITY—THE KEY TO CHANGE

My recent experience in Tuscany only confirmed the value of these week long residential programs. And the need to establish a better global support network.

As a part of my next move I would like to establish a small centre, a place where people come drop in for a day, a week, or longer, to reconnect with other like minded travelers. This has always been the individuals greatest challenge down the 'clearing' road. When leaving a workshop, be it a week long program or a weekend, each of us returns to the 'old' world and the expectations and conditions associated with that world. It is hard to maintain the energy and clarity of a workshop when all around you have different ideas. The pull back into 'past' is so strong many people find it too hard to continue.

Some people counter this by attending at least two workshops a year, not necessarily to hear the information again, though that always helps, but to reconnect with like minded souls, to reinforce their own change. Others form small communities who meet periodically for 'clearing sessions'.

I would like to see small centres appearing around the world where there are people who are on this path. As pressure to change builds (and remember pressure can only build where there is resistance to change) the need for local support will grow. Never underestimate the power of spending a few days in a non-judgemental environment, the best holiday you can give yourself.

I cannot do this alone and am asking for your help in creating a network of support centres around the world. This can be a small, personal venture, you may have a spare room in your house and would welcome the opportunity to have someone come stay for a day or two, to reconnect. You may know of other properties that would suit a larger gathering. I am thinking about establishing a not for profit company to allow those who can to contribute towards the creation of such places around the world. I will support as I am able, traveling around the world and training those who would staff these centres. This is a community effort. If you would like to be a part of this please let me know.

Another Day, Another Thought

> Since all things are naked, clear and free
> from obscuration, there is nothing to attain
> or realise, the every day practice is simply
> to develop a complete acceptance and openness
> to all things and to all people so that one never
> withdraws or centralises onto oneself.

THERE REALLY IS NOTHING MORE TO SAY. I HAVE SPENT years saying this in different ways, approaching it from one 'point of view' and then another but when all is said and done, this is it.

I think one reason why I have spent a lot of my writing time going over and over this is that the concept is so 'alien' to our collective way of being that we have little or no practice of this approach to life. No practice and perhaps no reason either. I see many people caught in the busy-ness of life, not particularly interested in accepting 'all things....' Sometimes quietly, sometimes not, going about the business of living a life on planet earth, people get lost in the demands of the day where there is no time or interest in extras. We often fail to question most things, we accept things are as they are. We accept the 'truths' handed down to us by our parents, by society. We accept the written word, simply because it is written and those who came before us accepted it.

It appears to be enough, for most people, to accept the information handed down to them without questioning. I don't think this 'acceptance' is what is meant in the quote above. Thee quote refers to an acceptance of all things. No exceptions. Most of us have a limited range of what we are able to accept, our conditioning by the society we were raised in, our belief in what we have been told, our need for something to believe in all serve to restrict what we are able to accept. Even when we do question what we have been told, the questioner is still limited by their expectations.

The difficulty with total acceptance is that we have our own ideas of right and wrong and cannot accept that which we believe to be wrong, and rightly so. For me the acceptance is more of an internal process, I wrote about this in *Loving Who Shows Up* (*Amar lo que se Dé* in Spanish). By accepting all feelings and emotions with equanimity the 'charge' that we hold around certain issues and emotions gradually falls away.

IS YOUR RECEIVER OPERATING AT FULL CAPACITY?

I particularly like Dr. Bruce Lipton's comments about becoming aware on a cellular level. When the thousands of receptor sites on the membrane of the cell are dominated by one or more specific frequencies, then there is little room left on the membrane for other, more varied frequencies. This can be likened to your TV before cable. You were limited in what information (programs) you could receive, even with cable you get what you pay for! The attention of whatever you focused upon in the past, consciously or more likely sub-consciously, has limited the programs you are now able to tune into. No sports receptors, no sports programs. No 'Jazz' receptors, no interest in 'Jazz'. No 'spiritual receptors' no interest in spirituality (I simplify of course). So then it doesn't matter what questions you ask, if you don't have the receptors you won't even be asking the question, the questions you do ask will be limited to the information you are picking up. A real 'Catch 22' situation. And around you go.

As those who have the necessary receptors that allow them to even be interested in accepting all things and all people begin such a journey (and 'clearing' is all about supporting that journey, making it easier to both understand and attain) the variety of receptor sites shift (remember *What the Bleep* when the cell divides there are more receptor sites on the 'sister' cells for that which we have given our attention) creating a more aware cell. Thee broader the range of receptor sites, the more self aware the cells becomes. As within—so without.

Without the required receptor sites much information is not even on your radar. Most of us give our attention to the basic survival skills because that is where our focus has been in the past. We are conditioned by our parents and society, as they were conditioned by theirs, the buck is handed down through the generations and little really changes. Because we cannot give our attention to anything else. Simple.

Yet when we practice clearing we are practicing accepting, when we practice acceptance the addiction to old conditions falls away, more space on the cell membrane becomes available for different receptors, we receive a broader range of information, which in turn, allows us to accept more. The more we accept the more variety of frequencies on the cell the more self aware we become.

I suspect the biggest challenge in acceptance is the deeply rooted belief that we are our emotions and our feelings, and our thoughts. While we believe this to be the case we are caught in internal conflict. The simple fact that we judge one emotion as being better, or worse, than another keeps us in a state of inner tension. If it is peace we are looking for then it has to begin within.

IDENTIFYING

Sub-consciously we all identify with certain beliefs and expectations. This behaviour allows us to 'collect' energetic charges that exist within this sea of consciousness in which we exist (why do some places tire you out more than others?) Like a magnet attracting metal objects we attract charge that supports who we believe we are (sub-consciously). These charges accumulate and create further problems; ill health, stressful situations etc., in our future.

For those of you practicing the clearing you may have noticed when you first clear a person, and in the first few sessions, there is a lot of energy being released. If you work on that same person every day, soon the release reduces until it is hardly noticeable. This is because the main charge, once released, takes time to build up again, you may also have noticed that the longer between clearing sessions, the 'more' shows up to be cleared.

With regular clearing the charge will not build to its original intensity, this allows the system to settle, to relax and begin to change, on a deep level. When stress is not allowed to build other possibilities are allowed to manifest.

So, a clearing a day keeps the stress away.

Ponder This

CHANGE—NEEDED, OR NOT?

I don't think there is any doubt that we live in times of great change. Depending upon when you were born you will remember different things, but even the younger readers will have seen change in their time on planet earth.

Television, I can remember the early black and white models. Now you get full colour TV and films on your cell phone! Cell phones, remember when they were the size and weight of a house brick! Technology has come a long way in a few years, no telling where it is going to stop, if it ever does.

Perhaps a shame that humanity has not evolved as rapidly, we still behave much as we have always done, at least we do if historical records are to be believed. Certainly advances in the arts, in science, medicine, but not much in the way we treat each other and the planet that we live on. There are of course exceptions to any 'rules'. But when evolution to some means more legislation, more rules, stronger borders simply because the few want to continue to exploit the many, well that's hardly evolution. There's nothing new in that, things haven't changed for a long time.

I use the image, in workshops, of a brown paper bag. When we are born we all get a brown paper bag put over our heads. The amount of light that gets through the brown paper depends upon the 'charge' each individual brings in with them. The more charge, the less 'light'. With this brown paper bag on our heads, we are fed a diet of history, basically 'fairy tales'. We are told how things have been, and because our parents were fed much the same diet, how things are. We 'learn' how to relate to manifesting reality and we support that reality by adding our belief to that of our parents, siblings, and the social expectations of the time. We unconsciously adopt the judgments and values of the society in which we grow, we may 'rebel' against certain conditions and expectations, but our very polarisation supports the old model because we assume that the old model is 'real' and needs to be changed.

This has been happening for millennia. Rebellion, revolution, conflict, to change one system and replace it with another. *If* everyone got a brown paper bag at birth then we have to ask: "Who is trying to change what?" It seems as though to become a politician a pre-requisite is a serious brown paper bag. If it weren't for your own brown paper bag you would never trust a person with a more serious brown paper bag to lead you out of danger.

The desire may arise within us to change things, does this mean we should swap our paper bag for another one? If brown paper bags are a bit hard to accept, try little carpet squares. Plain ones, fancy ones, welcoming ones, dirty ones, silk ones, rag ones, patterned ones, plain ones, get the picture? You are born, for whatever reason on a particular carpet square. This is your world, your life, you accept this (the social conditioning, political history etc) as being the way things are. Later you might question some of the beliefs, but remember you question them from the point of view of the carpet, so you are already biased and limited in what answers you may find. So, what do you do, renovate the carpet, add on a garage, weave a few more threads into the carpet to make it larger, or just trade the old one in and go looking for a new one (commonly experienced as death of the physical body). Ever try carpet jumping while you are still alive? Very unsettling.

NOW WHO AM I?

According to certain beliefs, the Merkaba, or light vehicle is arranged in a certain way, one way for male, one for female. When we checked this on a gay friend of mine, it was 'reversed' which wasn't really surprising. Realising the co creative nature of who we are, we changed it, with his agreement. He lasted two days, the 'new' reality was just too weird. So we become accustomed to the reality we are born into, we empower it on a daily basis, as we do this we are energising the opposite, for how can we know ourselves if there is no mirror to reflect that which we are not!

I 'think' that the reason evolution of humanity is caught in the current cycle of systems collapse countered by more legislation and control, is because to 'dream a new dream' someone has to have the vision. From what I understand, those with the 'vision' still have brown paper bags on their heads. They are no more able to dream a new dream outside of their current piece of carpet than anyone else is.

We approach 2012, darr dumm, darrr dummm, darrr dummmm (an attempt at the music from *Jaws*) I have been asked what do I think, or believe about this upcoming, 2012 winter solstice event. In a few words, I don't. Perhaps a part of me hopes for cosmic intervention but, that is not something to bank on, mind you, finding a trustworthy bank could be a bigger issue. I have heard a lot of stories about 2012, a lot of projections, some positive, others less so. I cannot helping remembering though that the projectionists all have brown paper bags on their heads.

A bit of a joke really. Next time you go to the shop/store imagine seeing everyone with a brown paper bag on their head, ha. And then remember that you are seeing everyone through your own brown paper bag, ha ha... Then look at those who are in your government, and see the brown paper bags. It just goes on and on. Who can see where they are going?

EXCUSE ME, IS THIS YOUR BROWN PAPER BAG?

So, assume everyone has a brown paper bag over their head, remember there are exceptions to every rule. Part of the brown paper bag concept is that you are the only person without one, ha ha ha.... For change to arise we need to work at making holes in the bag, something to let more light in, something to allow us to see 'more'. Work is probably not the right word, but it will do for the moment because those within the bag always feel the need to 'do' something. How do we do that? A little like the dog chasing its tail, round and round we go, trying to change something that we have given so much energy to that it has become 'real'. The more energy we give to anything, the more 'real' it becomes.

I am noticing, through the support network that I am currently establishing for fellow travelers wanting to trade in their old brown paper bag, that the longer the period between 'clearings' the more charge builds up. Charge can be seen as energy empowered by conceptions, beliefs, judgements, emotional conditioning. The 'Clearing' can release the charge, so I (or whoever the 'clearer' may be) can facilitate the release of charge from another. After a 'clearing' the individual feels much more at peace with themselves, more energised. But one clearing is often not sufficient to actually change the cellular memory, (the old carpet will pull you back to 'reality', its reality, not of course the bigger picture. So, having been slowly, unconsciously, pulled back, the old charge builds again. If there is no 'clearing' for this charge it will express, either externally, creating difficulties with others around you, or internally, creating imbalance in your physical or emotional health.

With regular and frequent clearing the charge never builds, when the charge doesn't build, the individual gradually finds themselves in a very different place, a more peaceful place, a more relaxed state. When the individual is not under self imposed pressure, they begin to feel 'safe', their system can relax, when they are relaxed they can begin to see and understand things differently, perhaps then, they can dream a new dream. Who knows?

Did You Know?

ABANDON HOPE?

Have you any thoughts on what could happen on the Winter Solstice in 2012 (the end (??) of the Mayan Calender???) Has anyone asked you what you think? They have asked me, many times.

My answer: 'I have no idea whatsoever, nor do I spend time imagining what could possibly happen'. I might have some wishful thoughts, but recognise them for what they are—in no way related to what is really going down at the end of 2012.

Some people would have us believe it has already happened, the accuracy of the timing is open to interpretation. Well, if it has happened, then it must have happened at night wherever I was because I slept through it.

I think the big issue here, as in all issues, is just who is interpreting the data? Who is looking for what? And where are they looking? And perhaps, why are they looking. Many of us have come to realise that you find what you are looking for, the simple act of looking affects the outcome of any 'study'. If this is true, that the observer affects the outcome, again we come back to who is actually observing, who is it who is affecting the outcome. If we all came to observe the possible events of solstice 2012, would we all see the same outcome? Well, it seems obvious that is not the case, there are so many differing interpretations, so many differing points of view.

I don't think most of us can get past our hopes and fears, all of which is based upon our past, conditioning, experiences, preferences etc., We project, based upon our limited understanding, a future, which must arise out of our past. Meaning, whatever we associated with, identified with or judged in the past, created the personality through whose eyes we 'see' the world. So of course, my 'past' is different to your past, so I see the 'future' differently than you do. Who, if anyone, is right? Well of course, everyone and no one.

The future may well be a product of the past, and may continue to remain so as long as the observers all agree. We are certainly given enough encouragement to continue to believe how the future will unfold, constantly supported by mainstream media, we are led to believe that answers to the present conditions are found in the past, which is carried forward, as though the past really had the answers and there is no alternative. One can only imagine that if the past did indeed have any answers of any value, conditions in the world would by quite different than they are, or as they appear to be. Even the appearance of issues is a product of who is looking, the observer affecting the manifesting reality once again.

DID YOU SEE WHAT I SAW?

I wanted to include this little clip, taken from the movie *What the Bleep* as it describes this approach so well, take a look and then come back to the 'story' here.

http://video.google.com/videoplay?
docid=-4237751840526284618#

We see from the little clip, that simply having an observer affects the outcome, something else might be happening but the observer cannot see it. We are limited to what we can see by our own expectations, and those expectations arise out of our past. Something else is happening but we cannot see it. Maybe many other things are happening, but we cannot see them. We see what we focus on, the more people focusing on 'something' the more 'real' it appears to be.

As an example, several years ago, at a space clearing workshop, one person noticed a transformer atop a power pole, and stood there, looking up and, perhaps, tuning into the energy field of the transformer. Other people, as they passed, stopped to look at the transformer. Soon many people were gathered all tuning into the energy field of the transformer. It was felt, among all those present, that the more people who 'tuned in' the more obvious, or intense were the feelings associated with the energy field of the transformer. So, the more observers the more powerful the effect.

Take a look at religions for example. The more 'followers' the more powerful the religion. Why do leaders of any group want more followers, well perhaps they think they have found 'the way' and wish only to save the rest of us, that is one point of view. Another is that they, the 'leaders' realise the power in numbers (not to mention the financial rewards of a huge following), so, the more followers the more powerful your group becomes.

The more people tuning into the transformer on top of the pole, the stronger the energy of the transformer appears to be. When people give their attention to 'something', no matter what it is, they may empower that 'something'.

A collective holds similar values, similar points of view, so the collective sees the world in unique ways, convinced of the 'rightness' of that view, they want to share it with others, most of whom may have a different point of view, the result, conflict. Nationalism is another example, 'right to life', pro abortion, political parties—all thinking they are right—They all have one thing in common, growing up in an environment that arose out of the past, a past that was created out of a past, supported by individuals who believed what they were told, and passed that belief down to their children, thus perpetuating the same old.

AS I THINK—SO I BECOME

All too abstract for you, well how about your thoughts? We need not go into where your thoughts came from at the moment, but when a thought does 'pop' into your mind, what do you do with it? Hang onto it, run away from it, laugh at it, feel sadness because of it? All sorts of possibilities. A lot of people I know take their thoughts seriously, when you take something seriously, you are giving it a lot of energy. Maybe you try to find out where it came from? Try to find solutions? (That's a big one!) If this happens, then does it follow that 'that' will happen, and if that happens, then I will have to do, or say, this, or, what would happen if I said that instead—get the picture?

Same thing, you give energy to your thoughts, or emotions, and they create your reality. If the personality consists of a whole collection of points of view, all based upon a story it was told by another personality, then that personalities perceptions of the world will be a carry over from past perceptions, even though something else is happening it is not seen (the particle or the wave question) the focus is on a story from the past.

So, if this meandering is true, projections for the winter solstice 2012 have to be based on the perceptions of those reporting on the possibilities. There is one thing I would like to add, perhaps something for you to 'do'. No matter what happens in December 2012, or tomorrow, the practice of compassion is the key to moving through change. Clearing frequently, noticing often and not judging that which you notice helps develop a compassionate heart, when the heart is in alignment, no matter where you are, no matter what happens, you are in the right place. Don't wait for December 2012 to start practicing!

And This!

"WHO DO I BELIEVE?"

Some people we just have trouble believing a word they say, it used to be simple, don't believe anyone from outside of your village. Certainly don't believe someone who spoke a different language, even dialects were suspect, and never ever believe someone from a different religion. And those whose ideology differed from your own, well, they were the enemy, everything they say is lies and propaganda.

Now it is not so easy to 'choose' who to believe, in fact it is becoming increasingly more and more difficult to believe our own leaders. If you have found this to be the case, extend the argument and look at what we read, why should anything that has been written be any different? Why should we accept the written word, simply because it managed to get into print (and survive). The 'truth' is that it isn't different. Everyone tells a story based on their own perceptions—perceptions which are influenced by their environment, their understanding, their beliefs at the time.

We have been imposing our perceptions on others, as they have been imposing theirs upon us, for aeons. Imagine, a time long ago, in the dark and distant past, a time without the Internet, without TV (I can hear the gasps now), no mobile telephones, no telephones at all. No newspapers, no printed word whatsoever, not even smoke signals. Can you imagine that? Hard I know, but try.

ONCE UPON A TIME

In our dark and distant past, there was a village whose water supply had failed, giving only enough for a little drink each day. This village was in a hot part of planet earth, and as you might expect, after a few weeks the population began to smell a little strong.

One day, out of nowhere, a stranger appeared, a stranger with a weird shaped head and funny eyes. This stranger took one breath and realised these people could use a bath. The people weren't so smart, no newspapers remember, and the stranger told them where to dig for a good water supply. The stranger was pretty tall compared to the villagers, and when he/she (the villagers had trouble telling which) looked at you, there was no question of not believing. The villagers found the water, and began bathing regularly so plentiful was the supply of water. Meanwhile the stranger had gone off looking for other villages needing a hand with general hygiene.

Back in the village with the plentiful supply of water, the villagers remembered the stranger differently, depending upon who you spoke with, the response was always a little different. This gave rise to several factions in the village which previously had lived in harmony, if a bit smelly. The factions, over time developed into quite well defined groups, those who thought the stranger was a water diviner, those who thought he/she was just plain lucky, and those who thought he/she was a god.

The different groups each got upset with the other two, how dare you insinuate that our god was just some lucky stranger, or some simple water diviner! How can you expect us to believe that some guy/woman who found water is a god? Do you think being lucky conveys godhead? And so it went.

Time passed, as it does, and the group who thought they had been visited by a god went off in search of their god, after all, if he/she could find water, then maybe they could find food as well, maybe even a little cash to help out now and again. Of the two groups who remained, the water diviners began practicing looking for water, had moderate success and became very popular with the neighbouring villages and eventually made enough money to leave the village and set themselves up as a specialist service in the city, making even more money.

The group who felt the stranger had been lucky stayed in the village, glad that the other two group had left them in peace, because the water supply was beginning to slow down and fewer people meant their luck would last a bit longer. And there they stayed, until their luck, the water, ran out.

More time passed, as it keeps doing, and the 'lucky' people had to break up into smaller groups and go live in the villagers that still had some luck, all the time telling their new neighbours how lucky they were. The water diviners continued to make lots of money. They kept finding water for those who needed it, and could pay, mostly increasing their popularity. They began traveling farther afield in their search for water and more money. Those who felt they had been visited by a god were still on the road. They had split up into smaller groups, they thought they would have a better chance of finding their god if they looked in lots more places.

WHO WAS THAT MASKED MAN?

After some more time, which passed mostly uneventfully, the 'Searchers', now in their own 'sub-groups' developed their own ideas of just what type of god they had been visited

And This!

by. One group thought the water most significant, another thought that the person who had believed and dug the well obviously had a special connection to the god and became a sort of go between, someone you could ask to speak to the god on your behalf. Time continued to work its magic. Members of the original three groups began to write about their experiences, or perhaps it would be more accurate to say, about their remembered experiences. The written word had been discovered and developed by now.

Many generations later, the various followers looked at the books, for printing had also been discovered, but only for 'important' books, no fantasy or science fiction allowed (or so they thought!) And some of those followers had a little trouble reconciling their memories with all that was written.

So, the scholars took upon themselves the task of rewriting the book, cut that bit out about the strange head, and the eyes! Well who had ever seen weird eyes, no one of their generation, so, must have been a fairy story to scare the kids. And while they were cutting that out, what about this bit? And that? Make it a lot easier to understand if this part was rewritten, and so it went.

Time waits for no man, or woman, and marched on. Science exploded onto the scene. The followers of the Great Diviner, for so he/she had become know amongst those very affluent types who found the water were under pressure from the disbelievers, and from the Searchers, the Lucky ones didn't give a hoot, they were enjoying a lucky life. The diviners had discovered more talents along the way and were performing all sorts of 'miracles' which had not been, unfortunately, recorded in the original books, so this was seen as a sort of one upmanship by the searchers and condemned.

The scientific group were getting stronger, so much fun playing with all this stuff, no one knew where it was going, but, hey, who cared, it was fun and there was money to be made.

| And This! |

The searchers ganged up on the diviners, they were thought to have too much money and power to be good neighbours, and really, they were non believers so they deserved to be punished. And punish them they did, for a very long time the diviners were persecuted almost to the point of extinction. That just left the increasingly wealthy science faction in competition with the searchers and laws had to be passed so both could live in relative peace. But always, behind the scenes, each conspired against the other, believing that they and they only had the truth.

With science came radio, TV, telephones. The two main groups quickly discovered the power of the media, the lucky ones operating behind the scenes started buying up as many media outlets as they could, once lucky always lucky. Science and the searchers had to earn lots more now, the cost of using the media was very high, so competition for the money grew.

People had been taking themselves seriously for a long time, so much time had passed that everyone had forgotten about the stranger and the water, all they could see was what was shown on the media, manipulated by the lucky ones, stay lucky or go under was their new motto. Now people were believing what they were told, what they were seeing, what they were taught.

And all because some stranger arrived in a village one day, thought they smelled a bit strong and showed them where to find water, which anyone could have done had they taken the trouble to look. The villagers however, like most members of the human race at that time were pretty lazy folk and were always looking for the path of least resistance!

Believe it or not.

Musings

> You will not be punished for your anger,
> you will be punished by your anger.
> —Shakyamuni Buddha

I SAW THIS ON A CALENDAR AT A FRIENDS, AND THOUGHT TO share my thoughts on what this means to me in this newsletter. Most of us have known the feeling of anger at sometime in our lives, it can take many forms but I suspect always arises from the same place.

We need not limit this to anger—there are many other emotions which can, when expressed inappropriately, or internalised, cause problems in health or relationships with others.

So, where do these feelings come from, and why do some people experience them more than others? I believe that anger is felt when the personalities needs are either not met or are challenged.

In the workshops we discuss how any feeling/emotion that we identify with gains energy to the point where more healthy functions of the body are impaired. By our continued association with any particular point of view that we have either inherited or acquired along the way we appear to need the world to be a certain way in order for us to feel safe, satisfied, valued. Invariably this point of view is in opposition to other points of view so we are constantly challenged, whether we are aware of it or not and have to either make adjustments or 'take a stand' to defend out point of view.

We may have been conditioned socially to not express our feelings, for fear of what others might think of us, we may have been taught to express those emotions no matter what others may think. Or, we may simply lose control and explode in emotional outbursts, unable to manage our own emotional body.

We can see around us people from different countries, different backgrounds, some repress or do not appear to be in touch with their emotions, others seem to be able to express their emotions freely and the third group, the minority, seemingly at peace with the world, will, of a sudden (road rage!) explode, sometimes to the point of violent behaviour. The first group, by not expressing their emotions often internalise them, the result of which is often health issues. The second, those who express freely often create animosity within their society and find it hard to forgive, and the last group in this mini study, experience total loss of control during which anything, including violence, is possible.

TO FEEL IS TO BE ALIVE

Our ability to feel is a very important part of what it means to be 'human', it is through feeling that we experience ourselves. The body has developed as a feeling organism. This 'space suit' of a body we inhabit picks up information, much like a radio and interprets that information, via neural connections which produce neuropeptides, which in turn produce various amino acids which then cascade through the body, which we then interpret as feelings and emotions. It is suggested that the more we identify, or personalise, such feelings and emotions, the more we become, on a sub-conscious level, addicted to those 'chemicals'. This applies to denied feelings and emotions as well, the more we deny something, the denial of which arises out of judgment which in itself is often based on fear (of the unknown!), the more energy we are giving to that emotion. Those emotions may not present or manifest obviously in our lives, they can be very subtle, but they are like a time bomb, ticking away in the background, creating their own form of chaos, until, given the right stimuli, explode.

So feeling is not really the issue here, without feeling we would not be able to relate to the world at all. Rather it is the misguided belief that we are those feelings. That they belong to us, and by that continued identification, become 'ours'.

Like the radio picking up signals, the body picks up information, like the radio the body interprets that information, unlike the radio though, we believe the product of the internal chemical reaction belongs to us. The radio is under no such delusion, it is simply the device that picks up and interprets signals. Which in fact is all the body is, a device that picks up and interprets signals.

By our identification with emotions, we tend to, subconsciously, create more of the chemicals associated with those emotions, thus generating an even more intense feeling/emotion. The more we believe ourselves to be 'angry' (for example) the more 'angry we become. The more angry we become the more chemicals that are identified with anger we create in our body. These chemicals are not particularly healthy, in fact they can and often do cause considerable dis-ease.

If the body, without conscious effort, produces a lot of the chemicals that we call 'anger' then there is less ability, within the body, to produce more life enhancing chemicals, this is one down side of identifying with and creating more chemicals associated with anger, the loss of the ability to produce a healthy body. The other downside is that the chemical of 'anger' creates, within the body, a flight or flight response to a situation. Essentially this condition diverts the blood from the viscera, the vital organs in the body, into the muscles of the arms and legs, preparing us to fight, or run away. There may be times this is appropriate, but more often than not it is a self generated response, based on a misunderstanding (that the chemically created feeling belongs to us!)

PRO LIFE—ANTI LIFE?

Every time the blood is diverted away from the viscera, the body dies a little. It is in a survival state, even though that survival state is often not appropriate. So, internally, we can well begin to imagine what our identifying with the chemicals of anger is doing to the body.

If you get 'angry' with someone, effectively because your perceived needs are not being met, that person may react in anger, whether that anger is expressed or internalised, it doesn't matter, the internal effects are the same. This results in your body being inundated with what are essentially toxic chemicals. Your anger generates a response/reaction in another person, and, while they too identify with the chemicals as being theirs, create a toxic internal environment in their own body. This release of toxic chemicals creates an unpleasant feeling, the more we identify with this unpleasantness, the more we create.

This is one of the ways that we are punished *by* our anger, the internal, destructive nature, of the chemicals associated with anger. The other is when we identify with anger and express it, we cause stress, not just in our own lives, the lives of those around us, but also our environment. My experience in 'space clearing' has shown that our environment is very responsive to the energy of those living in it. The more angry/stressed we become, the more the environment reflects that back to us. This has the effect of creating an 'external' state that then supports our perceptions that 'we' are 'angry' making it more difficult to stop identifying with the anger/stress, whatever.

An answer? Recognise what identification with anger is doing to your body, notice when you feel you are becoming angry and then, to the best of your ability, don't go there. Do whatever it takes to 'change' your mind, stop energising the more destructive emotions. Easier said than done? That's why there are workshops offering you an opportunity to put this into practice.

Remember, keep practicing, there will always be anger around in this world while people identify with it, if you lose yourself in anger, you are part of the global problem. Learn to be that which you seek in the world.

Something to Think About!

SUSTAINABILITY

WHEN OUR MANIFESTING REALITY SHIFTS, PRIMARILY because it had been built on a non sustainable foundation, what do we do? When it appears as though forces outside our control are shaping our destiny and that direction runs contrary to our deepest desires, what can we do?

Fundamental to our personal view of the world are the unique ways we all have of identifying ourselves. Our language, nationality, job, religion, friends, foes, hairstyle, lifestyle, the car we drive, our likes and our dislikes all contribute to how we picture ourselves and our 'place' in the world.

These are all aspects that we have either inherited or acquired along the way. Through the process of association with the body we mistakenly assume that the feelings experienced by the body belong to us (when in actual fact they are simply chemicals cascading through the body, the result of an interaction with an 'external' stimulus, which produce, within the body, that which we call a 'feeling').

The more we identify with the phenomena that is a product of this chemical process the more we become addicted to those chemicals, (remember, this is happening on a sub-conscious level) the more addicted we become the more the body demands its fix. Our personal world is the creation of our expectations, the majority of which are sub-conscious, this sub-conscious drive would be the result of the inherited patterns and those patterns subsequently acquired as a result of the foundational inherited conditioning.

And you thought you were free to choose your path! Any 'freedom of choice' only exists within the conditioned parameters of your inherited and acquired conditioning. At least it does while you are still a victim to that past conditioning.

For most people the choice is what to have for breakfast, assuming there is a choice and even any breakfast to be had, what clothes to wear for the day, assuming there are clothes to choose from. Essentially we are choosing from conditioned options available within the greater illusion of our perceived reality. This is not freedom of choice, this is habitual behaviour. Don't fool yourself, and don't let others fool you either.

Waking up from the illusion—the dream time—that we inhabit can be sudden, and may lead to psychotic episodes, or it can be gentle. There is little choice, your manifesting reality being self created, self supported and clung onto for dear life is in itself the limiting factor. The more you cling the more energy you give to an anxious future, fear of the unknown keeps most people happily asleep.

SO, WHAT HAS THIS TO DO WITH SUSTAINABILITY?

Any reality requires a certain amount of energy to sustain it. The difficulty arises when the internal reality/expectations do not match with the manifesting reality. This situation will arise when the internal self is in conflict, we saw in the workshops, how the blood samples taken from a random group of people all showed significant signs of internal conflict.

Internal conflict arises, again, from inherited and acquired conditioning.

Through the process of continued identification with phenomena we learn early on to judge some information/feelings as good and some as bad. This 'judgement' leads to a polarised state, a state within which we seek out the 'good' and deny the 'bad'. The more judgmental we become, the more polarised we are. The more polarised we are the more we exist in a state of internal conflict.

When there is internal conflict the 'external' world will reflect that which only serves to add to our state of inner conflict Because we continually find ourselves trying to 'do' something about the manifesting reality we end up spending all our time in damage control mode. The more we try and 'fix' the external, the more energy we give it, the harder it becomes to 'fix' anything. This is truly a non sustainable path. People are wearing themselves out in pursuit of something, perhaps called happiness, or security, in an illusion that, because of its very nature, cannot provide these things.

If your old, often unrecognised, conditioning is sabotaging your desires your reality is not sustainable, you will use all of your energy trying to create 'the perfect world' (from your perspective) and achieve little because your 'shadow' will always undermine your efforts. When your internal state is at peace, then, simply by being, your reality will shift into a more sustainable, peaceful manifestation.

So! How to achieve inner peace, well I would suggest you develop your clearing practice, as often as you can throughout the day, notice what you are feeling, recognise it for what it is, a conditioned reaction producing chemicals in the body, and stop giving it energy.

Easier said than done, especially when you are even more 'lost' in the drama than usual, but if you do not begin, then progress is unlikely. Don't be put off by imaging the big stuff confronting you, start with issues that you are not so attached too, those that generate a less intense feeling. 'Clearing,' after all, is not about emptying the back pack as much as it is about changing your relationship to the stuff in the back pack.

And this is the time to practice, no putting this off till tomorrow, there is no mañana, if you fail to practice now, as the pressure builds it will be harder and harder to see beyond the conditioned reality.

I once described the process of the death of the physical body in terms of sailing in a boat. While we are alive we feel we have some control over the direction we go in, a steady hand on the tiller, (though remember your freedom to choose directions is a product of your personal history). When you die the boat (your consciousness) no longer responds to your control and you are at the mercy of the winds and the tides, a metaphor for all the unloved parts of the self, the emotions and feelings you were identifying with up to the point of death. Where will your attachments take you?

CHANGE = ?

I don't think there is any question that we are living in interesting times, the problem is, 'interesting times' often means rapid change to old systems as they, being unsustainable in the first place, fall away. I have heard so many people tell me they are ready for change, but this is, apparently, not true, they may spend a lot of time talking about change but as far as real change goes. When we are ready for change, change arises.

People may want change, but are often unwilling to pay the price of change which requires releasing attachment to old concepts of self. Perhaps though, our hand will be forced, as we are live in a fast changing world, anytime we think we have a handle on it, it changes, the goal posts move and we are left wondering what happened. The old and familiar is no longer there to support the old way of being.

I suspect the reason we find this so uncomfortable and challenging is because we are always wanting to be somewhere else, with someone else, in a different job, different country, different reality, all the time looking for that elusive state of peace, of happiness, of wealth, of fulfillment. We notice the things in our manifesting reality that confront us, we take those more seriously than the parts that are in harmony, we give energy to the conflict and wonder why we are discontent.

To develop the ability to simply 'be' in the moment, no past, no future, does not mean that you will continue to allow chaos to manifest in your life, accepting the chaos as it arises (no longer continuing to energise it) will allow it to fall away. There will be birth pains for sure, because your established way of being is challenged, but if you can ride those waves the future will be very different, a future you cannot even imagine. And don't try to imagine it, you'll create it, and if you are still imagining from a place of discontent, well, no prizes for guessing what sort of reality you are going to create.

And This!

SEE NO EVIL , HEAR NO EVIL, SPEAK NO EVIL

Okay, where do we start. First, what does the word 'evil' mean, well you can look in many places and find variations, but basically these few words are common descriptions: morally bad; harmful; causing misfortune; malicious (Wow, that covers a lot of ground).

We, as a society, normally associate 'evil' with obvious acts, as defined by the words above. Things we see, things we hear about, things we personally judge as fitting into the category of evil. But what about the less obvious acts, those that go by other names, are we even aware of such acts, or is the smokescreen of 'might is right' so strong we don't even notice these things?

Imagine, two ideologies, each believing it is right, which, by their own standards, are 'evil.' If one ideology feels threatened by the other, or needs the resources possessed by the other, of just plain doesn't like the other, the first thing to do is label the other as 'evil.' This will guarantee support among the respective population. Meanwhile, the 'other' is doing the same, and labeling the other as 'evil' thereby gaining support among its own population.

So, we have two quite different ideologies, each believing 'god' is on their 'side' (just how many 'gods' are there? I know certain cultures have many sub-gods, but really?) and the other 'side' is 'evil.' As we are now fighting 'evil' then we are allowed, morally, to use any way to combat it. Those ways we employ, according to the above definition, are in themselves often evil. So we justify our behaviour by the labeling of the other as evil. The whole world does this in greater or lesser ways.

On a more personal level, our own judgements, often handed down to us by parents, society, organisations, become entrenched in our perceptions and allow us to happily commit acts which would, in another society, be defined as evil.

WHAT A MESS

Imagine, growing up in a house, on a street, in a town in some country somewhere in the world. Most of us did that. We were born into a household that had certain values, which were passed down from those who came before, and these values are embedded in us, with or without our awareness, often without. We end up carrying a torch of personal righteousness that came from someone else, who in their turn ended up carrying the torch of personal righteousness, which was handed down to them ... and so it goes.

We may have friends across the street, they may go to the same school as us, assuming we went to school. We share certain beliefs, the street, the town, the language, the school, the social environment, but at home, well our home is different because it is ours, we are 'special'. Just the way of things. In our town we have a sports team, which is also special. Now, the town on the other side of the hill, which also believes it is special, and that their sports team is really special. And now and again the two teams play against each other.

Now, as teams develop in a world that is pretty much dominated by money, good players are demanding more money. The team with more money can buy better players. The more 'better' players your team has the more people will come watch you and support you, each paying lots of money to see the game, so money begets money. (Don't lose sight of the bigger picture here, the 'sports game' is only a metaphor for the bigger 'game'). The more supporters each 'game' has the more powerful that team becomes. As we each subscribe to a particular team (sports, political, religious, environmental, whatever) the more energy we give to that team.

If we are convinced that our 'team' is right, then someone else's team has, by definition to be wrong or of lesser value (keep this thread going and evil is not so far away, though I have yet to hear of a football team being called evil!! Not yet anyway… But remember a sports team is still only an example). It stands to reason then, if any organisation is to become more powerful, gain more control, it must have an enemy, and the more 'evil' that enemy, the more supporters it gains. For example, the Crusades, way back, not the more recent ones!! Gather an army, at the request of a leading religious organisation and go off to fight the evil occupiers of a land. The occupiers of the land gather an army, at the request of a leading religious organisation, and fight the evil invaders. The more evil the opponent the more justified the invasion.

LIFE, AS WE SEEM TO KNOW IT, IS TRULY CRAZY

We may not think we support an 'evil' ideology, but that is only because we are delusional, believing what we are told by those we have come to accept as right. Yet, as long as we are divided internally, polarised and controlled to a large extent by shadow aspects of ourselves, aspects that have yet to be brought into the light—we are as responsible for the continued conflict as anyone else.

| And This! |

'Clearing' offers a way out of judgment, a way of being in the present without the past controlling the future. By practicing noticing, by developing awareness, by understanding the nature of thoughts and feelings, emotional or physical, we can free our selves from the game of good versus evil. In doing so we can reduce the conflict, firstly within us, and subsequently without.

A Piece to Start the Day

WHAT *IS* IMPORTANT TO YOU?

'Clearing' is not just something to do now and again when we are particularly stressed, it is a way of life, that, if followed and practiced regularly, and frequently, will lead to a very different state of being. The many benefits are beyond most people's imaginations simply because most people are locked into certain perceptions, a result of their past, and they cannot see outside of the box that has been created. This is just how it is, neither good nor bad, right nor wrong.

However, for those who do practice often, the results become more and more obvious. It is inherent in clearing, that, as we work clearing the energies of others or the environment, in reality we are embracing more and more of the otherwise hidden (shadow/back-pack) aspects of ourselves. With this embracing we change on a very deep level, perhaps only a little at a time, but, continue the practice and change becomes obvious.

Yet it is always difficult to notice the change because we have become the change, and it is not so easy to always be objective about our own drama. As we change, on a cellular level, and the body begins the journey of healing and becoming more self aware, our perceptions shift, some points of view that we held are no longer quite so important, we

| A Piece to Start the Day |

develop more spaciousness inside, which in turn leads to a greater sense of peace. With this shift comes an increased ability to see more, to understand more, to hear more, to be more without getting quite so lost in the story.

And it seems to be the story that is important here, why people have less time for philosophising. It is because the most important thing we can think of is the story, the drama that, because of conditioning, we take so seriously. We try to discover ways to make the story more comfortable, more healthy, more abundant, and in the early days of the practice of clearing, this seems to be what it is all about. To make the story easier, less stress, less worry, less conflict.

How many people studied space clearing with me intending to apply it to some aspect of their lives whereby they could make money? And how many just did it to learn about their environment, do something for themselves and their family? Maybe a piece of both? How many people attend self development courses designed to break free from the past? I once heard Dr. Deepak Chopra say that only 5% of workshop attendees followed through. What happened to the other 95%? I guess they went off looking for something that they felt they still needed.

Everybody, well almost everybody, is looking for something, be it a roof over their head, the next meal, a relationship, more money, more clients, spiritual progress, whatever. And all the time 'we' are looking, we look for the things that we imagine would make us happy, safe, at peace, the very nature of which is illusory. So what is it we hope to find? Given the fact that we are so involved in our personal drama it can only be something that meets the demands of the personal drama. And philosophising is not high on the list for most.

So, back to the grass roots level of clearing. What is it you want? (Do you even know?) What feelings arise when you think of this thing/person/place? Remember, clearing is about noticing, understanding and not identifying with that which you notice, not taking it personally, not denying the feeling nor judging the feeling, simply noticing. Sounds easy, just try it!

Clear the feelings that arise. Most feelings arise because of a build up of energy/charge in the system, a result of past conditioning. Notice how you feel when the feeling has been cleared, the charge dissipated. Do you still want whatever it was you thought you wanted when you began noticing? If so, notice the next feelings, and so on.

WE ALL WANT SOMETHING!!!

We all want something (most of us anyway) yet what we want is very often more of something that we believe will make us happy/content. Yet when we clear all of the feelings associated with that desire, we find that perhaps we didn't want that in the first place, 'that' has been replaced by something else, well, clear the feelings around the something else, and see what arises then.

It appears to be natural, that we desire that which will make us happy, and we spend much of our lives in pursuit of that happiness, or settle into a compromise. If Dr. Bruce Lipton was correct when he said that of our consciousness, only 3.5% (or thereabouts) was truly conscious. The rest, automatic pilot would not be far from the truth, though Lipton did not say that. So, who is making the decisions, who is desiring 'something'? How can you be sure which part of you it is? The conscious 3.5%, or the unconscious 96.5%!

Have you ever noticed that when you got something that you thought was going to make you happy, the happy state doesn't last too long? And then it is something else, a later model, a different colour, more/less. And so it goes. This is particularly true of relationships. Want one? Get one! (or not!!) and after the honeymoon, well, there is a can of worms you weren't expecting, not always of course, but you get the sense of where I am going with this.

Most people's desires are insatiable, they just keep on and on, due, I suspect to inherited patterns, which were then reinforced in early childhood. As we are not yet able to turn the clock back, we cannot 'make things right' from the past. What clearing can do though, is to reduce the intensity of the charge around old conditions. As the charge reduces, and you stop feeding it, the need for whatever it was that you thought you needed also falls away. And then what?

Well, you won't know till you get there, so don't be asking me, clear clear clear. And find out for yourself.

Sleep on This One

UNDER PRESSURE?

It seems that many people are under quite a lot of pressure lately, nothing new there really, just coming to my attention more these days.

Pressure builds as a result of many factors, financial is a big one, for in todays society, financial security seems to be the key to peace/happiness/safety. Of course, it doesn't matter how much money you have you can still get sick, and you will die, sooner or later, just the same as everyone else.... No matter who you think are, you still have to share the road. No matter where you think you might be going, you still have to share the journey. Doesn't matter how much money you have, you still have to share the planet.

Pressure can also arise from health issues, from relationships, from responsibilities, you can probably think of other sources of pressure. Anxiety would be another big one, though it may not be seen as the cause for a pressure build up, when the body becomes anxious, pressure builds. Anger, how about anger? What happens when you get angry? Pressure that has built is released, often in unhealthy ways because it leads to more conflict, which in turn allows more pressure to build up, and, steam needs to be vented.

Imagine a pressure cooker with a faulty valve, there is a limited amount of water in the cooker and when heat is applied, the water turns to steam, but cannot escape, so pressure builds up. That's the problem in a nutshell, if energy is contained in a small space—pressure cooker or human body, and there is no release valve, watch out, an 'ex', or 'im' plosion is about to happen. We know that when pressure builds and we explode, we often 'vent' our feelings, this just means we are expressing the result of a build up of energy/information. We can just as easily implode, meaning we fail to express so we internalise, this often leads to serious health issues.

Looks like there is no winner here. If we 'explode' not only those around us get 'hurt' but we pollute our body. Getting angry with someone is like drinking poison and expecting the other person to die…. Bit of a joke really, and the joke is on the person getting angry! If we internalise, and implode, then by putting a lid on our feelings, we are just shutting off the release valve and building even more pressure inside, the results of which have to be obvious.

The human body has ways of dealing with stressful situations, and that can often mean the production of a lot of adrenalin. When the stressful situation is over, assuming the body survives, then the body needs to get rid of the adrenalin because it is quite toxic, it has served its purpose but cannot remain in the body without causing harm. Getting angry is the same; feeling as though you are under pressure is the same; getting anxious is the same; all produce various chemicals in the body which are good for certain situations, but when the situation passes, need to be released and the body brought back into a more calm and peaceful state.

HANGING ONTO THE PAST

It is our rather misguided ability to hang onto the past that perpetuates the build up of chemicals in the body that are not always appropriate. I wrote a while back about research on the polar bear. When faced with, what seemed like a life threatening situation, it 're-lived' the stressful situation and rewrote the script so that it came through the stress, survived, with no trauma, almost no memory of the stressful situation. It did not 'carry' the stress into its future. Unlike most humans I know who carry all sorts of trauma with them wherever they go.

Pressure can also be seen as resistance. Resistance to the flow of information. What does that mean? Resistance to the flow of information? I have often used the analogy of a spider's web. Early morning the spider's web is new, uncluttered, no dead or dying insects, no debris. A gentle wind—read emotional charge in the environment, caused by??? a person sending out particular emotional signals—passes through the spider's web with no resistance. The spider's web may shake gently as it acknowledges the passing of the emotional charge, but quickly settles. As the day wears on, 'stuff' gets stuck to the web, twigs, leaves, insects, whatever. Later in the day, when a similar emotional charge passes through the environment of the spider's web, because of all the debris on the web, the web shakes quite violently and takes a lot longer to settle down after the passing of the charge.

This is due to the resistance generated by the debris. The human body is the same, only the debris in the case of the human body consists of the individuals attachment to conditioned 'points of view'. If we hold, consciously or otherwise, onto a point of view that is in conflict with the point of view of another, then our spider's web is going to shake and shudder, charge will be generated and at some point, will need to be expressed (or denied!). The body will take time to settle after conflict, like the spider's web takes time to settle after a charge passes through its environment while there is debris on the web.

We can use pressure build up to show us where we hold onto a point of view. We would need to catch that moment quickly though if we are even considering letting go of the point of view, leave it too long and the chemicals flood the body giving us no choice but to react. Many people, lost in the point of view, cannot conceive of letting go of their points of view, for without them who are they? You might spend years, lifetimes, developing points of view in order to define yourself, and all the while dealing with the conflict the generate in you and among those around you. And all the time paying the price of this addiction, either internally—creating even more chemical imbalance, or externally—dealing with the results of the conflicting points of view.

Until we can see that our 'point of view' whatever it may be, is of no more importance than any other 'point of view', we will remain victim to pressure build up and all its associated phenomena. Until we understand that letting go of an attachment to a point of view doesn't mean you become 'pointless', we will continue to stand fast in the image we have built of ourselves and face the consequences. One day you might question, "is it worth it"?

Another Day, Another Thought

HAUNTED BY YOUR PAST?

Do you have any 'ghosts' in your closets? Not real ghosts, though I have met a few people who do, though perhaps ghosts is still not the right word, demons might be a better word. Yes. Personal demons, not the sort you see in the movies, nothing as obvious or scary as that, but demons none the less.

I read, in a poem by the Greek, Constantine Cavafy, about personal demons, he called them 'Cyclops' (one-eyed giants), 'Poseidon' (god of the sea and earthquakes) and the 'Lestrygonians' (giant cannibals—now there's a bedtime story for the kids!!), all characters from Greek mythology. Briefly, he wrote that you would never find such as these on your path if your thoughts remain lofty, if a fine emotion touches your spirit and your body. You will never encounter these personal 'demons' if you do not carry them in your soul, if your soul does not set them up before you.

Nice to know, eh!

But how many people can claim, from way back, to have been able to maintain a state where lofty thoughts abound and where fine emotions touch the spirit and body. No little lapses along the way!

The 'stuff' that haunts us often arises from situations where we have reacted and done or said something seemingly in the heat of the moment. These words or deeds remain a part of our history, and possibly because those words or deeds created ill will, anger, fear or pain in another the memory just won't leave us in peace. We may be able to jam the ghost into the closet, along with all the others, and hold the door shut. But, sure as the chicken follows the egg (or does the egg follow the chicken!) those demons will escape at times to arise in your mind and take you back to the moment, and the feelings associated with the moment, to remind you that this memory is, in a way, unfinished business.

And there is nowhere to hide, you can only keep that closet door closed so long before the pressure bursts it open, and then how do you think you are going to be able to deal with the flood of memories that may well overwhelm you.

On my personal journey there have been many times when memories of past events return, with associated emotions, creating feelings of discomfort in me, at first I would just fling them back in the closet and firmly close the door, but this did not make them go away, not really, it was just a delaying tactic.

JUST HOW MUCH OF A CHOICE DO WE REALLY HAVE?

Firstly, I don't think most of us had a choice in how we dealt with the original situation, we are, like all others, subject to the patterns we were born with, that we were born into and those we acquired along the way. Points of view, judgments, 'values' etc. Even if we can think before we speak or act, that thinking is limited to our personal experiences and perceptions and is often not rational at all. We are who we are, we do what we do, we say what we say. We may regret saying something but only regret it because it continues to taunt us from the closet and will not leave us in peace. If the memory left us in peace, then there would be little or no charge around the original situation, and therein lies the answer.

We cannot undo the past, returning to the moment where we did or said something that we have since come to realise is going to haunt us but we can begin to face up to that past. If we simply jam the ghost back into the closet, and many still do because they don't have a choice, we are doing many things. One; we are keeping buried a part of ourselves that needs to be healed (why else would it keep showing up?). Two; because the buried emotion often consists of the more 'negative' or destructive feelings, those feelings, as chemicals in the body, are slowly poisoning the body. Three; past events colour our perceptions of the now, the more ghosts in the closet the more trouble we have seeing the present for what it is, free from the veils of the past. And four; all those ghosts are going to come tumbling out of the closet when the body dies, this is the movie you will experience, filled with people, events, words, deeds from your past, all unresolved. Maybe that is when they do indeed become demons!

So, no time like the present. Maybe you aren't ready to invite those demons to the dinner table all at once, but you can, when each arises, simply stop, and take notice. The situation is past now and the memory is unlikely to kill you, so, to the best of your current ability, say hello to the demon, make friends with the thoughts, feelings, emotions, and words. Accept that you are human and out of the mouths of humans comes at odd times, all sorts of weird stuff.

Do your best to simply acknowledge the memory and sit with it, let the emotions come but try not to judge them, or fear them, or run away from them. You are simply experiencing a cascade of chemicals in the physical body, associated with a past event. And we know, at least those on the 'clearing path' know, that if we deny those feelings, if we run away, shut them back into the closet or personalise yet again, those feelings, we are giving them energy, we are giving them power over us. Beware of the dangers of closet control!

You might be an expert in closet control, denial is often one of the only defences we have against a painful past, but sooner or later nothing you can do will keep that closet door closed. I believe that only when we feel safe can we address the past in a manner that will discharge the energy that has built due to denial. Safety comes from the realisation that the past is the past, the emotions associated with that past are simply a biological function of the body, re making the chemicals and thus recreating the feeling around the memory. While we take those chemicals personally, believing them to be who we are, we remain a victim to the ghost in the closet.

And This!

AUTHENTICITY

MEANING, AMONGST OTHER THINGS—TRUE TO ONE'S own personality, spirit, or character.

Authentic, a word that 'popped' into my awareness recently, and the awareness of one or two others that I know about. How many of us are truly authentic? And what the heck does it mean anyway.

Interesting.... Well, for starters I do not believe it is possible to not be true to one's personality, after all the personality is something that has developed as a result of being born into a human body. We have identified so strongly with who we believe ourselves to be, the personality, that we cannot be anything but true to it, even when confusion and conflict keep showing up, for if that is what we, the body, has become on a cellular level, then that is what we will experience, authentically!!!

Character next, well one's character arises out of and is interwoven with the personality, so no difference there. What about the Spirit? The immaterial essence, animating principle, or actuating cause of an individual life (one of many interpretations according to Merriam Webster). Is then being authentic to one's personality or character the same as being authentic to one's spirit (soul)? If the soul/spirit, is the 'driver' and the body the vehicle (a rental, so make sure you return it full of gas!!), and the soul/driver has become confused and now believes itself to be the body/vehicle how on earth can we expect to be 'authentic'?

Authentic to what? Your true self? Do you even know what that is? Or are you just guessing (or hoping!).

A simple example of a lack of authenticity (to personality etc) would be when we criticise a person for doing or saying something that we ourselves do or say all the time. Ever done that? Ever realised you were doing that?

Like "That person is a really fussy eater"! Yet the list of things you don't like or won't eat is a long one.

Or, "Just listen to that person—do they know what they are talking about"? When you, so lost in your own 'authenticity,' don't even know which way is up!

Or perhaps, "That person's political point of view is beyond bad"! And yours is any better???

You get the picture. So, what does it mean, and why bother to do it, be authentic, that is—and how would you know if you were or not?

I suspect when we comment on the behaviour of another, we are simply projecting our own 'shadow side' onto that person, after all, why is this type of behaviour in our face in the first place? What buttons are being pushed to make us react in certain ways? If it is indeed the shadow showing up, then, maybe because of the very nature, and reason for the shadow, is that it is hidden, unknown, unrecognised. We just play the part without stopping to question who wrote the script!

As I sit and write this, it is October 28th, the 'end' of the Mayan Calendar, according to those we would hope know more than we do on the subject. Not sure what it really means or what impact whatever it does mean will have on our lives, but at the very least it is something to talk about. What I find interesting is the build up to this date. Just how, observing what goes on around me, change seems to be the order of the day. I suspect that has always been the case—throughout history, change the only constant—yet always resisted in some way, or manipulated for the good of whoever. Yet now the heat has been turned up and the pressure has built to a point where change can no longer be denied. This is something that has appeared out of the various interpretations of the Mayan Calendar, the speeding up of change, what may have taken years in the past takes weeks, perhaps only days, now.

What has this got to do with authenticity, pretty much everything from my 'point of view' (remember earlier comments about 'points of view'—not to be taken too seriously!). *If* the pressure is building, *if* change can no longer be denied, in spite of the best efforts of some, then that which has been hidden will be exposed. I doubt you can take your shadow, your backpack with you into a new future, unless you plan on your new future being more of the same. Your shadow can either get dragged kicking and screaming into the future, or it can simply be acknowledged and released, easy once you understand it. So is this a wake up call to authenticity? Authenticity to the soul, not the personality. Easy or hard, up to you.

WOULD YOU KNOW YOUR SELF IF YOU MET 'IT' ON THE ROAD?

If you find your self (good luck with that!!) confronted by people, situations, emotions, with which you are not comfortable, best see them as wake up calls. Maybe don't try to understand them, after all, who is it who is trying to understand what (personality at a guess). Hard to change other people, unless you happen to be in the legislative arm of government when you can pass laws to make people behave

| And This! |

according to your wishes or the points of view of those paying for your lifestyle. Harder still to change the self. Easy to be 'true' to the personality for while the driver believes itself to be the vehicle it must be authentic to that vehicle. But anything beyond that can be challenging.

Hopefully you are familiar with the 'clearing' approach. What to do when confronted by such emotions, people, situations. A reminder … when you notice a change in how you are 'feeling' particularly emotionally perhaps even physically, you recognise that the body, your rented vehicle, is simply reacting to external stimuli. If you continue to give energy to the feeling, then the feeling will get stronger. If you deny the feeling, well just stuffing it to the bottom of the backpack isn't going to work, it will still be there tomorrow, influencing your future. So, stop giving it energy, notice it, accept it, don't judge it, don't deny it. Just let it be, doing your best to remain centred, at peace with whatever shows up.

And maybe, just maybe, the shadow will be exposed, embraced for what it is, the mistaken identification with the body/vehicle. I read recently "You don't have a soul, you are a soul who has a body." And if you didn't read the contract when you rented the vehicle, well, the rental company is hardly to blame.

Don't be true to yourself until you know who you are. And then, well it won't matter anymore, just live you life, breathe and smile a lot.

A Piece to Finish the Day

A MORE COMFORTABLE ILLUSION ANYONE?

THERE CAN BE LITTLE DOUBT THAT WE LIVE IN A TIME OF rapid change. A lot of people, it seems, are totally fed up with the management of planet earth and those who live upon it. A lot of other people are totally fed up with those who are fed up. Nothing new in that.

If history is to be believed (hmmm??) then those people who get fed up with systems are forever in conflict with the people who want to hold onto the existing system and this breeds revolutions of one kind or another. Again—if history is to be believed—all a revolution does is change one system for another (assuming the revolution succeeds). The new replacement system is still a polarised point of view which, in its turn, will set the scene for another revolution.

Revolution, be it armed or peaceful, is met with violence. Our TV screens have been showing us this for a while at least as long as the violence is not within the borders of our own country of course. The www is a little less biased, a little less fussy what it shows. Not being 'owned' as such the control is not there, yet….

The problem, as I see it, with revolutions is that nothing really changes. Still, revolutions are ultimately good for business because they still come from the belief that a new system is better than the existing system but still exist within the basic structure which is the real problem.

AND THEREIN LIES THE DILEMMA

So, what do we really want. Many of us know what we don't want, but what is going to take its place?

The nature of the world, as perceived by individuals, or groups of individuals, is pretty much dependant upon their collective conditioning. We see what we expect to see, feel what we expect to feel. The choices available to us are also products of that conditioning. So, with choices limited by our past, what could we possibly imagine we want. We may know what we do not want, but revolutions aren't the answer. They never have been anything other than a temporary solution to a much bigger issue.

In my understanding all the time we come from a place that personalises with thoughts, emotions and feelings, we will remain in conflict. Conflict that begins internally, which, in its turn, is a result of our likes and dislikes, our judgements, our association with the body as being who we are. This internal conflict presents itself on a daily basis, who we meet, the situations we find ourselves in, the judgments we hold consciously, or more often than not sub-consciously.

We may want change, but if our progress towards change is based on internal conflict, then we will meet conflict, no matter how peaceful our attempts to bring about change. And then, success, for we have someone, something to blame for our condition.

Until we can be the change this will always be the case. Us and them. Me and you. My people your people. My religion, your religion. My skin colour, your skin colour.

This is the real problem, our conditioned past and our blind obedience to it. The programming we experienced way before we knew we were being programmed. Who ever stops to question, truly question, all the stories we have been told, stories that have been paraded as the truth.

If we continue to seek change before we have become change then all we are really doing is empowering the shadow, whatever name you want to give that shadow, police, mayors, presidents, corporations, protesters, money, greed, the list goes on, and on and on.

Our past needs to be embraced, loved into acceptance until we are the peace that we seek, anything else is an illusion. Anything else will continue to demand struggle, the more we struggle the more we empower that which we oppose.

I tell a story in my workshops—this particular theme can be seen on "Weapons of Mass Hallucination" on my channel on YouTube—about anxiety. When you can see the body as the interface between the inhabitant of the body and the 'external' third dimensional world, you will see that the body is interpreting data that it is picking up. You, the inhabiter of the body then interpret that data as an emotion, for example. You think the emotion is 'yours' and thus give it energy. The more energy you give it, with or without conscious awareness, the more intense the emotion becomes.

If you pick up a signal that you interpret as anxiety, and then you identify with that emotion, you give energy to the feeling of anxiety. The more energy you give it the stronger it becomes. This changes the chemistry of the body, to a point where you not only take in, but also transmit the energy of anxiety. Now you have become a relay station, picking up, adding energy to and forwarding on, the feeling of anxiety. Now those around you feel anxious, and as a part of their own conditioning, they identify with the feeling, energise it and pass it on to even more people. Anxiety pretty soon reaches epidemic proportions.

And people will do some pretty weird things when their body has been taken over by the chemicals of anxiety.

Do yourself and the world a favour. Stop feeding the drama. Stop being a part of the problem. Be at peace with your self.

There is nothing more important that you could possibly do with this lifetime. When you 'know' this you will be the peace that you seek.

Ponder This

WELCOME TO 2012

IS THIS THE YEAR WE HAVE BEEN WAITING FOR? OR NOT!

Ever since more people became aware of the Mayan Calender, 2012 has been *the* year for change. In spite of more recent updates claiming October 28th 2011 to be THE day, many, particularly as little actually seemed to have happened in October (big shift wise), are still pinning their hopes on the winter solstice of this year.

Personally, I have no idea what, if anything will happen then, other than the sun begins its welcome return journey into the northern skies. It seems as though many people are hoping for some sort of divine/cosmic intervention to help put right a world gone mad. To me though, it is the concept of the world gone mad—something that needs to be fixed, and all those working out how to fix it—that is the issue.

We may believe that we are victims of a global conspiracy, in which case the responsibility for change falls—where? We may believe that the external manifesting reality is a product of our own imaginings (remember there are billions of people imagining different scenarios) in which case any responsibility for change falls upon our shoulders. We may believe that we are powerless or powerful, we may think that everything is perfect or we may think that all is totally screwed. We could all be right. We could all be wrong.

No matter what we 'think' is going on we are left with trying to make sense of a world consisting of so many opposite points of view that we tend to withdraw into our own world and get on the best we can.

Wherever we look, in the western world, people seem to want more. More security in the form of money, better health, more happiness, clients, clothes, food, power, peace, spirituality— in some parts of the world many people want just one meal for the day and clean drinking water! That shouldn't be too much to ask for. But still many are faced with how to attract more into their life. The 'Law' of Attraction is the current flavour of the month, mostly of course, in westernised countries. Few people in the more affluent countries seem to 'have' enough of whatever it is that would make them happy. At least, what they think will make them happy, for no sooner do many reach one goal than another takes its place.

For the most part my needs are met now. If my past tells any story at all it is that my needs have always been met, with or without any striving or desire on my part. Not always what I thought I needed, or wanted, often quite the opposite. Yet, my past also tells me that who I was/am just keeps on showing up. Sometimes who I was/am is not so nice (a judgement arising from a conditioned past!), there were/are aspects of who I thought I was that I may have preferred were left behind in all senses of the word, yet we can never hide from who we are. We just keep on showing up in our lives.

IT MATTERS LITTLE WHAT I 'WANT'

My 'reality' doesn't only depend upon what I want or what I desire or even what I think is going on, it just happens. It is not important if I think that I am a master of my destiny or a victim to my past, it is not relevant if I believe in global conspiracies, in winter solstices, in Mayan calenders, in divine intervention. I will keep showing up and until the messages—conscious or otherwise—that I put out, are no longer driven by any subconscious aspects of my conditioning, that which shows up will continue to offer polarised views of the world.

My past has also shown me it is how I deal with/react/respond to that which showed up that determines what will show up tomorrow. If I put fear into the soup, then fear will show up, anxiety, worry, frustration, conspiracy, alien invasion, then all of these will show up. The more people agreeing on what to expect, the more likely it is to happen that way. The challenge for a lot of us is to see exactly what we are putting into the soup. So lost are we in this cosmic soup that we can no longer tell where 'up' is anymore, who is putting what into the soup. We are in damage control, all the time trying to fix something, to change things for the better ('better'—a personal opinion of course, for there are many opinions about what is 'good' and what is 'bad' that differ from our own).

While we are running around trying to put out all the fires that we personally judge as 'bad' we often miss the bigger picture, and that is that we lit the fires in the first place.

A challenging aspect of accepting the part we play in the manifesting of our world is that we need to move through all the stuff that appears to happen to us without giving it anymore energy. At first this is hard to do as we are still in an internally polarised state where our conditioning leads us to judge situations, people and things as good or bad. If we remain in that state, then the world we pass onto our children (divine intervention/alien invasion/conspiracies/solstices notwithstanding) will be more of the same.

As we understand, more and more, that by giving any thought, feeling, emotion or thing energy, we support it. We pretty much guarantee it's future. No matter what that feeling, emotion, thought or thing may be, whilst we consciously or sub-consciously energise it, we are ensuring it will continue.

To be without desire for more doesn't mean that you are going to starve or go without, or even suffer any lack whatsoever. As you get closer to this particular 'desire-less' state, your needs will naturally reduce, and your fears/anxieties will be replaced with greater internal peace. Your shadow may continue to show up, but by recognising this you can slowly stop giving it energy and stop empowering it. Not an easy road for it seems to go against all that you think you are. Remember though who you think you are is just a product of conditioning, let go of the attachment to who you thought you were and find out who you are. When you are without desire there can be no disappointments, there simply is what is, and rest assured stuff will still show up in your life. In fact, life is more 'full' and all you need comes to you, effortlessly, and therefore more sustainable.

Clearing, of course, is my preferred method.

Be well? Be happy? Face your past without judgement, nothing I can say, or wish for you about a new year is of any use whatsoever, you are still going to meet yourself regardless of my good wishes.

Something to Think About!

HOW IS LIFE TREATING YOU?

Or perhaps, "how are you treating life?"

So much talk these days about being in the moment, I even wrote a book many years ago, "The Moment That Matters." Nothing new of course, my first exposure to this, this time around, was reading Ram Dass, *Be Here Now*, that eclectic mix of stuff that came out of the '60s and was printed in '71.

Amongst the things I have noticed, over the years I have been practicing/sharing/teaching 'clearing' is that for most people it is easy to be in the now (or so it seems at the time) when things are going your way. Meaning the experiences, emotions etc you encounter all fit within your comfort zone. While you have your health, while you have money, friends, a "good" job—just as long as your points of view are not being challenged, as long a your reality goes along in an easy going manner—all is well, and you don't even have to think about being in the moment.

It is when you are confronted by 'stuff' that makes you feel uncomfortable—insecure—that the real test of your ability to be in the moment arises. One would have to question whether you were actually in the moment before you were challenged, before you became uncomfortable, insecure. Had you truly been living in the moment, it is quite possible that challenges would not have arisen, for what is a challenge other than a reflection of your own limitations.

To be consciously, here is the rub—to be *consciously* in the moment—one needs to learn to accept that which arises, without judgement. Meaning that whatever happens is no better, nor worse, than anything else that arises, all arises and passes. But we have preferences, we want things to remain the same, or better yet, improve, according to our desires and expectations. We always want more. Not the first time I have brought this up in the newsletters. Now, I believe we are all driven by our desires, conscious or sub-conscious. Sometimes those desires are quite destructive. Driven by a force that we cannot begin to comprehend we blunder through life. Often we will choose a path of busy-ness, keeping occupied, after all sloth is one of the deadly sins!!!

So involved are we on our path, so intent on do-ing something all of the time that we rarely pause to think, "what the heck is going on in my life." All the time we are busy there is little time for reflection, all the time we are driven there is no thought of stopping and asking why. Just keep filling the blanks with more stuff. This isn't being in the moment, this is fleeing from the moment!

Nothing wrong with desire, as long as you recognise it for what it is, the energy that drives you to do, to achieve, a 'charge' that you likely were born with that needs to be expressed (karma!). Until the charge is exhausted there is little likelihood of your being able to stop and begin questioning the world you live in. In fact the idea that you can question never even arises, so full of do-ing are you that there is no mental space to even question why. If you understand that any desire is charge to be released you will be on a path towards personal harmony and all that entails. If you don't understand this then you will continue to add 'charge' by your attachment to outcome, by your judgements, your attachment to points of view. The more you personalise with the feelings associated with the experience, the more energy you give to those experiences, the more energy they have, the less 'free will' you have. It is this that makes us a victim to our pasts, our inability to see beyond the immediate experience.

This is all part of the charge though, the old 'Catch 22' situation. Attachment to the emotions, thoughts, perceptions, judgements by its very nature dictates our reality. While we are lost in this charge we are continually trying to work out ways to make the manifesting reality 'fit' into our own comfort zone. Like a kids 'merry-go-round' that never runs out of energy and keeps going around and around.

So, back to the moment, and a personal story.... For much, if not most of my life, I have been busy. Not busy in most peoples understanding of the word, but, perhaps 'occupied' would be a better word. A very full life no doubt about it. So it has been an interesting time for me, living out in the Irish countryside, alone for most of the week, no personal transport, nor desire for transport. 'Work' has slowed down, always does around this time of year, but work has been slowing down for a few years now. The door that opens now is one of not moving, not do-ing, not preoccupied. That took a week or two to get comfortable with, after a lifetime of do-ing, even though that do-ing involved lots of be-ing (clearing etc).

Resting the body, long overdue, becoming used to my own company, with no distractions. There could be various ways of looking at this change of course. Based though upon my past experiences I am seeing this as the next step, the winter where I can hibernate and allow the remaining past to catch up, without giving it anymore energy, a big clean out in a sense. I will still go out into the world and teach as required, but I am no longer driven to do this, the charge has been exhausted. At last! This self imposed isolation allows me to see, with even greater clarity, what is going on around me—to share that clarity. Don't think I am too old to travel, but the desire is no longer there. I remember from childhood a strong desire to travel, to see the world. Well, I have seen it now. If I travel in the future it will not be because of any sub-conscious personal desire.

More and more I speak with people who are still on their personal treadmill, what most people fail to understand is that the treadmill is their path, at least until the charge is exhausted and new ways, new opportunities arise. No problem, nothing right, nothing wrong, no this way or that way. Acceptance of all emotion, all thought, all experience without personalising with those emotions, thoughts or experiences is the path to self awareness.

Don't worry—as the song goes, be happy. And if you can't be happy, then just be and stop worrying about it.

And This!

RESISTANCE IS USELESS

WELL, PERHAPS NOT USELESS, MORE LIKE COUNTER-productive. I refer to resistance on a 'cellular' level, not the Taurean approach to life (which I am) nor the Chinese year of the Bull, which I also am!!! But resistance to change on a more subtle level.

Resistance in itself causes all sorts of problems in all sorts of aspects of our lives... In fact I would go so far as to say that resistance is the underlying cause of all difficulties we encounter in life. When people tell me that any particular 'clearing' job is/was more difficult than another, I recognise that any sense of difficulty arises out of the resistance of the individual 'doing' the clearing that is the issue.

We all encounter resistance on a daily basis, though we may not see it as 'resistance' for it is something that we have become so familiar with we can no longer observe these parts of our make-up objectively. Often when disease manifests it is a symptom of resistance of some sort. For example, when, due to early childhood conditioning, we hold particular beliefs about ourself, those beliefs are often very limiting. We can do this, but not that, we like this but not that. As we tend to try to experience more of what makes us happy and avoid that which makes us uncomfortable we are creating, internally, a greater polarity, i.e., charge between one thing and another.

| And This! |

This charge, on a cellular level, creates imbalance, and any imbalance affects the healthy working of the cell. The greater the imbalance the greater the likelihood of disease manifesting.

When we are 'clearing' what we may judge to be a powerful charge, something that the body experiences as very intense, is more often than not an indication of the resistance the body holds towards a particular energy/frequency/feeling. We may not know why there is resistance, it is not necessary that we understand. It is enough that we notice and stop energising the old patterns. This process alone will help us be less resistant to the flow of information/energy through the body opening us up to a much broader range of experiences and a greater sense of personal peace.

It isn't only through clearing or manifesting health issues that we experience the results of resistance. If there is a task to be done, something simple like cooking a meal, or washing the dishes after a meal and we think of all sorts of reasons why we cannot/will not do the job, then this is resistance, quite obvious really. The cause of the resistance may be lost in the mists of time, you may think you understand why you don't want to do something but this thought is only a justification for your lack of interest in getting the job done. And who really knows the cause? For while we are lost in the dictates of the personality, a personality that arose out of the past, much of which was absorbed sub-consciously, it is not really possible for us to understand why we do anything, why we react as we do, we just do it.

A lot of resistance arises through thinking about the task before we actually have to do it. We spend a lot of time justifying why we cannot do something, so by the time we should be getting on with the job we have built such a high wall there is no getting over it. There are many tasks with which

| And This! |

we might be unfamiliar, this sense of uncertainty will often prevent us from taking on the challenge. Often simple things have such an aura of difficulty around them, built from our own perceptions, that we cannot even consider doing them. And so much of life passes us by simply because we cannot take the first step.

Clearing is a wonderful means by which we can overcome resistance, starting with simple, abstract stuff we gradually open ourselves up to having more experiences, find ourselves doing things we could not have considered previously. Yet another of the significant benefits associated with practicing clearing regularly and frequently.

A Piece to Start the Day

THE I'S HAVE IT

AND IF THEY DON'T HAVE IT YET, THEN THEY WANT IT SOON. Last month I spoke about the challenges that arise from resistance. Resistance to the flow of information on whatever level. Yet resistance is just a symptom, not a cause. Why would we resist information/energy? And what is the big deal anyway?

The opposite of resistance could be seen as open-ness. When we are open and available we experience all things as they are, not as we might like them to be. So, immediately another challenge arises, why would I not want to see things as I am accustomed to seeing them. How can there be another way of seeing things?

Perhaps, if we look at what happens when we fail to see things as they are and instead insist on seeing them through the eyes of expectation, of limitation imposed by past beliefs we might be more inclined to move towards seeing things as they are. Our perceptions colour the world we live in, we can divide that world into parts that we like and parts that we do not like. In the middle there lies the grey zone, neither strongly for or against. Our conditioning tends to create a polarised world which then fragments into ever increasing parts, all of which the polarised consciousness has to judge and then take sides. Once we have assumed a side, which we believe is right, then we put our energy into making manifest our point of view.

This is fraught with disappointment, for the more energy we give to our point of view the more energy the 'opposition' gains, leading to, eventually, more open conflict. For most of us the majority of the energy we are giving to a cause arises out of our sub-conscious conditioning.

Look around, there are so many 'causes' to fight for the choice is overwhelming. One could argue that the winning team gets to write history, that the team with the most money, people, power gets to rewrite the rules, which always leaves the disenfranchised feeling more helpless and frustrated. The dolphins are killed, the seals slaughtered, the butterflies exterminated, the pollution increases, the children taught to use firearms, the women abused, the rape—pillage and plunder of the Earth continues. These can all be seen as issues worth fighting for.

IS THIS THE REAL ISSUE?

Are these the real issues though, or are they distractions, we might say that everywhere we look there are distractions, for while we are fighting for this, then what gets missed? What falls down the cracks? What is the fundamental issue, assuming there is one, that would make the rest go away? Surely, if there is anything to do it is to see through the distractions and go to the heart of the matter.

How many times have we heard the saying, as within, so without. How many of you are saying, right now, "yes, I have heard that, but…." Where does the initial 'problem' arise? If we truly felt the interconnected-ness of all things, all life, could we still, in all honestly abuse any part of the whole? Is the Earth really a planet of conflict? Is that all there is to life, a life spent in conflict, the 'i' trying to satisfy its perceived needs, to work more, earn more, have more, or are they just more symptoms, like resistance, not the cause, but arising out of something else?

Whilst we are subject to the sub-conscious desires of the personality, which in effect could be understood as chemical addictions to certain ways of being and the amino acids those ways produce, we will remain a part of personal, community and global conflict, feeding the very issues which we struggle so hard against.

Sleep on This One

CHOP WOOD, CARRY WATER

As promised. Following up from last month's 'story' where I spoke about our being victims to our own subconscious conditioning, 'Chop wood, carry water'.

If you are familiar at all with Buddhism, in particular Zen Buddhism you will have heard the saying "Before enlightenment chop wood—carry water, after enlightenment chop wood carry water. (Not as I have said on occasion, "before enlightenment chop wood—carry water, after enlightenment get someone else to do it for you"!!!)

For years I don't think I really understood this. Little did I realise, in the past, that while there was someone asking the question there could never be a real understanding of the question. I am not claiming to understand now, just offering my experience. There is another similar Buddhist saying, "It is not what you eat—it is who is doing the eating." Again, who is asking the question is the challenge here, not the understanding of the question itself.

Through my years of teaching 'Clearing' and putting into practice all that I teach I hope I have come to a better understanding (? knowing) of the meaning of these two phrases.

Essentially the 'who' is doing is the issue, who is chopping wood, who is carrying water, who is eating? This can best be understood by reflecting upon certain tasks that you need to do either on a daily basis or even infrequently. Tasks that you do not particularly enjoy but are often necessary in your life, (cooking—washing the dishes—cleaning the car—visiting the dentist—exercising—getting out of bed on a Monday morning, etc.). As you think about having to prepare a meal, or go to work, anything in fact that you do not look forward to, you mentally create lots of excuses to put the job off. You create a huge amount of resistance, all sorts of reasons and excuses not to go ahead and complete the task.

IS THIS RINGING ANY BELLS WITH YOU?

As you allow the excuses to build, the task seems even more unattractive and impossible, justifying your original resistance. We are, most of us, experts at justifying our resistances. It is only when we are confronted with a task that we find uncomfortable, challenging or downright distasteful that we can see that we still have resistance in the body.

Resistance is something that we may have been born with. Perhaps carried over ancestral stuff that has not been worked through, or we may have been indoctrinated into certain beliefs by our parents, relatives, peer groups, schooling simply because of when and where we were born. We will, depending upon that early conditioning, develop a 'personality'. We tend to get lost in the personality, because it is, or so we believe, who we are. Any change, from within this perception of personality, is by its very nature, doomed to failure. For we have been taking ourselves seriously for a long time, we believe that we are our personality and it is from that place that we try to manipulate the world, and those around us to conform to our expectations.

We should be able to see now, that the 'who' who is chopping wood, the 'who' who is carrying water, the 'who' who is eating is personality based. The personality, that has acquired likes and dislikes, for's and against's, is in charge. So, when something arises along the path that the personality has resistance to, for whatever reason, we immediately go into a conditioned response that leads to excuses and judgements around doing the particular job.

All the time we remain a victim to conditioned personality, the 'who' will be in resistance to many tasks, feelings, emotions and situations. Resistance it is simply a product of an internal state of polarised values. We can see that alternative points of view exist, and many people hoping various beliefs different from our own cope with life quite well, yet we maintain our own point of view, only because we are habituated to do so.

When, through 'clearing' or any other process we feel comfortable with, we begin to face up to the limitations those personal points of view impose, we are more inclined to begin the process of detaching ourselves from a point of view, even if only temporarily, to observe what would happen *if*.

As we train ourselves to notice points of view before they become manifest in our lives, it gets easier to observe and, for the moment, let go of that point of view (i.e. not energise by giving in to it, not allowing our thoughts to dwell upon it). We may need some 'device' to help us as we start this, because this process itself is not exempt from the old patterns of resistance, but given practice this does get easier.

If there is anyone at all chopping wood or carrying water the 'who' can be evaluated by the amount of resistance the 'who' has to the task. The more resistance the more uncomfortable the task. When there is no more resistance, then 'who' is left to chop wood or carry water?

A common misconception here is that if there is no one to judge, to protect the self from external forces, then one has weakened oneself and put oneself at the mercy of others, or the more negative experiences the personality imagines to be 'out there'. Not true, a 'negative' experience is only something that we hold as a belief pattern, the stronger we hold onto such a thought, the more likely it is to show up in our lives, simply because we have the 'buttons' that are triggered by such an event. When we no longer have the buttons, because we have accepted those aspects of personality, then the situation is much less likely to present itself before us. Even if it does, then because we no longer have the buttons we are no longer affected by whatever it is.

So, who is chopping wood and carrying water in your life?

Musings

SO EASY TO GET LOST!

For those of you who have been to a 'Clearing' workshop, or had a clearing session with me, you will recall a state of peace, a calm, that followed the workshop or the session. You may have your own description of the post-workshop experience, however you describe it though, it was 'different', different to the pre-workshop/session state.

Simply put, you were reminded of something that you have known, deep down, forever. You were allowed to find sanctuary, safety, amongst a group of often unknown people, and release a significant amount of stress, anxiety, tension, pain that you had been carrying for quite some time.

The relief this experience brings may last a day, a week, a month but, sooner or later the past returns to claim your world. The way you see and understand yourself, particularly in relation to those around you and your environment reverts back to its habitual ways. It is hard to hold the peace, because, inside, we are still not at peace. Our external reality being merely a reflection of our inner state.

For many years we have identified with the body, with emotions, with thoughts and feelings, not questioning where those thoughts/feelings/emotions came from, they simply 'are'. And they, those thoughts/feelings and emotions are who we believe ourselves to be. We have a deeply established way of looking at the world, we have come to expect the world to be a certain way, and that is what we see, our conditioned expectations.

The brief insight gained, after a workshop or clearing session, into something beyond the conditioning is both refreshing and enlightening but it is not sustainable. For many, this let down post workshop drives them to look elsewhere for the answers to whatever questions they may have. For some the post workshop experience simply fades into the background, a memory, perhaps good, but losing whatever impact it once had, like most memories. For others it is a wake up call and they continue to practice what they have learnt at the workshop/session.

Even the most devout practitioner of 'Clearing,' because they have 'lives to lead' obligations to family, friends work, will gradually slip back into the embrace of their past. This leads them to try to deal with life's issues, from the past points of view. They may have remembered, albeit briefly, that those old ways are not particularly effective, but still they persist, this is, after all, what they have become accustomed to, how they are conditioned, and constantly reminded, to manage their lives.

OUR TOTAL ENVIRONMENT SUPPORTS WHO WE THINK WE ARE

After all, everyone around them is trying the same thing, the same approach, with variations, to making their lives better, healthier, happier, more successful, wealthier etc. Supported by the media, friends and family, colleagues and memories held in their home or workplace it is hard to remember the clarity and peace that was the post workshop experience.

Whilst we fall so easily back into past ways of dealing with life's situations our ability to remain present, to be in the moment, the now, can be seen as a struggle. Even assuming there is the will, or awareness to attempt to remain in the now, urgent matters arises, demanding our attention and we must 'do' something to make things better, right, easier.... Our will to remain in the present is also a result of a part of our past. The more energy and time we devote to bringing our awareness back into the present, the more 'space' arises to make this a little easier in the future. Brick by brick, piece by piece we can dismantle the barriers that we, consciously or not, have built around ourselves, to protect ourselves from real or imagined hurts.

We need to feel safe in order to open up and let go of our attachment to old conditioned ways. But because most people still live in the past or an as yet un-manifest future, their expectations, their projections all serve to keep them locked into their own past. So much so that very few people actually recognise this is happening. A lot of people are 'people pleasers' disliking conflict they do all they can to make others feel good so they themselves won't feel threatened.

This is not how we find ourselves, it is not how we remember to remain in the moment. While we remain lost, victims to our past, it is not even possible to question who we are, for the questioner is lost within a dream and cannot access answers outside of that dream.

For those whose inner scales are leaning more to being in the moment, reminders are always good. This would be one reason I recommend repeated attendance at workshops, or at the least, regular sessions with me. To remind us, to help us see things from a different, often 'clearer' point of view. To re experience the benefits of allowing all stress to fall away. Many people think that having attended a workshop that is all they need, perhaps off to the next workshop, perhaps to sit with what they have learnt, perhaps just to go back to a life they know so well. 'Clearing' is not like that, not something that once tasted can be left on the shelf with all the other workshop experiences, 'clearing' is a moment by moment practice. 'Clearing' is a way of life.

REMEMBER, REMEMBER

The more we can be reminded, the less we need reminding, for the internal workings of the body begin to take over, finding a different way of being that arises out of all that we have been, all that we knew. Effortlessly, without prompting, without our knowing, other ways to be in this world show up. Futures that we could not even dream about offer themselves. Yet while we remain lost in the old dream, there is no one home that can dream a new dream.

Seek reminders where you can, put notes in your diary, on your calender, post-it notes on your bathroom mirror, take advantage of a Skype session once a month, attend a workshop whenever the chance presents. Re-connect with other 'clearers' in person or via Skype.

With pressures building, expectations changing, finances crumbling, a future seemingly more uncertain, it benefits us to continually bring ourselves back into clarity, into the moment and see things for what they are, not what we expect them to be.

And This!

THE PRICE OF PEACE!

IF YOU WANT TO LIVE A PEACEFUL LIFE FIRST YOU SHOULD TRY to live in a peaceful place. Not an option for most people. If this is not available to you then you must find the peace within. Again, not an option for most people.

As those of you who have attended a space clearing workshop with me will know, we affect our environment as much as it affects us. Where stress and tension exist in our home or workplace we are going to be affected by that, whether we are aware of it or not. Mostly not! Because if we were aware then how could it affect us in a negative way?

We may have the luxury of living in a calm environment, a place where the energies are harmonious and supportive of a peaceful life. We may have to 'go to work' into a less than harmonious environment. This may be more obvious now because of the financial chaos that currently exists in many countries. If we have something to compare our chaotic life with, a peaceful home, then it becomes obvious we are working in a very stressed environment—or vice-a-versa.

If we not only work in a very stressed environment but live in chaos as well, then how can we compare? What marker is there to say, this is chaos and that isn't. Only if we take a trip into the countryside, and spend enough time there do we begin to understand that much of our lives is lived in a chaotic environment. It is like someone who is depressed, and has been for a long time—they no longer have the ability to recognise a non-depressed state. They have become, in a word, depressed, and it is in this 'depressed' world that they exist. It is hard, if not impossible to be objective about our physical, mental or emotional state when we are lost within a world of chemical reactions that blinds us to all other possibilities.

And so it is with our environment. I am not limiting our environment to our home here, but our workplace, our social life, in fact, every part of our lives, our total environment. If that 'total' environment is chaotic, then how can we ever expect to be objective about that environment. Instead we become lost in that environment and all that it holds to be true. We unconsciously support the 'truths' that are generated within that environment. We get caught up in defending this, opposing that. We become those very 'truths' simply by the fact that we have become our environment. Then what happens of course is that our environment reflects back to us what we imagine ourselves to have become, further validating any perception we hold that this 'truth' is real.

A space clearing gives people a chance to take a peek outside the box. For most people this little insight is not of much value simply because it is so alien to them, they cannot comprehend a life so different. Add to this the physical bodies subconscious conditioning that supported the earlier chaos and the individual will return to the known rather than face the unknown. When this happens the chaos is quickly restored, both internally and externally. Our 'total' environment serves to keep us a prisoner to a way of being that is both limiting and dis-empowering. A way that doesn't even come close to our true nature.

MEET YOUR JAILER

Our jailer is our fears. Fear of change, even though when asked most people say change is high on their list of things to achieve. Fear of the unknown, fear of failure, fear of success. Fear of fear, that is a good one, and oh so powerful. Fear is a low energy frequency, it is fear that holds discarnate spirits, ghosts etc to the physical plane. When we space clear we bring a huge amount of compassion to the situation, this compassion encompasses the low energies and allows them to raise their vibration, to melt away, move on, whatever is required. This is applicable to those in a body as well, raise the vibration and open the door.

I recommend every person takes time out to reflect. A holiday is good, but what does it do really, give you the energy to carry on, for a little longer, living in some illusion that really doesn't have your best interest at heart. A reward for being a good worker … but no better than taking a handful of steroids and back to the fray.

If it is so hard for most of us to change our environment, simply because we have become it and it has become us, then baby steps towards greater self awareness may be the key to personal—and who knows—global transformation. I believe there exists in all of us, a desire to become fully conscious, to no longer depend upon a limited past to create our future. If this desire is nurtured, encouraged, loved, then it may just open the door to the unknown a little wider, may make the unknown less fearful, may help us step into another way of being.

Take whatever steps you are able, don't let your environment, those in your environment or the media tell you are this, when deep down you know you are not.

Be careful though, desire can blind us to the path to liberation, after all desire is nothing but a perceived need to be in a different state, a different place, a different reality. Once we begin the journey of self-realisation, acceptance is the key to allowing all to unfold. Acceptance will take the wind out of the sails of discontent. Acceptance will allow our past to fall away so that we can begin to see more clearly our true nature, free from environmental conditioning.

A Piece to Finish the Day

THE SEAMLESS PRACTICE

When I first began work as a Space Clearing Consultant I recall that 'conditions' had to be just right while I was working. By conditions, I mean no distractions whatsoever. No noises, telephones, radios, no babies crying, no neighbours cutting their lawn, everything had to be just so for me to 'do' the job.

I suspect that is the case in all fields of endeavour when we first begin, we need the quiet in order to concentrate fully on the job at hand.

There are several reasons for this need for optimal conditions. An important one being our 'new-ness' to the job, our lack of experience requires that we focus a lot more concentration on the process, make sure we get it right. Our minds are busy in the background checking and double checking, second guessing and trying not to forget the questions we need to be asking, the process we need to be applying. So easy to lose concentration and then we struggle to remember where we 'were' in the consultation.

As we become more experienced and more confident, so the mental chatter falls away and we are able to relax into the process knowing, from our growing experience, that all is well. This is true for all new skills we wish to learn, first the desire to learn (preferably!) then the language and mechanics of the new study area, then the practice. We often do not know where the new will lead us, we may imagine the results but truly are unable to grasp the totality of the new experience until we have become so familiar with all the aspects, which in turn open even more new doors for us to pass through.

Clearing is a classic example. First we have to come to terms with the language, often new or applied in a new way. Then the tools, the simple pendulum and L rod, which bring with them their own mind chatter, "Am I doing this right?", "Am I asking the right questions?", etc. the list goes on.

The more we practice clearing the more we understand that it is about a state of be-ing, not do-ing. Many people tell me they understood the information presented in workshops from an intellectual point of view but were unable to grasp it from an emotional place. They could not 'live' it. It is almost as though the two halves of the brain were in conflict, one side understands, the other looks on in amazement wondering what the heck is going on. The more we practice the less we question, because, by the simple act of practice we come to 'know' the truth, the value, the reason for the practice.

TO LIVE TO 'CLEAR' OR TO 'CLEAR TO LIVE' OR ???

The clearing process is a wonderful way to live because it offers us, always, a more objective point of view. We can begin, more and more, to notice how the body feels when its environment changes (people, places, diet, experiences etc) and we start to understand the nature of the change and the reason for the change. We start to see the connection between so called external phenomena and emotions/feelings. We can relate, in a new way, to what is happening in the body. The more we understand the less fear and anxiety we go into and the less we personalise with the phenomena. The less fear we go into, the less anxiety we experience, the more peace we feel.

The body starts to respond to stimuli instead of react. An internal peaceful state becomes the norm, and with this we radiate greater peace of course, which then affects those around us and our total environment. As we become the peace we experience less conflict, we 'attract' less conflict. Conflict ceases to exist in our reality. Conflict may well continue to manifest in the world, for the majority of people are strongly polarised and as such manifest that polarity 'externally'.

As the internal pendulum ceases its out of control swing from one extreme to the opposite so our view of the world shifts.

While we are constantly caught in a state of doing we remain in internal conflict, never finding or achieving the peace we seek.

> Do a lot—achieve a little; do little—achieve a lot;
> do nothing—achieve everything.

I have often mentioned, particularly in relation to clearing, that the practice is 'seamless' a Buddhist term for no beginning, no end—no object, no subject—no do-er, (the key to my recent article 'Chop Wood, Carry Water'). Recalling my need for great quiet when I first began space clearing consulting, there existed a separation between 'me' and the 'clearing'. Although I was not aware of this at the time it became obvious the more I practiced. Had it been obvious at first, then I could have changed, as we say in 'clearing' awareness is the first step.

I may not have noticed this separation of self from the task but the cats in the houses I visited certainly did. They would avoid me, walk around the edges of the room staring at me with great mistrust. Hardly a win-win situation. And the cats also told me when I had moved out of the do-ing stage of the clearing into the be-ing. Be-ing, from a clearing perspective, is simply where we just are, no longer feeling the need to do anything, no longer separate from the action. The cats welcomed me, came close, snuggled up, no longer wary. A major break though for me, to finally have realised that there was no longer anything to do, I had become that which I thought I needed to do. My practice was Seamless. There was no longer any difference between the me that walked down the street, the me that did the shopping, the me that sat at a computer, the me that cooked the dinner, the me that 'cleared' people or spaces.

I suspect we all experience such moments, though we fail to realise we are experiencing such a moment until we are back in duality. As our practice, our life, becomes more 'seamless' so we, and all those around us, experience the benefits. We are less liable to experience such dramatic mood swings, less anger, less fear, less anxiety. The body re adjusts to experience more while getting lost in less, our world view opens up, judgment falls away. And, if we are on the 'clearing path' then our way becomes more established, our lives reflect the peace and those we encounter all experience the benefits without us having to 'do' anything.

Nice one.... Enjoy your journey, it is unique and will pass soon enough.

Ponder This

YOU HAVE BEEN ...

According to words attributed to the Buddha: "You have been everybody's mother, father, sister, brother, child, uncle, aunt".

Whoa, you must have been busy, sounds a bit incestuous too. How could this be true? Especially if we imagine 'time' to be linear, then it is impossible that we have been all of these people.

But perhaps a lot of what we imagine to be true is simply a product of a collective belief, which has no basis in fact and is just a simple fiction that we have all subscribed to, including the concept of time itself. But here we go again, trying to understand the bigger picture from a limited point of view. For if we have, collectively, subscribed to a particular point of view about what is real and what is not, then all understandings of that point of view, all permutations, all analysis, all conclusions are based on and arising from a fundamental misconception. Wow!!!

One perception that some people have is that we are here, incarnate on planet 'Earth' to learn something! To strive, to improve. Yet, if this is 'true', "You have been everybody's mother, father, sister, brother, child, uncle, aunt", then how can there be anything more to learn. You have, in the words of the tshirt, "Been There, Done That". Been everywhere and done everything.

If 'time' is not linear, if there is truly only the present, rationalised into linearity to prevent us from going totally insane, then it is easier to see how we can be all of these people. I think the 'answer' though lies in the understanding that we are not who we think we are. We have a preoccupation with the body that we inhabit, we think it is who we are rather than the vehicle by which we are able to experience the wonders and delights of a third dimensional world. We think the emotions the body feels are who we are, we think the thoughts that arise in our awareness are ours, so lost are we in separation from our true nature. (Are we lost though? Is it our true nature to get lost in this world in order to fully experience duality?)

WE THINK, WE THINK, WE THINK

If we have been everybody's whatever, then what else is there to do/be? The only thing I can think of is to wake up to the fact that we have been there and done that already. There is nothing more to learn, nothing to do, nothing to achieve, nowhere to go. This sense of separation that drives us is perhaps the biggest obstacle we all face. No matter who we are, where we live, how much, or how little we have, healthy or not, happy or not, this idea that we are separate from all other creation is all that stands between us and omniscience, omnipresence, omnipotence.

> Since all things are naked, clear and free from obscuration, there is nothing to attain or realise. The everyday practice is simply to develop a complete acceptance and openness to all situations and emotions. And to all people—experiencing everything

totally without reservations and blockages, so that one never withdraws or centralises into oneself.

Or if that one doesn't do it for you:

Since everything is a product of ones own mind
Empty of meaning like a magicians illusion
Having nothing to do with good or bad—right or wrong
One might well burst out in laughter.

Yet all the time we take the manifesting reality seriously, each time we identify with a point of view (remember, points of view are based on a collective dream [*Having nothing to do with good or bad—right or wrong*]) we *empower* that illusion.... So as much as we might complain about this and that, taxes, poverty, social injustice, cruelty to animals, we are simply reinforcing that which we object to. Not only that, we give those who 'think' they are in power, even more power over 'us' further imprisoning us within a drama that is not even real.

WAKE UP FOLKS...

One more quote, before I wrap up this 'story', from Albert Einstein. (Remember you have been everybody's ... hmmm.)

> A human being is a part of the whole, called by us 'Universe', a part limited in time and space. He experiences himself, his thoughts and feelings as something separated from the rest—a kind of optical delusion of his consciousness. This delusion is a prison for us, restricting us to our personal desires and to affection for a few persons nearest to us.
>
> Our task must be to free ourselves from this prison by widening our circle of compassion to

embrace all living creatures and the whole of nature in its beauty.

And just how do we 'do' this? Well, funny you should ask. 'Clearing' is a means where, if practiced regularly and often, will restore an internal balance, a balance that by its nature will stop taking itself seriously, stop judging self or others, stop energising conflict. A balance that will be content, that will see clearly and develop greater objectivity around that which it experiences. A balance that will realise the value in acceptance that will see beyond the desire to learn, to accumulate, to judge or justify.

Whatever you 'think' is important, whatever it is that you 'think' you have to do is simply a product of a desire arising out of your belief that you are separate from all other creation. Whatever you 'think' is important, whatever it is that you 'think' you have to do is the result of an inability to see through the veil, for with clear vision there is nothing more to do.

I have 'thought (there I go again!) that there is nothing more important to do with this life than to wake up to a better understanding of my true nature. All that I have done has been slowly heading in that direction… A fun and interesting journey, but if there is nothing to do and no where to go, nothing to attain or realise, then what exactly have I been doing this for?

Think about it… or better yet, don't think about it. Ha ha.

TIME TO RE-INVENT!

In the 'past' that 'I' am conscious of living through this body, there have been times when one experience falls away and another arises to take its place. A pastime, such as a means to generate an income for example. Without my thinking about it, one way of being dissolves and another arises. One of the things I am very grateful for, my parents never told me I was limited in what I could do.

In a sense this lack or limitation reinforced an already inherent belief that I could do anything I chose (I chose not to do algebra or calculus!). How this manifests is interesting. As we develop our ability to live in the moment, there is less and less resistance to that which arises (acceptance). If there is no resistance then the 'new' tasks that arise are effortless. (See earlier articles, 'Chop Wood, Carry Water,' and 'The Seamless Practice'.)

Now, whether it is because of my 'self imposed' isolation, here in the Irish countryside, or just the times that we are in, the time seems to be near for another 'change in direction'. The old ways, not that old, perhaps better called, the 'familiar ways' just don't have a lot of energy around them anymore. This has always, in the 'past', indicated a change is imminent.

With one foot in the old and still not sure where the other foot needs to be placed, I am sitting, observing, and waiting.

If anyone has got any ideas, I love to hear them, ha ha.

MAKE UP YOUR MIND!

I was told once that the word 'Swami' means a self made person, one who is no longer dependant upon the collective to make up their mind. Yet how many of us realise that we are not in charge, that we are being manipulated, for the most part, without our awareness! If the goal then, is to wake up, then of course the manifesting reality is only there to help us, not something that we have to invest in, not something that we have to add our energy to. No matter what arises, it all has its foundation in the collective illusion.

| Ponder This |

Yet while we are still lost in that illusion we might as well make it a happy, safe, equitable one.... Just beware of who it is that is trying to make it happier, safer, more equitable.

And This!

THE CHICKEN OR THE EGG?

Which came first? Or perhaps it is more relevant than discussing chickens to ask about the thought or the emotion?

Apologies for the delay with this newsletter, had planned to write it before the week in Tuscany, but that was not possible, a lot of traveling and teaching a 3-day program in Holland. But, better late than never, maybe.

Back to which came first. In the more advanced clearing workshops we look at cause and effect without getting too attached to the concept that there is a cause or effect. My current point of view, and I know better than to claim anything as 'the truth' is as follows:

During the early years of my 'dowsing' around the body, using a simple L-rod, I found a field I called the Emotional Body and another which I called the Mental Body. These were well documented in other texts so naming them was an easy decision. I found other fields but they are not relevant to this article. We begin by taking the point of view that all is energy. Our bodies appear to us, and others, as solid objects. There is more, though, to us than our physical bodies. The Emotional Body (aka the Astral Body) is a finer, non-visible, energy field which contains all of our emotional experience.

Then there is the Mental Body, sometimes called the Causal Body, an even 'finer' energy than the emotional body. This is said to contain information about who we have been, who we are and who we will be.

My little stick figure diagram illustrates these fields in relation to the physical body. I have found the fields, particularly the Emotional Body, to expand or contract depending upon how comfortable the subject is feeling at any given point in time. The more comfortable or safe we feel the larger the Emotional Field.

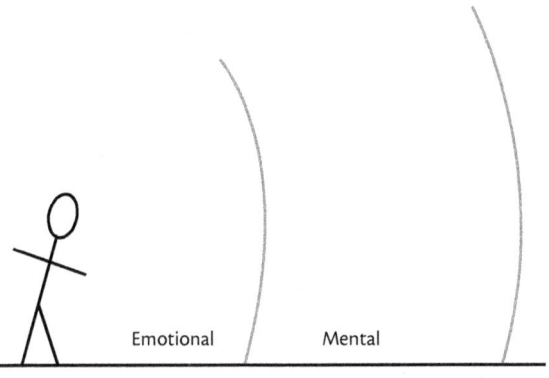

I have often been able to dowse physical sickness as having an emotional charge associated with it. I have also found that many problems can be alleviated by 'clearing' in the emotional body, but the clearing is not sustainable if the mental field is not cleared as well. Even 'clearing' the mental body is not necessarily going to provide ongoing relief from the symptoms if the 'condition' associated with the belief pattern is not addressed. Therein lies the biggest challenge the clearer faces in any attempt to support someone who is experiencing dis-ease or sickness.

A POINT OF VIEW

I have seen how some people, with long recurring problems make a dramatic shift after clearing the emotional body, then reject further treatment when it gets closer to the cause, the mental body. Primarily, I suspect, because the mental body, containing the "Points of View" (PoV) of the person appears, at least to the person concerned, to be sacrosanct, something that is an intrinsic part of who they believe themselves to be. This being the case any attempt to change this PoV is met with resistance, often on a sub-conscious level. We have simply come to accept this is who we are (this one PoV among many) and as such it cannot be changed.

We can easily, through 'clearing' take the pressure off a system, be it another person or an environmental condition but to re program someone requires something more.

If we assume that the work of Dr. Bruce Lipton and others is accurate, then an early developed (acquired or inherited) way of looking at the world shapes our experiences on a cellular level. As a result of this conditioning we find ourselves confined, locked into certain ways of looking at the world. We have certain expectations of how that world will manifest and unique ways of dealing with the situations that present. We are not aware of these limitations quite simply because we have become them, we can visualise no other way. These established "PoV" are then responsible for the quality of our experience in the physical body.

I believe that, arising from a point of view an emotional response follows. If the emotional response is not expressed in a satisfactory manner then pressure builds in the system. Too much pressure and the body begin to show signs of the imbalance which is being created on a cellular level. The body starts to malfunction and dis-ease manifests. Why we would adopt a "PoV" that was counter productive to good health is not really such a mystery. Most of this conditioning occurs while we very young and not ready to discern. A lot of the conditioning is acquired/learnt from our parents who were in their turn conditioned by their parents. Since, for the most part, we, as parents, are unaware of the impact our own sub-conscious has upon our children, we simply pass on the methods of being in the world that we learnt/absorbed in our childhood.

So, we truly become what we think, or rather, how we see our selves in relation to others and the world in general. These "PoV" collectively are called our personality and from them arise various emotional response/reactions to the situations we encounter. An emotional reaction supports the PoV, justifying our belief that we (our PoV) are right, which leads to further conflict, both within and without.

Personal 'points of view' are exclusive. Right or wrong (?) we maintain them because we know of no other way to be. Most points of view are based on judgement, the opposite of compassion, or unconditional love. Judgement arises from the 3 Buddhist poisons: greed, fear, and ignorance. If we imagine that fear in particular is a low frequency energy, then we can see how a being who exists in fear has a lower vibrational rate than one who exists in love.

It has been suggested that the body should be operating within certain frequency limits (62–72 Hz) in order to manifest in a healthy way. Colds and flu symptoms are more likely to appear when the frequencies lower to around 58 Hz. On much lower levels (42 Hz) Cancer will often manifest. By beginning to notice our P'soV we can see how they are affecting us. With this awareness comes the greater possibility that we can ease up on our attachment to a PoV that may well be harming us. Clearing supports a letting go of the attachment we have to our P'soV and as such, supports a sustainable release of any emotional charge we still carry.

Another Day, Another Thought

COMPASSION?

Continuing on from the 'Point of View' piece in the last issue. I finished up that article naming the three Buddhist Poisons: greed, fear, and ignorance as being responsible for the judgements we hold around ourselves, others and situations. It may sound simplistic and naive to think that we can be without judgement in this world. There are so many points of view that challenge us and we often feel, morally, in the right when we object to particular points of view. Yet this specific point of view, that we 'need' to stand fast to our own point of view (which we judge as morally superior to another) may well be the cause of continuing conflict. That conflict in turn demands that we expend more energy trying to create a reality where our point of view prevails.

I have heard it said that evil grows where good men do nothing, if this is the case then we are truly caught in a dilemma. For those of you treading the path of 'Clearing' will have found that the most benefit to self and others comes from a place of not doing. Yet many draw the line of 'not do-ing' when it comes to social issues, voting, condemning those who act in socially unacceptable ways etc.

We really need to question why we hold certain points of view and what we hope to achieve/attain by maintaining those points of view. Perhaps there are 2 major ways of looking at life. One, we look at evolution, how various species, humankind in particular, develop through the usual channels. Knowledge, power, control and wealth perhaps being seen as keys to survival. This is the materialistic approach which, if the history books are to be believed (!!) is 'the way'. Even so called religions employ knowledge, power, control and wealth to achieve their own goals, hardly a spiritual approach. What we can deduce from such a way of being is that life is full of conflict, various points of view battling other points of view for supremacy. And really, nothing changes.

We seem to continue down this path, probably because most people are easily led. Why is this? I suspect that most people feel a strong need to belong, to feel as though they are right, to feel safe in community. Which may explain the hugely polarised world of religion, politics, right to this, right to that. People have a basic need to feel as though they belong and will do almost anything that is required of them to continue to be a part of the group. That basic need can be summarised as a need to be loved, unconditionally, and to love, unconditionally—which, coincidentally, 'clearing' offers!

Now we are back to greed, fear, and ignorance. If we were to stop for a moment and reflect upon the chaos that our current subscriptions to organisations creates, the conflict that arises and the harm done to others because of this adherence to the need to belong we may question our point of view, we may question those who 'lead' us. But if the questioner is met with the threat of being thrown out of the group (excommunicated!) then it takes a strong person to stand away from the group. Often the threat of being shut out of the group is associated with violence, often the violence of others in the group, for the group cannot tolerate opposition.

By maintaining such a polarised state it is easy to control that population. And around we go.

SWAMI, A SELF MADE PERSON?

I was told once, many years ago, that the word 'Swami' refers to a self made person, one who is no longer dependant upon the collective to make up their mind.

Yet how would many know they are tools of the collective until they take a step outside of the group? Very hard to see ourselves from such a perspective for we are so lost in the beliefs that we are our thoughts, our emotions, our body that any alternative is not even on the radar let alone a realisable goal.

I have often quoted:

> Do a lot—achieve a little;
> Do a little —achieve a lot;
> Do nothing—achieve everything.

To remind those on the clearing path of the simplicity of this way of being. It has been a challenge at times, maintaining simplicity. In the many years I have been following this path many people offered more and more complications along the way. Yet an individuals need to complicate only arises from various levels of greed, fear and ignorance. So conditioned are we to do, in the material approach, that we have been seduced into believing it to be the way to personal happiness. The 'Clearing' practitioner will hold onto that particular point of view as they begin to embrace the alternative until gradually the scales tip and the world changes.

So, if there is an alternative to the 'material way' and it involves not doing, what is it and how can it work?

For a start while we hold onto the point of view that we need to 'do' something in order to achieve a goal we will continue to fall back upon the 'materialistic way'. It would only be through baby steps and constant mindfulness that we see the power of not doing manifest in our lives. A lot of people may think that not doing implies sitting all alone doing absolutely nothing, this being the case, nothing would get done, yet this is the argument used over and over again by the 'materialistic approach people' and which can only arise from, you guessed it, greed, fear and ignorance.

THUS THE DILEMMA

Go back and read the article on 'Chop Wood, Carry Water' if there is any doubt as to who is doing what. All the time we are driven by sub-conscious conditioning we remain a victim to our past and the collective belief in whatever. All the time we are driven by that sub-conscious conditioning we remain polarised, identifying with our point of view as being better (or worse?) than that of others. All the time we assume we are better or worse we will not find the peace that may have been promised, instead we struggle, albeit unconsciously, working for the goals of others.

When, through the 'Clearing' practice we see how any point of view that we hold onto affects our ability to be available for another we can see that by, even temporarily, letting go of that point of view, we can support the other (and by association—ourselves) why would we not apply that same approach to bigger issues.

Not only does our attachment to any point of view create conflict with others, it also creates imbalance internally. Sooner or later that imbalance, if not dealt with, will manifest as physical/emotional/mental dis-ease. When this happens we seek to 'do' something about the dis-ease which only creates further problems for us. Often, by the time any internal imbalance manifests then 'doing' something about it is the only option open to us. This is because the mental process that originally created the imbalance doesn't stop simply because there is a manifestation of that imbalance but continues down the same road and demands that we do something to fix the problem.

The other way of looking at life, the non materialistic way, doesn't imply that you are going to do nothing or that you will starve, or that you will be taken advantage of. Quite the opposite.

We will still 'do' stuff, but the doing arises less from a state of greed, fear or ignorance. When we personally experience the benefits of not doing then we are more likely to continue down that path, the more we walk that path the less greed, fear or ignorance remains. What this means on an individual level is that compassion replaces the greed, fear and ignorance. When there is more compassion there is less conflict, both internally and externally. Where there is less judgment of self/others there is more peace, when there is more peace a different reality presents itself, one that is not based upon conflict to be at peace. A strange idea that through conflict we will find peace!

When those traveling the 'Clearing' path understand that their ability to embrace the conflicting energies of those around them and their environment is limited by their own judgements, their own points of view, then it follows that the less they hold onto judgements the more available they are. The more available they are the more at peace they will be, the more at peace, the more powerful. For one in compassion knows no limits to what they can embrace. Through the compassionate acceptance of everything that arises conflict is no longer being fed or encouraged. Those with conflict in their hearts, knowingly or otherwise will all be equally affected by being embraced by a truly compassionate heart.

There are no limits to the amount of 'charge' a compassionate heart can embrace.

Just a thought really, do with it what you will, of course you will do that anyway—what choice do you have?

Sleep on This One

LETTING GO? OR ACCEPTANCE?

There comes a time, in the journey of those practicing 'Clearing' when it (clearing) becomes second nature. Something that you 'are' instead of something that you do. This often happens over a period of time, and sort of creeps up on you. Hindsight is wonderful! When you look back you can see that you are no longer quite the same person you thought you were in the past.

Which often leads us to think, well, if I am not that person, then who am I? Indeed who was I? And of course … who will I be? All totally useless conjectures. A waste of mental energy. Trying to know the self from within a belief—a set of 'points-of-view'—is like a fish trying to describe the sea within which it lives. We can continually come up with an 'answer' that may make us feel good for a day or two, but the answer is only relevant from within the framework around which we have built our lives. That framework is flawed at the best of times, that framework will change, as, through continual practice of the clearing, the old is allowed to fall away.

I guess if we, collectively, all go along with the same story, then we would agree on any 'answers' to problems. That doesn't happen of course, so many different points-of-view all contending for 'reality'. Yet none of them are real in any sense of the word. We discover, through clearing, that a point-of-view is simply a conditioned perspective, "having nothing to do with good or bad—right or wrong". So a world made up of points of view! Hmmm. I'll show you my point-of-view if you'll show me yours, I'll be polite and nod, but all the time I know that MY point-of-view is the 'real' one. So that's okay. Hmmmmm.

In the early stages of our 'Clearing' practice we still have at least one foot firmly in the world of the need to do. It is this foot that sustains the illusion that there is something to do, indeed, that there is some 'one' to do something. With one foot planted in the 'to do' world we cannot help ourselves, always something to do. Even when 'Clearing', "I have to 'clear' someone!" "I have to 'clear' an issue!" "I have to 'clear' around this!" etc. All imply that there is something to *do*. And, that there is someone who needs to be doing it.

Which brings us to the idea that we have to let go of something, a point-of-view, a feeling, whatever. As the lagging foot gradually begins to approach the lead foot, out of the to do world, into the being world there is less questioning. There is less to do. We find that we are that which we sought. The realisation is interesting, for the more we come into the knowledge that we are already that which we sought, (and we may have used 'Clearing' as the path towards a goal!) the more we know that we have always been that. As this concept firms up in our awareness of course there is less to do, and less 'someone' to do anything. From this point-of-view a more peaceful state arises.

And the more this awareness grows, the more acceptance is all that is left. When first asked to practice 'acceptance' most people find it challenging. "How am I expected to accept that!" Whatever 'that' is, which is often something that goes against our deeply established and often addictive, belief patterns (points-of-view). For, all the while we are lost in the illusion that our past is 'real', anything that challenges our status quo is seen as a threat. Whilst we remain lost in our personal reality our ability to understand, to accept, is very limited. If concepts do not fit into the paradigm that we have come to believe to be true, then we do one of several things. They include—deny it; fight it or manipulate it so that it does fit. Often we cannot even hear other points of view. It could be that we are so far removed from other possibilities that they never even show in our lives for we tend to associate with others who are more like-minded and support our general perceptions.

SOME OF THE THINGS I LIKE

Some of the things I like about 'Clearing' are that it does not require a leap of faith in order to feel the benefits, it does not require that we move into a state of greater acceptance, it does not require we do, or change anything. All it asks of us is that we notice how the body responds/reacts to different memories or stimuli. Add on to the noticing the development of greater objectivity around that which we notice and before we know it, we are practicing acceptance.

As our practice develops so does our ability to remain in the moment, to be in a more compassionate state, to move into a deeper personal balance, to hold this space for others, without our having to 'do' anything.

Another by-product of our practicing 'Clearing' is that our personal awareness begins to expand, our ability to hear other points-of-view without going into immediate reaction grows. Our tendency to judge self or others reduces. This seemingly new state affects all those around us, it affects our environment, it affects that which we see and experience, all without us having to do anything.

| Sleep on This One |

The more we practice the more we are able to observe the changes in the body when an old, deeply established belief pattern is challenged. When we begin, our lack of training in personal awareness requires some intense reactions to get us to sit up and notice. It takes us a while to return to a more centred state and we'll often judge and blame while in this state. With practice we start to notice those old chemicals getting up to their usual tricks a little earlier, we can catch them before they take over the body (and the heart and the mind!). This means that we can return to a more peaceful, centred state so much quicker, adding less aggressive, judgemental blaming energy to the mix, which in turn means less to clear up later! Which in its turn gives us more 'time' to enjoy life instead of being so grumpy that things are not going our way.

And, when we are less grumpy, why, what do you know! Those we meet are less grumpy. Wow, how did that happen?

Acceptance is the key to the door of a new world, you have the key, what are you going to do with it?

Ponder This

DECISION TIME?

As I understand things, on a very fundamental level, we have two main options—two seemingly different paths for us to walk. One, to try and 'do' something about the manifesting reality, and two, to wake up from the collective illusion.

Whether we are aware of this or not depends, I suspect, upon the bigger picture of our past. For many it is not even on the radar, for, in order to see the difference we must be able to look outside of the current collective expectations. While we are caught in the collective our goals are predetermined, our 'points of view' established, our thinking limited, our internal polarization set and our ability to think outside the box nonexistent.

If we look at the majority of main stream social media today we can see people trying to reshape society, to dream new dreams, to introduce a 'new' world, to 'do' something that will make a difference in the manifesting reality. We see many thoughts, ideas, points of view being expressed, for the most part, all in opposition to other thoughts, ideas, points of view. Those other thoughts, ideas and points of view are all held in place by the polarised thinking of the collective. Therefore, it follows, that any opposition to current thinking is supporting the current paradigm without conscious awareness that it is doing so.

An example: A friend recently asked why they were so tired when they took their holiday. If you are an experienced 'clearer' you will understand, but there are many people new to clearing reading this (I hope!) So an explanation (or reminder) will not be wasted.

Very briefly—for this could be the subject of a book, so much is involved—our environment reflects back to us who we believe our selves to be. Our home—decorated according to our taste, personality, budget—supports, on a daily basis, who we think we are. Our family is an ever present reminder. Our place of work and colleagues continue to support this program, which, because of the constant pressure this system maintains, doesn't give us a moment to reflect. For those who do dream a different dream the established order of our 'reality' will work all the time to bring us back into the collective thought causing us to question and doubt our own dreams. Effectively putting a lid on any escape plan we may have been searching for. (Pause for thought—'who' is dreaming the dream?).

Who we think we are is not necessarily who we are in truth, it just happens to be who we currently believe ourselves to be. Yet as our environment reflects back to us the energy that we have put into it, and the energy that we have put in is simply a belief that this is who we are, we are caught in a loop that keeps repeating itself. We have trouble reaching our dreams because our shadow, the hidden, buried, unloved, unaccepted parts of our self are equally responsible for creating the reality that we wake up to each morning. So we are caught in acts of self sabotage daily, issues that are buried deeply within us constantly attack any higher thoughts or ideals we may have, drawing us back, all the time to the collective reality.

And we do not even know this is happening, for so lost in the illusion that we live in are we that even if any questions arises, they arise from the illusion, and are answered from within the illusion.

This causes a state of internal polarisation which in turn causes stress, which in turn cause all manner of reactions. Many are physical, the body starts to malfunction and breakdown, because there is no inner peace the body can only sustain good health for so long before the pressure gets too much. Our emotional world suffers as well, because while there is internal conflict—whether or not this is known and accepted—the inner conflict simply is reflected back by those around us. It is often those closest to us that reflect us most intensely. We, in our turn, tend to blame them for our own discomfort. Another loop! And our environment, because we are in a very close and personal relationship with our total environment, the earth itself responds/reacts to the energies of those living upon it. While we remain in internal conflict the earth will reflect that.

| Ponder This |

All of this leads to our wanting to 'do' more to try and create a reality within which we feel more comfortable, safer, happier etc. The more we do, coming from the polarised state, the more conflict, externally, we create. The more challenges we then face on a physical, mental or emotional level. Yet another loop, for there is no resolution, no peace, no safety, no happiness while we remain caught in the loop.

We may appear to want change, change to the social order, to the economic disorder, to the political world. Yet all we are doing, at least until we have become the change that we seek internally—totally—is to simply support the current status quo by our opposition to it (which, remember, arises from our own internal polarisation). As within—So without. Nothing new in that idea.

Now, back to the tiredness. If we unwittingly keep ourselves lost in the loop, and, as mentioned earlier, this loop is never ending and self perpetuating, we are keeping our bodies in a state of tension. Stress that results from that tension causes us to do more, without any satisfying result. This leads to the body having to work really hard to maintain a healthy, balanced state. This is something that is not sustainable and the breakdown in the body, emotional relationships, environmental systems is inevitable. Look around, what do you see?

When we take ourselves out of the usual day to day expectations, for example when we go on holiday, there are no longer the old reminders surrounding us, the environment is unfamiliar, the routine changed. This change allows the body to relax, something it has not been able to do all the time it is held by its projections or the established order supported by all of those people in your world who are lost in the loop and reflect that back to you.

When the body relaxes, as we have seen from the research on blood work we have done, one of the first things that happens is, you've guessed it, exhaustion. The more internal chaos that existed, the more exhaustion the body experiences. If the body is allowed to process the cycle, meaning it has enough time and awareness to work through the process of chaos/exhaustion/re-booting/re-balance, then that person will be refreshed. Refreshed that is, until they go back to the old, the familiar, and is reminded of who they think they should be. Because the old patterns are so familiar any questioning the person may have about their reality is short lived. They fall quickly back into the expected and the cycle begins again—balance into chaos into exhaustion into reboot—if you are lucky and the chaos doesn't take you out!).

TIME OUT!

If the body is not permitted enough time out from the forces that maintain the chaotic illusion there is no time available when the person can question what is truly going on. Without the opportunity to question the body remains stressed, remains polarised in its thinking, continues to support the illusion that there is a better illusion to be had, if only it worked harder, did more, campaigned more, fought more. And here we are in the loop once more.

So, it is hardly surprising when we see so many people hoping for some 'alternate' reality, a new dream, some great cosmic shift, yet we are still caught in the loop, the loop of wanting something that we do not currently have. Something that we believe will make us happier, safer, healthier. There is nothing that will make you happier, safer, healthier all the while you fail to see the part you are playing in creating both your own, personal, reality and the reality of the bigger picture.

When you can stop judging and accept, stop struggling and let it be, stop wanting and start being, then and only then, will the manifesting reality shift. To what? Who knows, for the 'job' of the individual remains the same, loving acceptance.

Do not think that by loving acceptance you will support the old status quo, that is the thinking that caused the polarisation and has no place in a more peaceful, loving, safe reality. By accepting all that is you see through the illusory nature of the world you live in, you see things for what they are and you no longer support any reality, you no longer energise that which you believe to be wrong. As you do this, your body has less resistance to the flow of information, for you become less and less polarised internally. As your body has less resistance to all information so you become more balanced, as you become more balanced your health returns to a state of well-being, your emotional world stabilises and your environment, the earth, relaxes.

And This!

THE SHADOW: BLESSING OR CURSE?

YOU MAY HAVE READ SOME OF C.G. JUNG'S WORK ON THE shadow, if you have been to a workshop you will certainly have heard me talk about the shadow, or in workshop terms, the 'back-pack'.

The 'shadow' according to Jung, consists of the parts of the self that we have yet to accept or embrace. Often those parts from our past that we are still in fear of, ashamed of or afraid of. Jung's opinion was that until we can embrace our shadow we can never realise our true potential for the shadow aspects define and strengthen who we are once they are integrated. While they are denied, we deny aspects of ourselves. Simply put this could be understood that, until we are able to fully integrate the shadow aspects of our past we remain lost between two worlds.

Ever had a conversation seemingly in your mind, with two polarised points of view (the devil made me do it! Or god made me do it!!) Many people spend a lot of their lives dealing with this internal conflict, it is not apparent in everyone, but when it reaches extreme levels that person would often be diagnosed by modern medicine, as disturbed, or bipolar. Those swings of mood from one extreme to another, two worlds, so close together, yet a huge distance apart.

I suspect that most people on the planet are bipolar to some degree or other, most not having reached the stage where medication is recommended. This bipolar state, to whatever degree we experience it, is simply a product of our upbringing, which in turn is a product of our parents experiences, and their parents and so on. The moment we begin to learn the concept of 'me', 'mine', 'you', 'yours', we are on the path of becoming bipolar. In our very early childhood these concepts do not exist but are gradually introduced to us by our parents, siblings, peer group, social environment, etc.

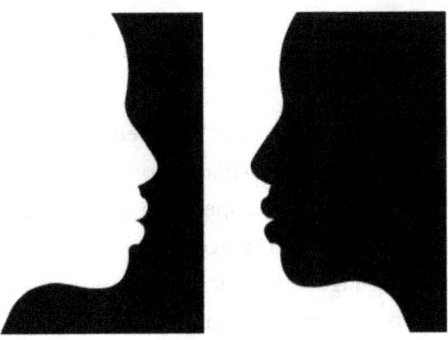

Along with these concepts we are indoctrinated into various points of view based on our parents points of view (which are often based upon their parents points of view…) The society in which we grow up, we are exposed, or not, to various religious points of view, social points of view, judgmental points of view. Being—as a very young child, non-discriminating—we copy the behaviour of our parents and those around us.

We learn to get on (or not!) with society depending upon how society 'treats' us. In effect we are being trained to have a unique experience while in the physical body.

We often judge some aspects of that experience as good and some as bad. Some we really like, some we like just a little, some are okay and some are, well, best not go there! Yet when we take a look at the bigger picture we see others in the world, who have grown up in different circumstances, with different points of view. It is this diversity that makes the world such a wonderfully interesting and exciting place. Yet certain points of view believe themselves to be better than other points of view, certainly better for a few individuals that gain the most from those points of view.

Then the collective belonging to one point of view try to impose that point of view on others whether the other collective wants it or not. We all know where that road leads.

MY SHADOW? CAN'T BE MINE, MUST BE YOURS!

While one collective fails to acknowledge their own shadow they will continually seek to blame someone, something, outside of themselves. This happens on global scales, religious differences, political differences, racial differences, colour differences, language differences, economic differences. Yet it also happens closer to home. Communities, particularly isolated communities that have a distrust of other communities. Distrust can often arise because of something that has been passed down through the generations. Whether or not this 'something' is valid or not is no longer in question. You were told it was this way by your parents, and if you were told often enough you did not question whatever it was, you just accepted, and then, in your turn, passed it onto your children thus often perpetuating the same illusion.

Yet even closer to home your 'personal shadow' can be sabotaging your best efforts at happiness. The internal dialogue, full of conflicting points of view is often a sign of an inner imbalance, a heavily polarised state that has arisen because of societal conditioning. Your shadow can be a major player in your well-being—physical, mental, or emotional. For the more polarised you become the more reactive you become, the more intense those 'feelings' associated with the reaction are. The more you identify with those feelings, the more chemicals the body produces.

I heard recently that the chemicals associated with any feeling only remain in the body for a short time (90 seconds?). What happens then? Well, if the source of the chemicals is continually stimulated, then the body produces more of the same, giving the impression that the feeling is continuous. Only when the supply is interrupted will the body be able to 'settle down' once again.

Our picture of the world is coloured by/influenced by our perceptions. Our perceptions can be understood as the points of view that we adopt, most often without our conscious participation. Any 'points of view' we identify with subsequent to our initial indoctrination have to be a product of that self same indoctrination. Whilst we continue to project the cause of any discomfort we may feel onto others we strengthen the shadow, causing the others to react to our blame and deepening and enforcing our own polarised state. This in turn gives rise to even more conflict, both internal and external.

We often refer to the shadow as being yours, but this can only be true from the personality, or an ego point of view. For as long as you hold onto the conditioned sense of who you are, there will remain the concept that whatever 'your' body feels actually belongs to you. In my experience this is so not true as to hint at a delusional state, the condition of someone not wanting to wake up from a nightmare because the nightmare is all they know.

But, don't believe a word I say, explore this for your self. Question where your points of view came from. Attach less importance to 'your' world view for by following this path it might just be possible that you become an agent for change, for a more peaceful, just society. Do not get sucked back into blame and judgement with the excuse that you will be disempowered if you don't. That sort of talk only arises from a fear based world view, a world view that cannot continue to exist if it is no longer fed.

Our next week in Tuscany will be devoted to shadow work. Uncovering it and embracing it. All in a very safe environment.

THINK ONCE, THINK TWICE, THINK THREE TIMES (AT LEAST)

Before allowing anyone to put (inject?) anything into your body. If the above talk about the shadow is anywhere near the 'truth' then those who think they know have absolutely no idea what is really going on. They may be convincing, they may be convinced themselves, but who told them, and why do they choose to believe? Question, always question. Until there is no one left in whom questions arise.

Something to Think About!

THE TRANSITION FROM 'DO-ING' TO 'BE-ING'!

I AM OFTEN REMINDING THOSE WHO ATTEND MY WORKSHOPS not to 'do' anything, the power and benefits of the work are in the be-ing. Easy for me to say, and often easy enough to understand intellectually, but to practice! That is a whole new ball game.

We are, all of us, so conditioned to 'do' that we don't know we are doing, whatever 'it' may be anymore—excuse the pun. Do-ing has become such a total part of the package of our experience that we rarely, if ever, question what we are doing or why we are doing it. We operate from within a certain structure. A structure that consists of accumulated judgements which are based upon points of view that we have acquired along the way.

This structure, as Einstein once said, "is a prison for us". We remain a prisoner to our own conditioned past without questioning the nature of the prison. Instead we become involved in various causes and give our energy to supporting one or more points of view. Yet these points of view that we energise are simply manifestations of the illusion that arises as a result of our being seduced into the need to do something all the time. What we do depends upon what we believe, or who we believe ourselves to be.

Most often I find that people are limited in what they believe. When people are introduced to my approach to Space Clearing they soon discover that things are not as they were told. In fact they find out that they are also not what they believed themselves to be. This of course can be the beginning of a very different journey, one that opens new doors. Yet most, if not all, people gaining this understanding still insist on holding onto the point of view that there is something that has to be done. Whether working with the energies of the space, or others, our conditioned response is always to do something to achieve a desired result.

I know that, for a while, along my path of a Space Clearing Consultant I was heavily into doing without realising it. It seems as though human nature, or perhaps the ego, has a need to be seen to be of value, to be acknowledged for its achievements. Many of us want to help, ourselves and others and I suspect this is why 'clearing' is so challenging.

'Clearing' is most effective when there is no attachment to the outcome, hard enough when 'working' for strangers, almost impossible when working on family members.

While I 'thought' I was do-ing something clearing people or the environmental energies I tended to get overloaded as 'my' body was unable to effectively process all of the information it gathered during consultations. Much of this was the result of my own shadow, the hidden aspects of the self. Of course, if it is hidden, how can we know about it, if we cannot know about it what chance do we have of changing it?

CAT—A—TONIC!

It was during one particular space clearing consultation that I was enlightened on this point. Previously, while working in houses, the resident cat would creep around the edges of the room, watching me with what appeared to be deep distrust. Happened all the time. I took little real notice of this, other than to acknowledge that the cat, being a very sensitive creature, didn't particularly like what I was 'do-ing'.

On this one consultation I had a minor epiphany, a brief moment of satori where I simple stopped doing. Immediately the cat came over, hung around, and wouldn't leave me alone! Subsequent consultations proved this point as all the cats now wanted to be my best friend, including one 'man hating' Siamese who amazed its owner by snuggling up around my neck, purring away and not wanting to leave. Ah Ha! One with the cats. Well, not trying to 'do' anything anyway. I had known for many years that dogs picked up on fear and other negative aspects and would react very quickly, but this newly discovered friendship with cats was really very enlightening.

I expect I was still 'doing' something for a few years after this experience, for we 'do' as a natural response. Yet the doing involved in clearing is simply the re education of the body to notice and not judge. This takes time and practice, at least it appears to. People often believe that the shadow—or backpack as we call it—is something that needs to be emptied, item by item. This would be a journey that would never end! Rather it is the realisation that whatever shows up simply needs to be accepted, unconditionally. It is the acceptance that takes any charge out of whatever shows up.

When someone tells me that a particular clearing was 'difficult or hard' I explain that degrees of difficulty are simply examples of the body/mind still in resistance or judgement. While we continue to feel the need to do something we must know at least two things, one, what is the problem, and two, how to fix it. Can we ever know the problem, or do we simply analyse the situation from our personal points of view/judgements and then apply what we have been taught to try to fix the situation?

Is this truly relevant to the situation or is it just our interpretation, which is arising from our own attachment to the illusion?

There is no good or bad in the doing or being, simply an acceptance that this is where we are at. For whatever reason we do what we do, we are what we are. Yet, as we practice acceptance and not doing our perceptions shift. Our points of view become less important, still relevant perhaps, but not something that we grasp quite so firmly. As we practice the clearing so we are able to accept more, the more we accept the less charge we give to that which arises. The less we energise that which arises the clearer we see, the clearer we see the less energy we give to supporting the old illusions, "… thus freeing ourselves from this prison." (Albert Einstein).

And This!

THE PROBLEM WITH CHANGE

How many people have told you they are ready for change? How many people have you told you are ready for Change? Has anything changed simply because you stated you were ready?

Before I get into my 'story' I would like to welcome several new people to this newsletter, many of whom come from an interest in Feng Shui. It may appear, from first reading, that this subject has little to do with Feng Shui, yet underlying any space clearing consultation is a desire, on the part of the client, to change. Change, as I hope to explain, is not so easy, in spite of people's apparent readiness.

There are many reasons why people may want to change: to improve their lives and the lives of their children would be for many, at the top of their list. Our conditioning tells us that to improve our conditions we need to work harder, longer, save more, do more, accumulate more. And it doesn't seem to matter what 'damage' we may do along the way, to ourselves, our family, friends, others and the environment. All in the pursuit of happiness??? Or wealth! Fame! Fortune! Or power!

One of the biggest challenges to change we face is the sacrifice it requires. We have become accustomed to events, emotions, relationships all unfolding in a particular way, a way that is unique to us. There are obviously many similarities in the way life presents to all, those similarities become more compartmentalised as we break up into various groups, each which their own specific perceptions. Religions, race, ethnicity, language etc, and then even further defined as we break into sub groups of the above.

Then we end up with a family unit, who bought into the local collective as a sense of belonging and safety is high on the list of priorities for comfortable survival. It is from this family unit that we get our own 'points of view' which we either reject or develop as we mature. Most people don't move far away from the tree and simply pass on their conditioning to their children without questioning the values or origin of the belief patterns they hold about themselves.

Change, for most people, can be best described as modified behaviour. Modifications to the human system, otherwise known as the personality, subtle shifts within the framework that has been established for many generations. Some people are resigned to the 'personality' being who they are and deny the possibility of change. Some people are determined to 'better' themselves, many are resigned, some are even happy.

It doesn't matter which category we fall into, we are still living within a dream world that has been created by previous generations, generations who themselves, were living in a dream that had been passed down to them by their ancestors. From my experience, working with people, it has become obvious that very few people actually question where the main aspects of their reality come from.

THE DREAMTIME

You may have heard people talk about changing the dream. Now, think about this for a moment. Who is it who is dreaming the current dream? (To better understand this explore the long term inhabitants of Australia, pre-European, and their 'Dreamtime', how representatives of the collective dreamed the world into being…). In the modern world, we are, each and everyone of us contributing to the dream within which we believe we exist. To change that world is to change the dream.

So, who is it, just who is dreaming the current reality? And who is it who is going to change that dream? If the 'personality' is the dominant force in dreaming the dream then that dream will be based on the desires of that personality and nothing of any fundamental value can change.

In an earlier newsletter I spoke of the two basic paths that are open to us, a) the modification or change of the dream or b) to wake up to the true nature of mind. Yet there is one more option, the middle way. We can settle on changing the dream, by following the path of 'clearing' the dreamer naturally dreams a different reality. As this shifts so the veil hiding us from our true nature reduces. Yet, as mentioned earlier, this requires sacrifice, for to change anything of fundamental importance we must first become the change that we believe we seek.

Becoming that change means letting go of who we thought we were, who we believed ourselves to be all of our lives. And therein lies the problem. To let go of who we thought ourselves to be requires that we are first aware of who we thought we were in the first place. To be aware of the personality, in an objective way, requires that we step outside of the self and observe the self from a place of non attachment. If we could all do that the dream would change very quickly, overnight we would wake up to a very different world. That doesn't seem to be happening though, instead we continue to struggle trying to right the wrongs, to modify the manifesting reality so that it will fit more comfortably with our own perceptions.

The dangers associated with this path should be obvious, it produces a continuation of where we appear to be now. Nothing more than and ongoing conflict as others seek to modify reality to fit their perceptions which are in opposition to our own 'dream'. We play our part in maintaining a dream that we seek to move beyond.

We cannot experience any fundamental change while we hold onto the past. So the sacrifice involves letting go of our past, a past that has been constructed upon nothing more than stories that evolved with our without supervision. How many of you are willing to release your past, unconditionally, no saving mementos, no hiding away little parts of an old self. Letting go of old hurts, old judgements, old conflicts, old loves, old expectations, old points of view? For without this commitment, little, if anything is going to change.

Perhaps the most exciting thing about change is that it can be instant, the moment the collective releases the past it makes way for the new dream to enter. If there are any attachments that you try to take with you, you are simply guaranteeing conflict in your future, and that is not a new dream, that is an old nightmare!

A Piece to Finish the Day

BEWARE THE GUNSHIPS

THE JOURNEY INTO GREATER SELF AWARENESS IS REALLY quite fascinating, providing of course you do your best not to take any of it personally. Those new to the newsletter may be wondering right about now, what on earth did I sign up for? Bear with me here, for all of this information is fundamental to how we approach life, what life gives back, and why.

I'll use 'Clearing' as an example of one way towards a greater understanding of the self. Mostly because those of you who actually read this have shown some interest in 'Clearing' as a way of be-ing.

Firstly, picture please, a great big sea, and in that sea the majority of life exists. We can call this the sea of consciousness, but that would not be even close to being accurate, best call it the 'commonly accepted' 'sea of consciousness' a big difference, as we shall 'see'.

People, amongst other life forms, are born, brought into being, in this sea, they know nothing else for the sea is their world. They swim in this sea, as do their family, friends, associates, in fact everyone they know or could possibly know, swims in this sea. It is only natural then that those in the sea take the sea and all conditions that arise in that sea seriously, personally. Become passionate about the events that present in that sea, take sides, according to their upbringing, to their sense of values.

There is something very special about this sea of consciousness, it is not like an ocean (or perhaps it is!) in that this 'sea of consciousness' is a connective, responsive field (*The Field* by Lynn McTaggart) that not only supports life in a three dimensional sense but is also the cradle for all creation. Imagine, sending out a radio signal (thought/emotion/action) into this 'sea' and having the 'sea' respond to the thought/emotion/action. Some of you may have made good use of 'parking spot angels' demonstrating the responsive nature of the sea and your ability to create your reality. Some of you have been a little more creative and have taken more responsibility for the world in which you live.

If it were as simple as investing energy into a though/emotion/action and reaping the rewards we would have to wonder why more people are not 'do-ing' it. Well, of course they are, all of the time, it is not possible that they are not. We are all, simply by existing, putting thoughts/emotions/actions into the sea the sea is responding.

Well, I can hear more than a few of you say, I never ordered this, I asked for a later model, better health etc. etc. Yet did you? Are you consciously creating the world you live in, or are you creating without awareness?

A good measure which you can use to determine how conscious you are in the world you live in is how content you are with that world!

A challenge that all face as they become more aware of this, is that with awareness comes all sorts of otherwise hidden information. When a part of us decides that whatever answers we seek are not to be found where we previously asked the questions we start to look elsewhere. Where can we look but in the same sea of consciousness that we have been existing within for a long, long time. Hmmm.

EVERYTHING EXISTS WITHIN THE SEA

I believe that all answers to all questions, all truth, all knowledge, exists within this 'sea', yet, like all areas, if we don't ask the right questions we are not going to get the right answers. We can spend a lifetime, or more, wondering what the 'right' questions are. Yet whether we ask questions or not, we still contribute to creating the world in which we live. It is no good complaining about that world if the part we play in creating that world is still asleep, not aware of the part it plays.

Take a long look at the world you are responsible for, if there is anything there that you are not comfortable with, then see that as a part of the self that has yet to awaken. See also, that every thought, every emotion every action is contributing to your world. Every judgement you make reinforces that which you 'oppose'.

As we travel the path of, in this example, 'Clearing' by practicing non-identification with, non-judgement of, that which presents itself in our lives, we gain greater objectivity. We take things less personally, we give less energy to various thoughts/emotions/actions. As we consciously reduce the amount of energy we put into the sea of consciousness, so we create less chaos. For most of us exist, to some degree or other, in chaos like it or not, realise it or not.

As we begin to take things less personally, we begin to feel safer with old thoughts and emotions. We become less likely to get lost in the drama. An apparently 'negative' side effect of this process is increasing paranoia, anxiety and fear. As we release control and attachment a lot of 'dark' primordial thoughts and emotions arise, stuff that has been kept under wraps for so long we never realised we had it. This seems to be a stage that we go through, sometimes called the 'dark night of the soul' it is like a test… Can you pass through this particular stage of the illusion without taking it personally?

As we seemingly awaken more information becomes available to us. It benefits us to remember that all is part of the illusory nature of the world in which we live. No exceptions. For those of you who came to earlier workshops, this stage was known as the 'gunships' (your worst nightmare lying in wait). They patrol the areas of your consciousness that, for most people, remain buried beneath layers of personality. Yet we meet your own 'gunships' everyday of our lives, and I suspect every day thereafter too! It depends on how much fear remains as to how you will experience these gunships, otherwise known as your personal demons, your dark side, the hidden, unloved aspects of yourself, you 'shadow'.

As we explore the final frontier (and it is not outer but inner space) the collective shadow arises, we must see this for what it is, not as some guardian of the gates but just another part of the sub-conscious, the collective shadow.

A final test? Perhaps.

Musings

THE NEED TO BELONG

It seems that a natural part of being human needs to feel a sense of belonging. A deep need to identify with something.

I do not know if this is inherent in the soul, a deep seated part of who we are that seeks to return to a sense of oneness, of connectedness to all things which we, as pure consciousness, may have been more aware of prior to being born into the human form. Or perhaps, is it a result of the conditioning we are subject to the moment we take on a physical body.

Is it that we feel safer identified with a particular group, whether we call that group a nation, a religion, a sports team or anyone of a number of other 'groups' that we feel we resonate with? Are we searching for a connection that we believe we have lost by passing into the body. Or is it that the society we are born into demands that we join it or be cast out. That fear alone, whether known or hidden deep within the sub-conscious, would be enough to keep us in the group.

It would be hard to tell which came first, societies needs or the deeper need of the soul. I suspect that, as all who came before us had the same experience, coming from a place of oneness into the separation of this 3rd dimensional 'reality' they quickly formed bonds and associations in order to fill the need to belong.

Or can this need to belong be traced back to the time of the hunter gatherers, when to be in a tribe meant a greater chance of survival?

Wherever, why-ever it came to be such a powerful part of our lives is not really the issue though. For most people it is something that is so deeply established, so much a part of their being that to consider otherwise doesn't even enter their minds. It has become how they identify themselves and is not something that is easily let go of.

In addition to these groups we associate with we have many other outward manifestations of our identity, sex, skin colour, language, job, home, car, hairstyle, clothes, partners. And then there are the more private 'objects' home furnishings, artwork, secrets, thoughts, beliefs and points of view. Whilst we are surrounded by all of these reminders, it is next to impossible to see beyond the 'box' that we live in. Our created environment keeps us a prisoner to our past. Those closest to us expect us to behave in a certain way, think certain thoughts, respond in emotionally predictable ways, (as we project onto those around us the same expectations). All of these external influences keep us marching in step, as we did in the past, as we do today and as we are expected to do tomorrow.

AS WE THINK SO WE ARE

I believe that our minds create the world around us and are capable of re-creating that world moment by moment. Yet we are caught in re-creating the same world that we lived in yesterday. Is this because of the need to belong and to not be different, to stand out from the crowd? Or is it simply because we are prisoners to our own routine.

Think back to when you were a child, you either had a stable home environment or you didn't. Either way that

| Musings |

experience has affected you on very deep levels throughout your life. You either came home to all that was familiar or to an ever changing world. Let's go with the familiar for the sake of this 'story'. You would come 'home' and home would contain all that you experienced every day. Parents, siblings, other relatives perhaps, even the furnishings and decorations would be familiar, the smells, the feel of the place, all familiar. Whether you felt welcome or not, comfortable or not, these were all things that, if they changed at all they changed slowly. Even going back to a friends place felt different, different people, furnishings, smells, feelings, you knew this was not home, not your home.

This was your world, if it changed it would take a while for you to readjust.

Sooner or later, most people move out of the family home, get their own place, decorate their place as they wish, as they can afford, and recreate a home of their own. They become, if not comfortable, at least familiar with their new environment. They may start a family of their own, they may not. If they do they pass on all of the learned patterns to their children, creating in their children this same need to belong although this may be done without awareness it will happen.

Each of us, sooner or later, creates a 'personal' environment and surrounds ourselves with furniture, objects, friends, work and social activities that reflect who we believe ourselves to be.

If discontent with this imaginary world should arise then we look outside of the self for answers. We seek support from other groups who may approach life a little differently than we have become accustomed to, though not too different of course. We may get temporary relief but, deep down, nothing has changed, we still inhabit the same reality with all its associated challenges.

We are still surrounded by 'stuff' that reminds us of our past, obviously we cannot surround ourselves with 'stuff' that reminds us of our future but we can learn to see things for what they are, reflections of who we thought ourselves to be.

While we are still driven by sub-conscious conditioning we will always seek to belong, a part of this 'belonging' demands that we follow the rules of the group. We may think we have the freedom to choose, but by joining a group we have relinquished that right to choose and instead, have the group choose for us. And the group may change the rules as it seeks to expand, and we are powerless to change the rules all the while we have this 'need' to belong.

It would seem that until we are able to step outside of this box we have constructed around ourselves we cannot take back control of our lives. Until the desire to do so arises from within us it will not be a part of our future, a part of our potential yes, but not a manifested reality.

Here is the dilemma that faces all those who seek to bring about change. If something needs to be done, then first we look at what it is that needs doing. The problem here is that the person who believes something needs doing is a product of the conditioning of the box. As such anything they 'do' is also a product of the conditioning of the box. You see the paradox? Doing something from within the limited awareness of the box simply perpetuates the reality created by the belief.

We are who we think we are. Or so we are told. Who do you think you are? And what makes you think thus?

I was told once that the word 'Swami' means a self made person, one who is no longer dependant upon the collective (groups) to make up their mind.

There is no safety in numbers, there is not security in belonging to a group that makes decisions for you. If it is safety you want, then you should not have chosen a human form. There is no safety here, you live, you die and stuff happens in between. When you let go of the need to feel safe all the time you begin to come alive. You move away from the groups that control your life, your world changes. When your world changes it allows others more room to breathe, more chance to see, for themselves, through the illusion of safety and to know, to really know, that they were never separate, never needed to belong to groups.

Wake up to your true nature, enjoy the experience of belonging, but don't take it too seriously, don't give away your power.

'Clearing'—of course—can help.

Did You Know?

STAND CLEAR!

For many 'Clearing' is a tool to help cope with life's experiences. By applying 'clearing' to our lives it is true that a lot of pressure falls away, there is a reduction of the stress held in the body and, by association, less build up of tension and all that entails on a physical, mental or emotional level.

If we are faced with situations that challenge us emotionally, mentally of physically, then finding a better way of dealing with those situations has to be a big plus and there is no doubt that clearing can be an effective way of dealing with life's ups and downs.

For many people it stops there, having discovered a process whereby life gets 'easier' many people are content.

While we are under pressure, whether we realise it or not, much of our life is spent coping. We manage situations (or avoid them!) often from the same model that allowed those situations to arise in the first place. It doesn't take a genius to realise that although this may affect the short term reality nothing is going to change on a fundamental level and at some time in our future we are going to re-experience the same situations often with greater intensity.

A lot of people may be familiar with the concept of infinite possibilities. At least they would have heard of this, whether or not they understand, and are living that life. If we imagine a being, free from the past and without any fear whatsoever, having the ability to choose, moment by moment, their reality then we may be able to see the potential and give it a go for ourselves.

The potential of infinite possibilities exists in every moment of every day. For most people that which presents has already been filtered through their own unique world views, which have been established over may lifetimes (generational). So infinity has been reduced to 'no choice', any choice we may feel we have being limited by our own considerably narrowed perceptions.

THE WORLD IS WHAT I EXPECT IT TO BE

In the workshops I use the example of wearing sunglasses to illustrate this point. They may be blue, they may be black, they may have spots on them, but each of us wears our own uniquely styled sunglasses and it is through them that we view the world. The world reflects back to us our expectations, our projections and we deal with that manifesting reality, as we have in the past. Nothing can change while we wear the same old sunglasses as they represent our expectations, and the world is always meeting those expectations.

Trying to 'get ahead' while wearing sunglasses (especially if they are sunglasses of self worth issues) is futile. Trying to achieve anything that is not already a part of the expectations of the sunglasses is futile. There is no way that, of the infinite possibilities available to us, the wearer of the sunglasses is going to be able to even imagine any alternative, such is the power of the sunglasses.

Imagine being free to choose. To select, moment by moment, from an infinite array of possibilities! Yet that is not even a dream for many for our choices have already been made by past decisions. Yet the potential exists here and now, always has.

'Clearing' is, rightfully so, seen as a tool to help cope, but it can be so much more than that. By developing the practice of not giving energy to that which shows up we are re-training ourselves to be more accepting and less judgmental. As we become less attached to any particular outcome so new doors open to new possibilities. We may not realise at first that we have 'chosen' a different path, for the chooser of the path is still wearing a pair of sunglasses and as such cannot be totally objective about possible choices they make. Rather we are still 'unconscious' but the sub-conscious has begun to move away from the conditioned path and is starting to make slightly different choices. It is not as though we are going to see the multiple choices before us all of the time, that may well be overwhelming! But as we let go of our hold on the past different futures can be allowed to show up, each time we 'choose' a different future that choice leads to an even greater range of possibilities.

It is in the letting go that new possibilities are able to present themselves. New possibilities are 'here' 'now' the only thing stopping them manifest now is your addiction to the past.

So, practice your clearing on a regular and frequent basis, practice noticing and accepting, practice non-judgement and non-identification. And see how it subtly affects the world you live in.

Take your power back, stop giving energy to the BS that is fed to you through the media, stop doing what is expected and open the door to a very new world. Remember, if you wear the sunglasses of lack, nothing you do is going to change that. If you wear sunglasses of inequality nothing will

| Did You Know? |

change that, fight, protest, campaign, all are actions of the wearer of the sunglasses and are doomed to failure.

Learn how to see the world without any sunglasses and make a difference that counts.

A Piece to Start the Day

LIVING IN THE MOMENT!

MOST PEOPLE TEND TO EXPECT LIFE TO BE A CERTAIN way, their past experiences dictating their current reality.

We may all hope things turn out for the best, and perhaps they do in the 'bigger picture' but the emotional rollercoaster many people find themselves on is often accepted as 'their lot in life'. We have conditioned ourselves to expect certain things to unfold and when they don't we get disappointed, perhaps this makes us try harder in the future, or try a different way to get what we think we need in order to be happy.

Last month I wrote about the many possibilities that were available, should we be free to select but our selections were pretty much set by our past experiences and expectations. I also wrote about the benefits of 'clearing' to help us be in a place where different futures were possible.

Yet this still requires us to 'do' something. To practice everyday awareness, the Buddhists might call this mindfulness, noticing, accepting and letting go.

No matter which path we take—wherever we may find ourselves—all the while we have any expectations about the future, all the time we have aspects of the self that have been denied, shut away, for whatever reason (the shadow) we will run up against challenges.

On the one hand—a common enough approach in the past—we can try to do something about that which shows up. Learn more, spend more, do more. Yet for those of us who have tried that in the past we see that it doesn't actually change very much, it is the slow road to a more peaceful state. It requires that we are in a constant search for another state of being. That path in itself is a trap because it takes advantage of a belief that there is somewhere to go, someplace to be, something to do. A lot of people who practice clearing may sub-consciously, follow that path. Yet, it can also be seen that this is a path with an end, for as we practice clearing, so we learn to take less and less personally. The less we take personally the more peace we feel, the more peace we feel the less there is to 'do'.

I used to be full of the need to do something in order to be 'enlightened'. I don't know if it is age, clearing, or just life's experiences that have taken the edge off that drive. Or possibly I have seen through the illusion of 'do-ing'. For now I am content with what is.

Often during Skype, or other clearing sessions, people tell me that their past still shows up. My reply would be that the past will always show up, especially while we give it energy, or deny it, whether consciously or otherwise. The past showing up is not a bad thing, not something to be avoided. It is what we do with the information that is the key. We know, through continual practice of the 'clearing' that we learn to see the past a little differently each time it shows up. Each time we become aware of it in our lives we develop the practice of stepping back and observing without getting involved.

AWARENESS

Awareness, again, is the key. Without being aware we remain victims to the past.

For many though, this still seems like a journey, a means to an end. Peeling the layers of the onion.

As we accept though, that there is nowhere to go and nothing to do then really what *are* we do-ing? And *why*!

I am reminded here of a delightful quote:

> Since all things are naked, clear and free from obscuration there is nothing to attain or realise. The everyday practice is simply to develop a complete acceptance and openness to all things and to all people so that one never withdraws or centralise onto oneself.

And that, in a nutshell, is it.

Certainly the 'Clearing' helps us to accept, and for many this is a gradual process, because the conditioning that holds us in the past is so strong. Added to which are the people in our lives, who in their turn are prisoners of their own past, each of them with their expectations of who we are, holding us in conformity.

Imagine a set of those Russian Dolls, the nesting ones, one fits in another, which fits in another, etc.

And there you are, born into a family.

Skin colour, one box, sex, another box, religion, another box, land-owner/non landowner, a box, wealthy/middle of the road/poor, another box. Education, another box. And so it goes. Each box nesting in the previous one. Following this model it is easy to imagine that it is a process, to be free of all the boxes, one by one, and many people take this path. Hardly surprising that this particular path could take many years, lifetimes even.

| A Piece to Start the Day |

Yet, if we follow the above quote: " The everyday practice is simply to develop a complete acceptance and openness to all things and to all people.…" There is nothing to do other than accept that which shows up. This is your life, higher vibrational information inhabiting a physical body, having an experience. Nothing more, nothing less. Acceptance, hard as it may appear to be at first, is the key to liberation from the cycle of birth, death and rebirth. Acceptance is the foundation upon which the myriad of possibilities become real, acceptance is the one thing that will change your life in the hear and now. No expectations which lead to disappointment, sadness or confusion.

Piece of cake.

Ponder This

WHO IS IN CHARGE?

MOST, IF NOT ALL OF US WOULD LIKE TO THINK THAT we are in charge of our lives, making decisions from, hopefully, an open and informed place.

My experience over the years teaching and consulting imply that this is not necessarily the case. Where we may think we have free will our past conditioning creates a funnel type effect where each decision, conscious or otherwise, reduces or channels each future decision in a particular way.

Our very early years of this particular human experience conditioned us in unique ways without our conscious participation. This conditioning formed the basis upon which we would go through life predisposing us to respond/react in particular ways without giving any thought as to why we respond/react in these ways.

The perceptions that we acquired, inherited or learnt along the way create within us expectations of the way events/people will appear to us. It is as though we are viewing life through a unique pair of sunglasses. They colour our view of the world, change the person or event into patterns that meet our expectations, block it out if it doesn't fall within our area of acceptance.

So much for free will. Trying to get to the bottom line here and realise who is making the decisions and why is the subject of many of the Personal Clearing Workshops.

It is challenging to take on board the fact that the decisions are making us, not the other way around. For even when we believe we are making a choice out of free will, we are actually only choosing from limited options which themselves are a result of past decisions.

Imagine being raised in a household that had very fundamental values. As you grew more mature those values may not have the same meaning that they did for your parents, yet they are still a deeply conditioned part of who you believe yourself to be. You will either accept them, fight against them or find a compromise somewhere in the middle. But much of your life will revolve around that childhood conditioning.

All the time we make decisions without recognising who is making the decision (ego/personality, genetic memory, spirit etc) our choices will be both limited and unsustainable.

I call this process putting out fires. We do this without realising that we were the one who lit the fires in the first place. If you want to see some real change in your life stop lighting fires.

This is also known as damage control, all the time trying to make decisions that will lessen the negative effects of previous decisions.

While we continue to deal with life's experiences as we have in the past, we can only expect more of the same.

Our problems cannot be solved from within the framework they were created.

A little lateral thinking can make the difference between a happy, healthy future and the continuation of old patterns and old ways of dealing with those problems.

Applying 'Clearing' to everyday situations allows both internal and external balance to be restored. With balance the need to do or fix anything falls away.

As with most of this type of information it is easy to understand on an intellectual level but the actual practice is a whole new ball game. For a start we need the intellectual understanding. To be able to recognise that the decision making process is not under our control is the first step towards liberating the self from the past.

Then we need to apply this understanding, obviously I would recommend a workshop for the training and support, because this path can be very lonely. Without the support of a community that follows this path those around us who are still locked into the old 'traditional' ways will try to keep you conforming to their views. This is not always a conscious effort on their part, again, we are all subject to the past conditioning, some people try to break away, some people fail to recognise this is the case.

Are you ready to step out of the shadows of the past? Are you even aware just how much your life is controlled by your past?

And This!

WHO IS IN CHARGE?

MOST, IF NOT ALL OF US WOULD LIKE TO THINK THAT we are in charge of our lives, making decisions from, hopefully, an open and informed place.

My experience over the years teaching and consulting imply that this is not necessarily the case. Where we may think we have free will our past conditioning creates a funnel type effect where each decision, conscious or otherwise, reduces or channels each future decision in a particular way.

Our very early years of this particular human experience conditioned us in unique ways without our conscious participation. This conditioning formed the basis upon which we would go through life predisposing us to respond/react in particular ways without giving any thought as to why we respond/react in these ways.

The perceptions that we acquired, inherited or learnt along the way create within us expectations of the way events/people will appear to us. It is as though we are viewing life through a unique pair of sunglasses. They colour our view of the world, change the person or event into patterns that meet our expectations, block it out if it doesn't fall within our area of acceptance.

So much for free will. Trying to get to the bottom line here and realise who is making the decisions and why is the subject of many of the Personal Clearing Workshops.

It is challenging to take on board the fact that the decisions are making us, not the other way around. For even when we believe we are making a choice out of free will, we are actually only choosing from limited options which themselves are a result of past decisions.

Imagine being raised in a household that had very fundamental values. As you grew more mature those values may not have the same meaning that they did for your parents, yet they are still a deeply conditioned part of who you believe yourself to be. You will either accept them, fight against them or find a compromise somewhere in the middle. But much of your life will revolve around that childhood conditioning.

All the time we make decisions without recognising who is making the decision (ego/personality, genetic memory, spirit etc) our choices will be both limited and unsustainable.

I call this process putting out fires. We do this without realising that we were the one who lit the fires in the first place. If you want to see some real change in your life stop lighting fires.

This is also known as damage control, all the time trying to make decisions that will lessen the negative effects of previous decisions.

While we continue to deal with life's experiences as we have in the past, we can only expect more of the same.

Our problems cannot be solved from within the framework they were created.

A little lateral thinking can make the difference between a happy, healthy future and the continuation of old patterns and old ways of dealing with those problems.

| And This! |

Applying 'Clearing' to everyday situations allows both internal and external balance to be restored. With balance the need to do or fix anything falls away.

As with most of this type of information it is easy to understand on an intellectual level but the actual practice is a whole new ball game. For a start we need the intellectual understanding. To be able to recognise that the decision making process is not under our control is the first step towards liberating the self from the past.

Then we need to apply this understanding, obviously I would recommend a workshop for the training and support, because this path can be very lonely. Without the support of a community that follows this path those around us who are still locked into the old 'traditional' ways will try to keep you conforming to their views. This is not always a conscious effort on their part, again, we are all subject to the past conditioning, some people try to break away, some people fail to recognise this is the case.

Are you ready to step out of the shadows of the past? Are you even aware just how much your life is controlled by your past?

Another Day, Another Thought

DO YOU EVER WONDER?

I have often been asked to answer "What if..." questions for people. What if this? What if that? If only. I never do of course. I mean, where do the 'what if's' stop? And really, what good would it do to have an answer.

Answers are statements that either fit our current perceptions/reality model or not. If they do, and we are happy with the 'answer' then it is the right one. If they do fit but we are not happy with the answer then we manipulate the 'answer' until it sits well with us. If an 'answer' lies outside of our current 'reality' i.e., something we are not at all comfortable with, then we just fail to hear it or we attack the giver...

So, we only hear what we want to hear/are ready to hear. And even then, what we hear may not be what was said/meant. And the same goes for seeing as well, we see what we want to see.

That which we see and hear are products of our past projected into the now. We see, and hear, what we expect (conditioned) to see and hear. There is a lot of talk about the need for change yet little understanding of what that word 'change' really means. If what we see and what we hear are all products of our expectations then the manifesting world is but a reflection of who we believe ourselves to be. Here and now.

| Another Day, Another Thought |

For change to occur in the outer world it must first happen in the inner world. Yet most people are so convinced their perceptions of reality are right there is little room for true change. All we get, when people hang onto their perceptions and defend their points of view is more conflict.

RUSSIAN DOLLS

Every morning people wake up and find themselves embroiled in conflict. Not always obvious for the conflict is simply a manifestation of who we think we are, not separate from that understanding. So, it appears to be an integral part of who we think we are. How then are we supposed to be objective about our perceptions, particularly when we take them so seriously and attack or undermine others with different points of view. Waking up within this 'perceived' conflict one does what one always does, cope to the best of ones abilities.

We do our best to manage life's situations, we spend much of our time in damage control mode without even being conscious that we are doing it. A little like the Russian Nesting Dolls, take the top off, and there is another doll, remove it, take the top off, and yet another doll, and so it goes. Now, in human terms, the second doll in may be aware that it is playing a part, that of the outer doll, but what about the next layer, or the next? How are they going to make themselves known to the outer doll all the while we give so much attention to the external layer, the obvious manifestation of who we think we are. Is it even required in this 'drama' that they become known?

If indeed manifestation follows intention and the intention is clouded, lost in the layers, then what may start out relatively pure, even with the best of intentions gets polluted as it makes its way into the outer world. We are still caught in damage control. Trying to 'fix' something that is not even broken, merely a manifestation of our own making. 'Fixing' something gives it energy, giving something energy aids in its manifestation. So, while we continue to wake up each morning to the dramas of life that we fell asleep to, nothing changes, other than perhaps our attempts to 'fix' something. We try to change something, all the time coming from the illusion that in order to change the manifesting reality we must 'do' something!

And most of the time the conditioning that holds us is so strong we cannot even pause and consider a different way.

Here's an example. If you celebrate(d) the New Year, you did so because, well, either you just like to party, or you believe there is something special about another year dawning. The calendar that has the New Year occurring when it does is based upon the shortest day of the year, when the sun begins to return to the sky. Pretty logical really. The winter begins to break, according to the slowly lengthening days. All well and good. But what happens when you live in the Southern Hemisphere. The sun is beginning to shorten its time in the skies from where I am sitting now. Hardly a time to celebrate a new year, we should really have our own New Years Celebration, if we still feel the need to, at our own mid winter solstice.

We go along with established belief patterns for many reasons. Mainly because we are still in damage control mode and anything outside of that is heresy. Or we may not want to feel like the odd (wo)man out, we have a need to belong, so no rocking the boat. Perhaps it just never occurs to us that current collective thinking is not the best way to go. What is good for the North may not hold in the South, what works for you may not work for me. Because we hold onto our perceptions of what is and what is not real, neither of which is ultimately sustainable, we simply perpetuate conflict.

We have found our niche and even though at times it might be uncomfortable, challenging, it is still 'ours' so we hang onto it, defend it, establish it. Meanwhile the world continues to move on, leaving us to struggle within an illusion of our own making.

For those of you familiar with clearing as a process, take a moment, sit quietly, and notice—do your best not to energise that which you notice. If you fight against that which manifests in your life you are fighting a battle with your self. Who is going to win? If you practice acceptance, hard as that may seem to do if you are lost in the drama, then you gradually disempower the drama.

Practice makes perfect.

And This!

UP OR DOWN!

DOES IT MAKE ANY DIFFERENCE? AS I CURRENTLY UNDERstand things, we are either trying to make sense of, and improve, the world we find ourselves in, or we are trying to see through the illusory nature and understand just what the heck is going on from a different perspective.

Imagine. We may believe ourselves to be on a journey, walking up the spiral staircase, or down. Down leads to more 'stuff', a search, a journey into the physical. A journey that, one hopes, leads to a happier, healthy, wealthier state. Or, just plain more. More stuff. More experiences.

Up, we believe, leads out of this cosmic soup. A journey 'home'. The spiritual path. Religions have perpetuated this myth. Heaven is up, and hell is, where else! But down. Choices, choices, choices. Do we really have a choice, or is the very idea of 'choice' a product of the illusion. We think we have a choice, but, if that were the case how many people would choose to live in anything but a more peaceful, harmonious environment? Choices are limited. You may think this, because, given certain structures within which you live, your choices are, well, limited!

Whether you are 'on the way up', or, 'on the way down' is not going to affect your peace of mind. It is not going to make the world a better place. It is not going to satisfy the personality that is on the journey.

All the time we think we are on a journey, or have a lesson to learn (that is a common point of view with those who believe themselves to be going up the spiral staircase home/to heaven?) we cannot be at peace.

If we are lost within the illusion, having no thought that we may be in an illusion, then our choices are certainly limited. Any choice we may think we have is contained within the manifesting reality. The manifesting reality is a product of our (the collectives) belief patterns. Where energy has been invested in an idea, so that idea takes form and becomes the 'reality'. Stop giving an idea/concept/belief pattern energy and it falls away.

The results of this simple idea, that giving energy to any point of view charges that 'point of view' and given enough energy, becomes the reality of the day, are easy to follow. Various invading civilisations in the past have imposed their perceptions upon the invaded peoples. Given enough time, energy (money/power) the invading perceptions become the norm, replacing the more traditional beliefs of the conquered people. Time and again history demonstrates this is the case.

GLOBAL/LOCAL/PERSONAL

This happened, is happening, on a global scale. It also happens on a personal level. We 'give' energy to ideas, thoughts, belief patterns that we currently believe to be 'real'. We are then left to deal with the manifesting reality that those belief patterns have created. You can see how easy it is to get lost in the drama.

- We believe something to be 'real'
- This something is a product of the collective

- We give energy to whatever this belief pattern happens to be
- The belief manifests, 'proving' that it was 'real' to begin with!!
- We then have to try to manage, come to terms with or improve the manifesting reality
- This only deepens the hole we have dug for ourselves

While we attempt to control anything that arose from a belief pattern, we are simply chasing our tails, around and around we go.

So, back to the spiral staircase. Going *up*? Going *down*? All the time we believe we are going anywhere there will be judgement/comparison/envy. All the time there is judgement/comparison/envy, there will be discontent. All the time there is discontent there will be judgement/comparison/envy. While we are not content, always seeking something else, new, more, less, better etc., there will be no peace. While there is no peace within, there can be no peace without. (Remember, if you are not at peace you are energising 'not at peace'.)

If there is such a thing as choice, then perhaps it would benefit us (all) if we chose to pause for a moment. Reflect upon what we are giving our energy to. Take a breath, look around. Just because everyone else is energising conflict doesn't mean it is the best way to go. Every time you pause, the choice is to either continue to give energy to a belief, or withdraw your energy, keep it for a rainy day, keep it for something worthwhile.

Choose clarity over confusion, freedom over imprisonment, life over death.

Choose 'clearing' as the tool to help.

| And This! |

There is no up, no down, no ladder, no here, no there, no 'spiritual, no material. There is no me, no you. Enjoy the moment without judgement/comparison/envy. Stop energising that which no longer serves you or the greater well-being.

Sleep on This One

THE DILEMMA CONTINUED

Where do you get your information from? And who do you trust/believe?

Many years ago, while sailing through the Arafura Sea, we picked up five radio stations at 'news' time. Five different countries global news services. All had one story in common, not a very important story—and each had a completely different take on the story! Who do I believe? Why none of course. Now my 'news' comes through social media and I don't believe much of that either. I don't have a television, don't listen to the radio, certainly never read newspapers. Recently, through the social media, attention has been brought to Venezuela and The Ukraine, both areas of civil conflict. Not so long ago it was other countries. And before that, other countries. We certainly live in 'interesting' times.

It is hard to see all that is happening around the world as the 'big picture.' We see small parts and then we react to those parts based upon our personal sense of good bad, right or wrong. We judge, we take sides. We may act in response to the situation, we may feel powerless. Different people have different points of view. Some support one side, others, well, they support the other side.

If we look back over history, at least the history that has been recorded, we will see countless wars and revolutions. An almost never ending series of conflicts, for various reasons, fought around the world. Having refreshed our memory of the rather violent known history of the world we should be able to take a step back and take another look at where the world is now! (Of course plenty of other stuff has happened apart from the conflicts, but let's just look at the conflicts for now).

What has changed as a result of these wars, these revolutions? Are we any closer to a peaceful state! We don't even have to look globally for an answer. Domestic violence—civil violence, all seem to be an ongoing part of everyday life for many people around the world, And not just in 'other' countries, in our own backyard. Violence may not show itself as open warfare—even economic control—wherever there is any internal imbalance, on whatever scale, the 'accepted' resolution is conflict of varying degrees.

Certainly some things have changed over the course of history. But there is one thing, one very important thing, that has not changed. The majority of people, including those who govern, remain in a state of greed, fear and ignorance. How can conflict exist without greed, no fear, no ignorance?

All this 'new age' talk of 'one-ness' is just so much hot air if those talking it are not practicing it. If indeed there is such a state (one-ness), then who is 'doing' what to who? Or are we not 'doing' this—whatever we perceive as being done—to ourselves?

I saw, many years ago, that there was a very long list of social and environmental injustices, nothing has changed there, perhaps the list is longer now, I don't know. Where to start? Which one to take a stand on. You have probably read recently, in your social media, something about 'good men/women doing nothing' as being the big problem. We see a social injustice and we need to 'do' something to make it better. This is the stock standard response today. DO something, to make it better. Yet which is better? Simply because it is your point of view (possibly shared by others) does that make it right?

And does exerting your point of view other another point of view solve any problems? Just take a look at the increasing amount of legislation being enacted, all, so we are told, put in place to protect us!!!

OR ARE WE TOTALLY MISSING THE POINT?

While we are taking a stand against one injustice what is happening behind our back? And, a reminder, if the state of one-ness exists, who is doing what to whom?

By remaining polarised, and caught in a lesser game, are you really making a difference. Has any revolution led to peace?

Or do we just swap one set of 'greedy, fearful and ignorant' leaders for another.

I believe that the only reason conflict continues to exist is because it exists within us. Whether that is a conditioned part of humanity or a fundamental state of being is the issue here.

If it is a conditioned part, then there is room to grow and change. If it is fundamental, then, well, just accept it.

If I say you are wrong, does that make me right? Or are we all just acting out our own insecurities, manifesting as 'greed, fear and ignorance.'

I was recently asked to post a request for clearing around the situation in The Ukraine. The difficulty with 'clearing' is that it cannot be attached to any particular outcome otherwise it falls back into the category of 'doing', and, as we all know, ha ha, clearing is not about do-ing, but be-ing.

So, what can we possibly focus on from a state of be-ing? It is intrinsic in human nature to want to help. This is a good thing, but often misguided. We want to 'help' based upon our values, and, as we can see, our values differ from the values of others around us. If we are ruled by our emotions we are thoughtless, if we are ruled by our head we are heartless!

My suggestion, to those who made themselves available to clear around areas of conflict was simple.

The basic premise was based on unconditional love, true compassion. A place where there is no judgement, no taking sides, no thoughts or right or wrong, good or bad.

But I have already written too much. This article to be continued next month. Stay tuned!!!

And This!

THE DILEMMA, PART 3

So, what to do?

Easy enough to talk about unconditional love—easy enough to pretend or intellectualize—that you are a compassionate person. A whole new ball game to actually 'be' it.

So much talk about 'one-ness' but scratch the surface, just a little, and you will find old, long established prejudices. How can we possibly expect others to lead us when those who would lead have their own hidden prejudices and we cannot even be that which we seek.

We live in a polarised world, without this 'polarity' it is quite possible the world would not exist, certainly not the world as we have come to know it. A good thing or a bad thing? Look at the symbol for the Ying and the Yang, the circle with the black and the white, each balancing out the other—the eternal conflict out of which arises the world we live in, and many others I imagine!

Through my exploration of this world through the path of clearing I have noticed there is always balance. Whether we look at the 'big' picture or a much more personal picture we see this balanced state. We may not agree with the balance as we see it, but it exists nonetheless. For example, on a personal level, when looking at the energy of a home in a space clearing consultation, the home reflects those living in it. When the people living in the house feel the need for a consultation it is often because they are experiencing some discomfort, either they are sick and need to try something else to get well or they are 'stuck' energetically. This often isn't indicative of an environmental imbalance, rather it is a shift in the awareness of the people living in the space.

As long as the energy around us reflects back to us the accepted parts of who we are, we are, for the most part, comfortable with that. It may well be that the environment is stressed, but that would only be because we too are stressed.

Yet often what is reflected back to us is made up not only of the conscious, accepting aspects of the self, but the hidden, the 'unloved' shadow parts of the self that have yet to be integrated fully. It is the growing awareness of these shadow aspects that give rise to feelings of discomfort. Because of our conditioning, we tend to look outside of ourselves for the answers to any problems that we face. We blame others, we blame our environment, we blame the weather, the tax man, the neighbours, the list is endless.

EXTERNALISING IS NOT THE ANSWER

While we continue to blame we fail to see where the real issue lies. While we blame and externalise we seek to 'do' something to change our circumstances. Yet always that around us reflects back who we are, shadow included. So our environment is always in a balanced state albeit a stressed, anxious, fearful one. The more stressed we become, the more stressed the environment (still in a balanced state) the more peaceful we become, the more peaceful the environment.

Now expand the picture a little. Imagine a conflict with your neighbour (or anyone else of course) the more determined you become the more determined the neighbour becomes. The angrier you get the angrier the neighbour gets. This, believe it or not, is a balanced state. We respond this way partly because when confronted, whether this is obvious or not, our conditioned reaction is to defend our position, strengthen our point of view. When we feel threatened, under attack, we defend ourselves, whether the attack is real or just perceived. The more energy we give to defence the more energy is given to the attacker.

We easily arrive in a situation of conflict with another, whether that is physical, emotional or energetic, because we are determined that our point of view is the correct one, the one that must prevail. The issue here is not having a point of view, nor even believing that it must prevail, this after all is just a reflection of the Yin and the Yang, energised by the parties involved. The issue is more the energy behind the point of view, the sub-conscious conditioning out of which the uncomfortable feelings of being challenged arises. We are, for the most part, very self centred beings. We attach great importance to the ideas, concepts and views, of the self. We see the world from within a conditioned framework and if something doesn't fit then we either ignore it, challenge it or manipulate it so that it does fit.

All the time we do this we force our perceptions of balance onto the manifesting reality, much of this, remember, is not done consciously.

It is easy to see how any 'balanced' state is precarious because it is not based upon solid ground but ideas that have been given life/energy by all who subscribe to them. It doesn't matter how much money or power is used to shore up a belief pattern, when it comes down to nuts and bolts, they are still castles in the air.

| And This! |

While people continue to subscribe to particular belief patterns, they energise those belief patterns, or perhaps, more importantly, they energise the opposites. So, even when we take a stand we are supporting that which we are standing against. Crazy eh!

WEAPONS OF MASS HALLUCINATION

Take, for example the feeling of anxiety—anxiety is an airborne dis-ease. It is a transmission from someone, somewhere, that triggers off in another the feeling of anxiety. The person picking up the signal assumes that the anxiety is theirs—a product of their past conditioning—their body develops the symptoms of anxiety and they, in their turn, radiate out the feeling of anxiety. This is picked up by another, or many. The degree to which individuals respond/react to the feeling depends upon their personal history. So, by our identifying with a feeling, in this case anxiety, we become a part of the problem of global anxiety.

Back to where I finished last month. By developing the ability to notice the changes in the body alongside of the understanding of what is happening and why, we can gradually distance ourselves from the feeling. We stop energising a particular feeling. This causes the wave form of that energy/emotion to collapse. When the wave collapses we no longer feed it, we are free from a debilitating feeling, which wasn't even ours in the first place, and we stop spreading the dis-ease to others around us.

A new balance is formed, based once again on who we are at any given point in time. Same as before, only now 'who we are' has shifted into greater awareness.

Try it for your self.

Something to Think About!

WHAT THE ****

Clearing—at its most basic level can be of immediate benefit to both practitioner and family member and friends. As with most things though, the more you practice, the more 'energy' you give to your practice, the more obvious, and powerful are the benefits.

Life can be challenging at times and many of us seem to be in a constant battle with our personal demons. The demons of depression, anger, frustration, envy. Problems in relationships, health issues, financial difficulties. Just 'life' really, and all that it has to offer.

We may often think that 'life' would be better if: if we were healthier, younger, older, wiser, wealthier, if we had that new car, new relationship, new job, new house. Always we look to the future as holding more promise than the world we currently find ourselves in. If the future is the attraction, the carrot on the stick, then we will have to do something to make that new future happen. Yet often the steps we take to create, what for us seems a better world, we simply strengthen the web that we struggle to free ourselves from by giving it energy.

As we continue to express ourselves, where social, political, financial or racial conditions prevail, we try our best to not only survive, but thrive. Are we really making our own choices, or are we being channeled into limited choice, believing that we have free will?

Do you live in some fantasy land or do you consider yourself a 'realist'? Do you live for a future that has yet to manifest? Whilst we give energy to whatever it is that manifests in our life, we will continue to add 'charge/energy' to that creation. All the time we energise the world we live in we will seek ways to improve it, yet the choices that we have are limited to the parameters within which live. This being the case our choices have already been made, for they have to fit into the model that we currently take to be the truth of our world.

I believe that it is only by thinking outside the box that genuinely new experiences can present. Yet most of us insist on trying to resolve any issues we may have from within the paradigm that created those issues, our efforts are not only doomed to eventual failure but actually reinforce the belief patterns that make the world what we believe it to be. We are kept in this polarised state by our own refusal to see things differently.

THE ETERNAL DILEMMA

And just how am I creating my world?

Have you ever hurt yourself, nothing major but painful? And then answered the telephone, a loving friend is calling, you forget all about your injury, until you hang up!! Then the pain comes back. See how your attention, and where you put it, creates your reality on this small scale. If everyone in the world puts their attention on pain, what do we all get! Are you totally conscious of where you put your attention, all of the time?

The fact that the more we focus our attention on any particular aspect of our lives, whether we do this with any conscious awareness or not, the more we support that reality has been demonstrated over and over again in the many workshops that I have presented. All the time we fail to 'see' this we continue to add energy to that manifestation. It is not so easy, to stop energising our 'reality' there are always little hooks, seductions, feelings, to pull us back. Yet without letting go of our judgements we are just guaranteeing more of the same.

If you find yourself caught up in this craziness, then join us for a week in France in September and see the world from a very different point of view. Discover just who it is who is behind the desire for more.

Ponder This

PONDERING ON THE IMPONDERABLE

Something to ponder upon. During the years I have been developing my understanding of 'clearing' it has become increasingly obvious that no state exists without its opposite. Where we hold extreme points of view we will find its opposite. This applies both on a macro and a micro level. It applies to individuals whose lack of internal peace shows as judgemental perceptions. This manifests initially internally, which, if not addressed early will result in physical health issues, emotional problems, psychological difficulties.

It applies to communities, to countries. To religions, to race, politics, everywhere you look you will see examples of a polarised consciousness. The more we, or our community, holds onto a 'point of view' the more we will encounter its opposite, the more radical we become, the more radical the 'opposition.' All the time you hold onto and defend a point of view you will continue to experience its 'reflection'. This of course justifies your point of view and you expend more time, money, energy, in defending it.

Along the way, on this journey of judgement, the issues of internal imbalance are often externalised. When we encounter people or situations that make us feel uncomfortable the habitual response is to blame, to strike out at those we hold responsible. Often those we are blaming are simply responding/reacting to their own sub conscious conditioning. They are, seemingly, as powerless as we are to handle the situation in any other way.

This is interesting because if we were not so polarised we would not have encountered the challenging person/situation in the first place. It simply would not exist—in our reality.

The 'stronger' we feel about an issue, any issue, the more energy we give to that issue, for or against. In fact, if no one opposes us we have no value, our point of view becomes meaningless. Our sense of identity, from this point of view, exists only to the degree that there are others who challenge us. Imagine, you identify yourself by your points of view. If no one opposes your point of view, there is no energetic support for you to maintain that point of view.

While we believe this, and remember, this whole reality only arises because we have the point of view, there is no alternative approach. When we allow, through past conditioning, the body to become inundated with particular amino acids, which we identify as emotions or physical feelings, we, in a way, become those feelings. We get lost within the feeling—physical or emotional, so much so that we believe that is who we are. When we are lost in a belief, and that belief is challenged, as it inevitably has to be, the increase in chemical production in the body generates an even more intense feeling, often one of discomfort. The more uncomfortable we feel the more likely we are to blame, the more we blame the more energy we give to that which we feel is responsible for our discomfort.

JUDGEMENT DAY IS HERE, AND HERE, AND HERE AND...

Judgement which begins as an internally polarised condition, once externalised creates conflict, it is inevitable.

Lost in this state, believing it to be real, we are faced with few options. Those options include, amongst others: 1) our remaining lost in the feelings, identifying with them and taking them so personally that ongoing conflict is guaranteed; 2) our behaviour becomes so antisocial, according to the values in the time and place, that we are ostracised, imprisoned, persecuted, which only adds to the charge behind the problem; 3) we seek help; 4) we exert even more control, through violence or legislation.

All of these so called solutions are short sighted attempts to continue to control the chaos that is manifesting, in itself a result of the internal conflict experienced by the individual. Society, any society, is the product of its past. If that past is based upon a fundamental misconception then all that follows is built upon an error in thinking. All solutions that arise from this error in thinking are simply compounding the error. To imagine that legislation is going to solve a problem is either naive or highly manipulative.

> When an inner situation is not made conscious it appears outside of you as fate.
>
> —Carl Jung

When a situation, that has its roots in your subconscious, manifests, it is too late to change things at any meaningful level. All you can do is struggle with the manifesting reality, adding energy to the fundamental issue.

The only sane option is to realise what is happening and why it is happening. To move beyond the idea that if you do not fight for your point of view the 'opposition' to that point of view will prevail. To truly know that it is only your opposition, the belief that you hold onto, that allows that conflict to manifest in the first place.

| Ponder This |

If you believe that we create the world we live in, then why do you persist in living in a world of conflict. The world of conflict requires you to continually be 'do-ing' something in order to survive. All the while you are do-ing there is no room within your awareness to see through the illusion that you are partly responsible for creating and maintaining.

Recognise that it is your own conditioned point of view that supports the reality you live in. If that is not totally to your liking, know that you can change it, but that change means that, well, you have to change. You cannot hold onto your points of view and expect the world to change. Surrendering your points of view will, initially, be hard for it will appear as though everything around you, everything that you are familiar with strives to keep you locked into the old, familiar way. But when you truly accept, no judgement, no resistance, then change will happen on such a deep level you will be amazed. Well, perhaps not amazed, because when you reach that level it will have become so obvious. This concept is extremely difficult to accept from within the collective belief of what is 'real', it is only by taking steps to see beyond the current accepted reality that we can free ourselves and experience a very different reality.

Musings

REALITY—YOURS OR MINE?

WITH THE HELP OF THE WEB AND SOCIAL MEDIA WE seem to be much more aware of events and situations than we were in the past, many things we never even heard about having to rely on the established media.

Often the information provided by contributors to the social media offers alternative points of view. Yet who is to say that the 'alternative contributors' are telling the truth? But then, do you believe the established media? And what is the truth anyway other than a point of view relative to the observer.

Through the years I have been practicing and teaching 'Clearing' it has become obvious, to me, that we live in a "makeit-up-as-you-go-along" universe. This applies whether we are aware of it or not. For most that means creating more of the same, or at the very least, operating within an old 'accepted' format. We try to make sense of the world we live in, we try to manipulate it to suit our needs. We oppose those who do not support us and give energy to those who do.

Through this same social media we notice how the few try to control the many. This knowledge causes us to react and try to 'do' something to change things. Yet we are trying to change a system that has been in place for countless years.

Simply because we have become more aware doesn't imply that this is something new. There appears to be a strong desire for change. In the past, if history is correct (!) then change was sought through revolution, new legislation, wars, struggle, the usual approaches one imagines when we talk of social change.

No doubt there have been changes as a result of this approach, yet has there really been any advance? We still struggle within a set of rules we probably never agreed to. We still seek change within a system that, by its nature, limits change according to its own rules.

Is there another way, another approach to change that, although it may have been staring us in the face, we have not yet tried! While we seek change from within a biased reality, we are still playing by the old rules, still working within current confines in order to achieve a 'better reality.' If this 'old' way worked there would be no need for further change, we would already have achieved a different state. Yet here we are, still struggling away.

Many will be familiar with the concept 'parallel realities' mostly from a science fiction point of view. Yet if we do truly live in a "make-it-up-as-you-go-along" universe, we should ask ourselves "what are we making up?" And why? When we subscribe to a belief, a point of view, we give energy to that belief/point of view. We subscribe because our parents did, because everyone else does, because it is the only/right thing to do. Yet if we truly seek change we are not going to find it in the stories of our parents, or the media, or even the collective.

If we want change then the first thing we have to do is stop subscribing to an old way that has proven time and time again that is simply does not work. It does not deliver on its promises, rather it continues to hold individuals and the collective prisoners within the same dramas they have been for a very long time.

EASIER SAID THAN DONE!

So, stop energising the past. Easier said than done. When all around you support the past it is hard for an individual to withdraw their energy. The system labels them and alienates them. The challenge here is that the louder you call foul, the more energy you give to that which you oppose and the more likely you are to be picked out from the crowd and treated like a pariah.

If you ever watched the movie, *What the Bleep*, you may recall a scene where the lead actress was passing by a basketball court when the young boy asked her to play. There were hundreds of basketballs bouncing around the court, the young woman just looked, confused. "Pick a ball" the boy said, "any ball". Out of the many balls, she chose one that, when thrown, landed in the net.

She appeared to have many choices, many balls from which to make a selection. We are like that, every moment of every day we have all those options. Yet we don't see them as basketballs, or even as options. We have so believed the collective conditioning that there doesn't appear to be any choice at all. We simply deal with what shows up. More or less effectively.

Yet the choices are always there, they may be unseen by us, but that doesn't mean they are not there. It is just that we have limited our options by choosing, without very much awareness, the reality that now unfolds before us. As we 'choose' it we give it energy, the more energy we give it the more 'real' it becomes. Once we have given substance to a point of view and it manifests we have to deal with the

| Musings |

consequences. So choices, if we ever had any, become more limited along the path because of the previous choices we have made.

The interesting part here is that we don't have to continue to live out the reality that we 'chose'.

We choose on a moment by moment basis. Our 'choices' are affected by the belief that we have a choice in the first place, by the knowledge that we can choose something that lies outside the current accepted paradigm and our imagination.

First, stop energising the past. If you find that difficult, come along to a workshop and get a kick start. Next observe the possibilities without grasping at any, and, finally should the need arise, give your energy to a reality that is so different, so much more in harmony with your true nature that you awake to find yourself in a very different world, along with others who agree with your values and dreams. Those who choose to remain will do so, those who have a different idea of what they want, will find their own place. It is not your responsibility to make it better for everyone, everyone needs to choose their own path.

It may be possible, that after you have stopped energising the past, observed the many options without grasping at any of the alternatives that arise in the vacuum left after the release of the past, you will have no need to select from the choices available, the natural state of who you have become will automatically select a new world for you. (This is happening now, it happens all the time, your future is automatically selected based upon deep down convictions you hold).

Above all, enjoy the journey, for life is an adventure, an experience.

If you are 'serious' about change then share this information with as many people as you can. Some will already be

| Musings |

aware, some will reject, others will embrace this information. While we assume knowledge of how others react to this sort of information we effectively keep them a prisoner to our own fears and limitation. Let others decide for themselves.

And This!

IS VIOLENCE INEVITABLE?

So much air time has been given, by all forms of media, to various conflicts around the world and other acts of violence that is very hard not to take sides. There is nothing new in this violence, humankind have become masters at it, but we see more of it now mainly because of the increase in social media as a means to share information.

We have the same talking heads discussing the issues, from the same tired old points of view. We imagine lots going on behind the scenes, we point the finger of blame, we judge easily, from the safety and comfort of our armchair, the parties our conditioning has informed as are 'guilty'.

I have observed in the years I have been working as a consultant and teacher of 'Clearing' that we cannot have one side of an argument, or situation, without having its opposite. We cannot have peace if we do not have war! Sounds a little strange but if we explore, for a moment, the forces that give rise to conflict we may better understand this point of view. Having a better understanding of the cause for all conflict is a great place to start to reduce the charge that creates conflict before it can manifest.

We are each raised within a set of rules and regulations, values and judgments handed down, often by our parents, who in their turn have adopted the values of the society within which they were born. We believe in right and wrong, according to the values of the society in which we grow up. Our values maybe different to the values of others, who grew up in a different society. Neither is necessarily good or bad, right or wrong simply because they are not the same as ours. We are not 'right' and they are not 'wrong'. Yet too often those with different beliefs, different values, are portrayed as evil, dangerous, troublesome, untrustworthy. There are lots of labels used to de-humanise those with different values and beliefs to our own.

This 'conditioning' that we all go through, sets the stage for how we are going to experience life, how we are going to react or respond. It also creates expectations. Our childhood experiences teach us that if this happens, then that will follow. We come to expect that to be always the case and are constantly on the lookout, particularly if the product of a certain situation ended in violence. So, without conscious awareness, we are helping to create the world in which we live.

Our expectations define the world. Our world, not necessarily the world as perceived by others.

If we have any fear issues that have not been brought into the open and resolved, any anger issues, any hatred, any blame or judgement then we, to some degree or other, live in a state of tension. This is not always obvious for it is hard to accept responsibility for the conflict one witnesses, much easier to point the finger of blame to someone else.

CHARGE MUST BE EXPRESSED

If we live in a state of tension, that tension builds and must express itself. In a 'civilised' society, and I say that word with tongue in cheek, for I am not convinced any of us live in a truly civilised society, then that tension is often not expressed and is therefore internalised. When we turn the tension inward sickness and disease are inevitable. The build up of tension, or charge has to be expressed or it creates a very unhealthy environment. When the charge is expressed outwardly as blame, then conflict is inevitable. For if we 'blame' someone for our own problems, then that someone will, with conscious awareness, react to being blamed. The obvious reaction is to blame back. Someone throws a rock (of blame) then someone is going to throw it back. And, before you know it, you have a war on your hands.

It may be a 'small' war, conflict between neighbours, it may be a large war, conflict between countries, but they all start from the same place. The individuals early conditioning where they were taught to personalise their emotions and given something outside of themselves to blame. But a war is a war is a war. And without two sides, cannot manifest.

If you think you are right because god is on your side, you are totally deluded, as most people who go to war are. Who, in their right mind, would go to war.

We may presume we are in our 'right mind' but that is just a product of the conditioning which is perpetuated, either consciously or sub-consciously, by the media associated with the society that we 'belong' to.

If you judge any act that you witness, be it direct or via a conditioned media source, you are adding your energy to one side or other and have become a part of the problem. No matter that you march for peace, that you 'desire' peace, if you have not found peace within you are not going to find it outside. Even more to the point, you will be partly responsible for any state of war that you judge.

It is hard enough for those of us not personally involved in war, for those who have family, and those directly caught up it is almost impossible for them to step back far enough and see what is really going on. So then it falls to those not directly involved to begin the process of creating greater balance within themselves, which, in turn will create an opportunity for a reality to manifest where all beings can be happy. This reality cannot be made manifest while you remain a victim to your own shadow, while aspects of your total self remain hidden, directing your life from behind the scenes.

Make the shadow conscious, confront your fears and move beyond the polarised thinking that makes conflict possible.

A Piece to Finish the Day

ARE YOU AWARE OF YOUR THOUGHTS?

Have you made the connection between your thoughts and your reality?

I mean really looked at how one thought arises because of an earlier thought? The conditioned mind is a very busy place, always thinking, thinking, thinking. Thoughts seem to just pop into the mind—wherever that might be—from? From wherever.

We easily become addicted to particular thought processes, we call that a train of thought. Sometimes when we are problem solving this train of thought can be a friend, more often than not though it is not our friend. We do it because we know of no other way. Is that the real reason why we fill our 'minds' with thoughts, one after the other, a non stop production which appears to be inside our head, because we have learnt that? And why would we learn that way of being? Who would have taught us? Likely it would have been people whose own 'minds' were full of thoughts, one chasing the other, they would have taught us. Had our teachers had quiet 'minds' then it is probable that we would have learnt to have quiet minds as well. Maybe, maybe not. Who can say.

Meditation would be a good way to quiet the mind. The many benefits of meditation can only be realised through practice. Many people are indeed drawn to meditation, some find it easy, some find it hard, many don't find it at all. It would seem that those who are not drawn to mediation are those who would benefit the most, for their busy minds are the very reason they are not attracted to meditation in the first place.

There may be many explanations for a busy mind. Take your pick, remember though that any reason you come up with is going to be a product of the already busy mind. This is not necessarily the real reason, rather it is one you are happy with for the time being. Really any 'answer' you get is just another example of how our thoughts are creating the world we live in.

Imagine a conditioned mind that resonates with anxiety. Anxiety is just an example, choose whatever keeps popping up into your mind with alarming frequency. It can be any thought or feeling that you cannot seem to escape.

So, for some reason the thought that you are anxious arises in your awareness. This is invariably due to external environmental conditions or the energy of others or, of course, a memory you have of being anxious in the past. It is not important, at the moment why you have the thought. The thought that you are anxious creates a chemical reaction in your body, this leads to another thought relating to anxiety. You may not be fully aware that you are giving energy to the thought, anxiety, but the chemicals are being produced nonetheless. Pretty soon your thoughts are so lost in anxiety there is no room for another thought. Your body has become very anxious. And you created this by your initial identification with the chemical, with anxiety, that led to the production of more chemicals which gave rise to a stronger feeling of anxiety in the body.

JUDGING THE THOUGHT!

So, a thought arises, maybe at first giving a slightly uncomfortable feeling, you judge this feeling as being unpleasant, at the same time your conditioned mind identifies with the feeling, you 'think' it is yours, and, as you think, so you become. The more you allow your thought to follow this particular train, the more anxious you will become. Realise that you are not deliberately making yourself anxious, why would you do that? This is an example of the conditioned mind running the show.

After one thought, the next thought is simply a product of the previous one, and so it goes. When you have enough thoughts on one subject, given enough energy to any particular thought, your body will become that thought, happy, sad, anxious, excited, whatever. When your body is 'full' of the chemicals associated with anxiety it doesn't take a genius to know that any thoughts that follow are going to be impacted by, and arise out of, an anxious state.

Such thoughts are not likely to be rational, assuming you were rational before! You do and say things based on your anxious state, this affects those around you who respond or react, depending upon their own conditioning. They may aggravate your anxious condition, they may alleviate it, they may take it upon themselves and become anxious, a common reaction. However those around you respond, they are responding to your anxious state. When they affirm your anxiety, you just get lost deeper in anxiety, and all subsequent thoughts are based upon the idea that you are anxious.

The world will react to this. Not because the world is judging your anxiety, but because you are now seeing the world as an anxious place. You are seeing the world though anxious eyes, so the world doesn't really have a choice other than to reflect back to you that anxiety. When you have a lot of people doing the same thing, identifying with a particular thought, which creates the next thought and so on, then collectively the world is seen as an anxious place, and the thought, that 'logically' arises next, is to find a safe place in this highly anxious world.

SHELTER FROM THE STORM!

Where are you going to find a safe place when the unsafe place that you seek shelter from is in your mind. So, the next step along this path is to externalise the danger, don't want to go looking for an answer in the mind, when the mind is so busy following thoughts of anxiety, it has become a troubled place and not one that is going to hold the answers. This of course is not true, but to a mind lost in anxiety it certainly seems to be the case.

When we externalise the problem we need to find someone to blame. If the person(s) that we blame are also lost in anxiety then conflict is going to result. It is inevitable. We gather together, with who we hope or believe are like minded people, all doing their best to defend themselves and their families from those who they see as the cause for their anxious state. Now, because they have spent so long in this highly anxious condition, it is no longer understood as something outside of the self, and all actions, reactions, thoughts and feelings arise because of, what is now a subconscious condition. Anxiety has become an accepted condition that is no longer questioned.

We are easily led into situations that we are told will alleviate our anxiety, but in actual feed simply keep on feeding it.

And all this started because you believed you were anxious, you took a thought and gave it a life of its own, and now you suffer the consequences without remembering the part you played in creating this world. One major benefit of a quiet mind is that you stop energising anxiety, so your future may take a different path.

Next month, another possible reason for a busy mind.

Ponder This

GET YOUR POINT OF VIEW HERE!

TODAY I AM SELLING POINTS OF VIEW. I HAVE NO INVESTment, you understand, in any of the points of view I am selling, I am just the middle man.

Take your pick from what is on offer.

It is always a challenge to understand why you have preferences for certain points of view. Why you choose one over another, why you believe that any point of view is more important than any other.

Most of the points of view on offer today are free of charge, at least initially. Most, if not all, are going to require maintenance. They are going to take time and energy to develop, without a doubt they are going to cost, money, sometimes lots of money. The ones to look out for, be a little wary of are those that come full of promise with no deposit required. They are the ones that are going to cost a lot, in terms of the financial obligations that follow commitment.

Also be on the lookout for those that offer you freedom, for those the cost is going to be higher, and not always financial, for those the price is your soul. These particular points of view are most commonly held by the collective and are thus not so easy to see through and avoid. In our naivety we accept these points of view, before we can even question the wisdom of our choice we are committed and sink deeper into the mire that is the point of view.

Often, as a result of our accepting a point of view, other points of view become available. Our choices are limited, based on some fundamental points of view we either inherited or otherwise acquired. These 'foundational' points of view are not so easy to escape from, we hardly realise they are points of view, so escaping from them is never considered an option. Instead, to make life more comfortable, we seek out other points of view, according to our desires, which are, invariably, based upon initial points of view.

So, when choosing from my Bazaar, my cornucopia, my suitcase of points of view, try to remember that the person choosing is totally lost in previous points of view, to the point where any clarity about which point of view would serve you best has been long lost. It matters little which one you choose, I am happy because you think you have what you need and, for the time being at least, are happy with your choice. We are all happy, wonderful.

Happy until your newly acquired point of view starts to age, to show cracks around the edges, starts to fall apart. Starts to make demands upon you, requires you spend more money to maintain it, or, worse yet, you see through the illusory nature of your point of view and question its validity. When you outgrow your point of view the initial feelings can be very confusing. What to do, hang on a little longer, in case the point of view was valid, you are just having doubts? Or walk away, leaving behind all those friends you have made along the way, friends who can no longer communicate with you because you no longer belong to the club?

Many points of view have back up plans for occasions just like this, they are experienced when doubt shows up and have whole packages of doubt busting points of view, each designed to encourage you to continue holding the initial point of view yet lead you further into the depths of that point of view making it harder to entertain thoughts of doubt.

For those lost in their point of view have become masters at justifying their point of view, at explaining their point of view with clever, smaller, points of view.

If we were to consider the point of view that subscribing to any one point of view leads to the adoption of other points of view, each taking us further from the place we thought we were going when we accepted the original point of view, then points of view are valueless. At least while we take them so seriously.

This world is made up of points of view. There is nothing that isn't a point of view. Even this statement is a point of view. They are everywhere, seemingly impossible to escape from, for each time I offer you a new one, or a remodeled old one, I am just adding to your burden, but hey, who am I to tell you which point of view is best for you. You have to try them all on for size before deciding which one suits you best. Or perhaps, you are tired of defending your points of view. What then?

You wake up one morning, if you are lucky, and say to yourself, this point of view no longer serves me. What then, do you cast it aside, like a worn out piece of clothing, send it off to be recycled, maybe someone else would like your used point of view.

IS IT SO EASY TO WALK AWAY FROM A POINT OF VIEW?

Whatever you are thinking right now is a product of a point of view.

Whatever you are feeling right now is a product of a point of view.

Even your emotional responses are the products of various points of view.

Walking away from a point of view means walking away from who you thought/think yourself to be. Most points of view are insidious, they creep up on you, entangling you in their web of points of view and sub points of view to the point you are no longer conscious it was a point of view that started this journey at all.

Disengaging from points of view is an art, a unique point of view in itself. For how does one disengage from something that permeates your total being, something that does not even appear on the radar of possibilities, for each point of view demands action, requires you to take it seriously. It holds you in its embrace so tightly that there are no alternatives.

Trade ins are always welcome. I will gladly take your old point of view and either supply a new one, the choices are limitless, but I might, if you don't mind, suggest one of the new, disposable points of view. They have a limited shelf life, presuming you take them seriously for long enough to maximise the benefits. Some of the later models, the improved points of view, have been designed to self destruct, so, no matter how seriously you take them they are guaranteed to blow up in your face before you get too lost in them, marvelous eh!

If you are interested in top of the range points of view then I suggest you start with one of the self destruct models. They prepare you for the rarified points of view that only those who have had points of view explode in their face often enough can handle.

If you are confused now, remember that is just a point of view. There is no charge for that one, as long as you don't think it is yours. Any claim to ownership of any of the points of view mentioned in any of my work requires you enter a contract and agree to abide by the particular rules of that point of view, sub sections notwithstanding. At some point in the future the price of that point of view will become obvious and you will be expected to pay it.

In the meantime, the Bazaar is always open, feel free to step in, have a browse, try one on, see how it fits. Everyone is trying to sell their favourite, few offer unlimited choices.

Another Day, Another Thought

PARALLEL REALITIES

The world we live in is a pretty amazing place. But, there is always room for improvement right?

The natural world is fine as it is, well it would be if greed fear and ignorance didn't rule the day. Same with the human perceptions of the world, could it be improved if there were less greed, fear and ignorance around? Is greed, fear and ignorance a set condition for life in human form… If it isn't, how are we going to sidestep it?

Do we need to work within the confines of our current 'reality' to create something new and more sustainable, or can we step outside of this reality, jump tracks as it were, to travel down a totally different path?

Of course, if anyone has already jumped tracks and exists in a parallel reality how could we possibly know? Without feedback we assume, rightly or wrongly, that there is only the one path, make the most/best of it while you walk it. Unless you know anyone who has simply disappeared, gone over to a parallel reality and kept in touch (not from a psychiatric hospital!).

It is conditioned thinking that maintains this reality, but is conditioned thinking the only way to go? Thinking outside the box, we are told, can solve problems, problems that were created inside the box. But just how far out of the box can you go without being locked up or losing it completely?

An interesting challenge, the box within which we currently operate cannot provide answers to problems that are created from within the box. Always assuming there are problems to be solved. Another dilemma. Are there any problems? If there are, the chances are they were created from within the box. No answers, of any lasting, positive, sustainable nature, can be found within the box, it is not the nature of the current box to be rational, logical, compassionate. Rather, it appears to be just the opposite. Although it contains elements of every imaginable aspect of humanity, unfortunately a limited, small box, point of view, maintains such a strongly polarised perception that reality follows, or fits within, these extremes.

How far out of the box do we need to go to find answers that are more rational, logical and compassionate? And, on those out of the box explorations, unless we take a bunch of people with us, there is not going to be anyone out there, as far as the limited 'box' thinking allows us to know, who is going to be able to understand the out of the box language.

So, in order to communicate effectively we need to keep one foot in the box. But if we keep one foot in the box it will anchor us to the commonly accepted reality. This, by its nature, prevents us from truly exploring out of the box and at the same time maintaining a level of communication that can be understood and appreciated by those who remain in the box.

If we manage to escape our box yet still exist within the greater reality, we are likely to be shut away or disappeared, not in a nice way, for there would be no one to understand our new point of view. If we manage to really reach escape velocity and jump tracks, then any trace of our existence in the old reality, the one you are reading this in, without communication between the realities, would no longer exist. At least I think that would be the case. So I, or whoever manages the jump, will be unable to share what they have discovered, assuming they can even remember what life was like before they jumped.

I think I am getting a headache.

To be clear, I cannot escape the box and communicate to those left in the box. I am not sure, because of my conditioned existence, that such a place as 'out of the box' even exists. Does madness await me out of the box, or am I already mad within the box but have not, as yet, realised it?

I think, at least I think it is me thinking, that for the time being I will be content just expanding the box. Putting a few feelers out, testing the limits, before taking the plunge. Assuming a plunge is possible. So many unknowns. Part of the fun I guess, the total uncertainty of the unknown.

A bit like dying in a way.

If you don't receive anymore newsletters from me, you know why.

See you on the other side.

Ponder This

ARE YOU FOLLOWING YOUR HEART OR CONVENTION?

I notice, quite often, those who ask me for 'help' are often caught in a pattern of convention. There are certain things that dictate how we live our lives, one of which is money, or, in a more general sense support. We need money to eat, to have shelter, in short, a comfortable lifestyle. At least we believe we do, and we all know what a belief will do!

We are, or appear to be, born into a system that has particular requirements. Our parents, our society, siblings, friends, colleagues, all support those requirements. They were born into the same 'world' as we were and follow, to varying degrees, the same rules.

When convention opposes our heart's desires we get sick. Either that or we act out the imbalance and create chaos around us, affecting all those in our environment, and the very environment itself. When, for whatever reason, we fail to follow our heart we often internalise, without conscious participation, that struggle. The longer we internalise these feelings the more likely we are to create an internal environment that reflects that struggle and dis-ease is inevitable. The longer we do this the more established the state of dis-ease becomes, the more likely it is going to manifest as sickness.

Convention dictates how we live our lives. Regardless of any deeper, energetic, desires we may have, we follow convention because, well, what else can we do. Lost in convention it is hard to see what is happening. Convention supplies answers to all our questions, questions that only arise because we are lost in convention.

Because we often fail to follow our hearts desires, through either fear of being 'unconventional' or of the possibility of lack of support, money, food or shelter, the 'charge' that is the desire of the heart fails to express. This can be referred also as a karmic charge that is not being expressed. If our parents, for whatever reason, failed to express this charge it is passed down the family line. We inherit the charge. Are we able to recognise this for what it is, or do we accept this as a part of the 'convention' into which we are born believing there is nothing we can do to change it?

The desire of the heart, like a karmic charge, is just that, a charge that seeks to find expression. Not necessarily an internalised expression, and not in a way that hurts self or others, but as a creative force. Once the charge has been released in a safe manner we are able to see beyond the conditions imposed upon us by the charge. As we awaken to the idea that this is charge—this heart's desire—that needs to be expressed we may think we have found our life's path. Yet we are simply expressing a charge. Until this charge has been expressed we cannot even begin to understand our life's path. Not to say that expressing the charge is not a part of our path, perhaps there is no path, no 'on' the path, no 'off' the path. Life expresses, it is our perceptions that control our response/reaction to that expression.

While we deny charge because of, for example, conventional thinking, the pressure builds and creates new charges. If these are internalised, i.e., not expressed, they create sickness. This state of 'sickness' creates its own charge, based on the way we deal with whatever and however is manifesting in our lives. If we continue to deny the part we have played in creating this state (by not following our heart), if we continue to blame, to judge, to 'personalise' with the symptoms, then we continue to energise the 'conventions' that created this personal reality.

The road to recovery, if that is indeed possible and what you seek, starts when we begin the journey into the heart. We can use the mind to help us along the way, but we should not become slaves to the mind, which, for the most part, follows convention. The conditioned reality that we subscribe to is not the only reality available to us, yet we continue to limit ourselves by our addiction to the path laid out by convention.

Any journey into the heart requires either totally exhausting any other options!! Or, a great deal of safety. Safety is not found in conventional thinking, nor amongst 'conventional' or judgemental or fearful surroundings. We must seek out a place of safety, nurture it, develop it until it completely embraces us. Find that place within us. When we achieve this we discover many things. Perhaps most importantly, that there was no journey, no path, no goal.

We have arrived. We never left. And all things return to a more balanced state.

And This!

BEEN THERE DONE THAT—OR NOT

DO YOU EVER BELIEVE YOU HAVE DEALT WITH SOMETHING only to have it show up again, and again? How often have you said to your 'self' I thought I had finished with that *stuff*?

I find a good measure of whether I have indeed 'finished' with something is how much I still talk about it. How much I continue to justify certain patterns of behaviour, how I 'feel' about old situations, people, places. How much energy I am giving to the past.

Often we cannot just conjure up an old situation to check out how much charge is left, we just have to wait until circumstances are right and we are triggered into an old pattern, so it is not so easy to notice how you are doing.

When I began my 'clearing' journey there was a lot of my past that I was not aware of, without an awareness of this it is almost impossible to step outside of the old patterns. So I was stuck, at the time, in old conditioned ways of being and 'doing.' Being stuck in these patterns without being consciously aware that we are stuck tends to attract others who are also stuck in similar patterns. Of course when they show up the tendency is to blame the other for all the bad *stuff* that happens. A consequence of not being aware of our own *stuff*.

| And This! |

During this stage of the journey we lack the awareness to 'do' anything about our situation. We live it, we are it. Crazy *stuff* happens for which we blame those around us, often those closest to us.

For whatever reason we may, sooner or later, awaken to certain patterns of behaviour and realise that if we continue to follow that path then we are more than likely going to experience all the crazy *stuff* again, and again. At this stage of the journey we look for things to do to help us out of this place. This is "the answers out there" stage. We spend a lot of time talking about *stuff*, and a lot of time learning what to do with the *stuff* but very little time actually understanding the *stuff*. So it keeps showing up, the *stuff* that is.

And we keep thinking that because we had been to a workshop and learnt some more *stuff* that we had dealt with this old '*stuff*.'

Eventually it becomes obvious that we haven't even begun to deal with the *stuff*, we have just been running around in circles avoiding the real issues, still believing that the answer is 'out there.' When we exhaust that stage, we reluctantly turn the direction of our search inwards. I say reluctantly because this is the hardest aspect of the journey to accept, that we are responsible for all that we experience. This is not quite as overwhelming as it sounds. Because these many aspects of ourselves that we are still not consciously aware of remain hidden there is nothing we can do to change them. They don't show up on our doorstep all at once, this gives us a chance to catch our breath before more *stuff* makes itself known to us.

Yet still we talk about situations, people places, experiences, we talk about the problems we have with others, how challenged we are by the behaviour of others. All the time justifying our own behaviour believing that because we have some concept that we are responsible we are dealing with the past. Wrong.

When even this road doesn't lead to the peace we think we want/need, and we are exhausted, our defence is down and we are open to not only seeing through the veils of the past, but open to all sorts of other weird stuff as well. *Stuff* that has been oppressed, with or without our awareness for whatever reason. Oppressed *stuff* has to be exposed to the light of our awareness. Often the manifestation of this oppressed *stuff* is very uncomfortable and appears to be circumstantial, having nothing to do with 'us' at all. We still talk about this *stuff* and wonder why it keeps showing up.

We don't always need to become aware of our past before moving beyond it. If we can just imagine, for a series of moments in time, that everything is just *stuff*, neither good nor bad, right nor wrong, neither better nor worse we reduce the judgement we hold around *stuff*. This simple act of acceptance will reduce the charge which in turn increases the likelihood that when it returns it is with less and less intensity. When we stop feeding the drama the drama will fall away. With the reduction in the intensity of the drama we naturally talk less and less about the drama.

Then we truly know that we have dealt with it, we no longer feel the need to talk about it, we don't even think about it for it has stopped showing up in our life.

Musings

WELCOME TO THE DARK SIDE

Have you noticed how everything is relative. For example, whether we are able to respond to a situation or we react is relative to our emotional attachment to the situation. The limits within which we respond or react are dictated by our past conditioning. So, either response or reaction is relative to any experiences from our past. We may respond /react in such a way that we barely notice the situation, we attach very little importance to it. We may respond/react in an intense way, generally meaning that we have a strong degree of attachment to the situation, one way or another.

We can keep traveling back in time to find primary cause and never come to a satisfactory conclusion, always something beyond what we think is going on/went on, in our personal history. We can be sure though that no matter how we handle situations it is relative to how we have handled, or failed to handle, similar situations in our past.

You may believe that one person is totally obnoxious, another person may think that person to be open, relaxed and very friendly. Each response/reaction is relative to the individuals conditioning. Neither is right or wrong, they are just different, personal, takes on information that they experience when confronted with the third party.

If we continue to blame our past for our present circumstances we remain lost in a world that is cyclic, in that the patterns keep repeating. This process can unfortunately strengthen the belief that we have to continue to blame external people or phenomena for our troubles, or blame ourselves for something that we think is 'wrong' with us. Neither of these approaches are designed to liberate us from this patterned behaviour.

A SIMPLE EXAMPLE OF MANIFESTING THE DARK SIDE

A common condition is arachnophobia, a fear of spiders. Who knows where this comes from, often there is no rational explanation. No need to try to analyse any cause, we just need to focus on the manifesting issues. I live in an area of Australia that could be designated as 'the bush' plenty of trees and other plant life, and wildlife. The ideal environment for spiders, amongst other assorted creatures. We see the occasional spider, and it generates no reaction, other than the thought perhaps we should put this one outside. I have lived in a similar environment where one of the others living in the house was terrified of spiders. This person would see spiders everywhere, yet I only saw one or two.

It is the same with anything that we fear, it just keeps showing up, relentlessly. Any manifestation is relative to the fear we hold around any particular phenomena. The more we fear something the more likely it is to manifest. We have to question here the abundance of spiders. Are there really that many spiders in the house? Why can I not see them? Why does this other person see so many? Don't get me wrong here, if there is a spider on the wall I will see it. But I see very few.

| Musings |

Is it possible to 'manifest' spiders? Like a magician pulling rabbits out of a hat! If the number of spiders a person with a great fear of them sees is relative to the fear they have around spiders then there is a direct relationship between fear and manifestation. This 'relationship' is not limited to spiders. Anything that we have a deep fear around, a strong judgement, a powerful aversion, will have a similar effect.

Assuming there is some 'truth' in this 'theory' then that which we experience in our world is relative to the charge/judgment/fear/aversion that we have around the phenomena.

Since much of this charge is sub-conscious we are not aware that we have it. Only by seeing what 'shows up' on a daily basis can we begin to recognise the part the sub-conscious plays in creating the world around us. If it works for spiders, why not for health, happiness, wealth, peace? Think about it.

While you are thinking about that, remember that it is the sub-conscious conditioning that is helping to create the world you live in. Even if you 'want' a different reality you will be sabotaging yourself 24/7 if you do not address the sub-conscious.

It is also worth keeping in mind that the desire for something (more of this, less of that) arises only because of its opposite which is the conditioned response/reaction that exists, mostly, in the sub-conscious. The personality feels the need for something that it believes will make life easier, more pleasant, healthier, wealthier. The personality however is mistaken in this belief. If we can expose the sub-conscious conditioning that continues to bring 'spiders' into our awareness, then spiders will no longer be a problem. When spiders (read also fear, anxiety, resistance, aversion to just about anything) are no longer a problem they cease to exist in your world. They may show up now and again, you are not going to be responsible for the disappearance from the planet of all spiders, but when they do show up, because you are no longer arachnophobic, they will not trouble you.

When spiders are no longer an issue there will be no reason to worry about them, to 'defend' yourself against them, to even think of them. So many 'things' fall away when the cause is released.

And so it is with all things, not just the spiders. When that which causes you distress is understood and released there is no need to seek its opposite. As you release old limitations and fears your body, as an energetic system, will come into a more balanced state. When you are more balanced there is less need to seek change outside of the self. You will automatically begin attracting a very different reality.

If you believe you still have to 'do' something to create a 'better' reality you have not yet released the old conditioning from which the perceived desire for change arises.

Think about that for a moment or two.

Sleep on This One

BELIEVE IT OR NOT

WE ALL BELIEVE WHAT WE WANT TO BELIEVE, WE ALL see what we want to see, we all hear what we want to hear.

Sometimes it may not seem that is the case, but, because of conditioning we are limited in what we can believe, see and hear. We have come to think that what we believe, see or hear is the truth of the situation, not from a judgemental point of view, but from a place where we have believed, in the past, what we were told simply because we trusted those who told us.

As a child our mother may have told us not to touch the hotplate when it was turned on or we would burn ourselves. Okay, so child A just accepts this, because mummy said so. Child B, being the rebellious type, didn't believe it so touched the hotplate, *whoa*, that hurt, mummy was right. And child see, more interested in discovering its own truth, gradually moved its hand closer and closer to the hotplate, feeling the heat increase the closer the hand got. Hmmm, that will hurt if I touch it, mummy was right.

A few of these lessons and we are more likely to accept our parents word at face value. But what about the less concrete examples. Did your mother every tell you that certain neighbours were 'weird', 'strange' or 'different'? Every time you walked past their house you would think, that's where the weird people live. You may not have understood what 'weird' meant in this situation, but your imagination was more than able to fill in the blanks. Those were definitely weird people, their house even smelt different, you got the goose bumps whenever you passed the house, and at night, when it was really dark, you would run past the house of the 'weird people.' Rushing to get home to the safety of your own 'weird' household, though or course the familiar is not weird!

If the weird people kept pretty much to themselves, their children went to a different school, that's really weird. You rarely saw the parents, probably at work before you left your house, but what did you know, they were weird, it explained everything. Maybe they went to a 'weird' church, maybe they worked on a holy day, maybe they dressed differently. Any behaviour that does not fit into your conditioned perspectives is classified as weird, so you avoid contact with the weird ones.

Your neighbours weren't alone in their weirdness, we are all weird, in our own idiosyncratic ways. We tend to hang out with others whose weirdness we can relate to, safety in numbers. Not just physical safety but psychological as well. For we need to feel as though we are right in our weirdness, never truly accepting our own weirdness because we surround ourselves with like-minded folk.

Having believed our parents, and lived in an environment that supported that point of view, you are going to continue to believe the neighbours are weird and, depending upon whether you are a type A, B or C child, you will pass on your own stories about the neighbours to your children. And so it goes.

We 'learn' something from our parents, that 'something' is continually reinforced by our parents and siblings as we grow up. The something becomes embedded in our being and after a while we no longer question it. This allows us to pass that information, about weird neighbours or whatever, onto our children. We may learn to be outwardly polite to others, but deep down there is a mistrust that we are hardly aware of.

Rarely would we stop for a moment and question, who told our parents that the neighbours were weird? If your parents did not have direct exposure to the real reasons for their passing information on to you, it may have been something they were told by their parents. So you question your grand parents. If you are lucky you may eventually find out the reason, and it could have been something so simple, so nonthreatening, so quickly misunderstood that you are able to easily see through the drama that has built up over generations.

You still have to deal with the results of your conditioning and the years of mistrust that have grown but at least you now understand.

Having questioned one piece of information you may begin to wonder how much more you were told that was based on some misunderstanding in the long forgotten past. Really, who told our parents the stories? Whoever told them, who told them in their turn, and did any of them really know what they were talking about or were they simply repeating something they had been told but never bothered to check out?

Is it enough that someone in the distant past had 'written' down something. Are we to believe that someone from the past 'knew' what was going on, or were they, in their turn, simply passing on something that they had heard. How can we be sure they heard/remembered correctly. And can we be sure of their motives in writing down information?

Be like child C, accept nothing, try it out, question it. Examine it, does it hold true for you now, today? Then take that information, but don't get too attached, tomorrow may bring a new realisation which reveals the previous 'knowing' to be false. Nothing is as it seems. Believe no one, no media, no written information. Check it out, and where you cannot directly confirm just put it into the yet to be confirmed basket.

Which is why, at my workshops, I tell people to not believe a word I say, take it, if it fits, try it out, see if it works for you. Use it as long as you feel it helps, but don't get too attached to the process.

Did You Know?

THE CONDITIONED MIND

The conditioned mind will continue to find reasons to deny any other possible reality. By its very nature, the conditioned mind can only accept that which it has become comfortable with, the familiar.

It will not put up barriers to learning new ways, new ways will simply not be within the realm of possibility. The conditioned mind will be incapable of viewing the world in any way other than that which it has become accustomed to. So it will endeavour to rationalise any new information from within the confines of its own experience.

It is this fundamental issue that prevents 'us' from realising the true nature of mind, the unlimited potential that is who we are. 'We' cannot realise this true nature of mind while we continue to run questions through the same paradigm that prevents us from simply being in another state. We cannot even begin to comprehend what the true nature of mind is, for those caught in the conditioned mind this 'true nature of mind' remains some vague concept, not accessible, or knowable.

We have been conditioned to look outside of ourselves for answers, for goals and objectives, to always seek to create, or manifest based upon the desires of the conditioned mind. Invariably the conditioned mind is polarised, being brought up in a world of separation, of judgements and blame, continually externalising. In such a polarised state there will be a constant need to question, to sort through various options in order to select the best path. We will be caught in a never ending story, looking for a way out but looking in all the wrong places.

The reason we keep looking outside of the self for answers, the reason we try harder to achieve more is the constant association with an 'i.' We have become so conditioned to associate phenomena, thoughts, emotions, feelings, to truly believe that they are 'our' thoughts, emotions, feelings, that we spend our lives trying to satisfy the perceived needs of this 'i.'

For someone who has glimpsed this true nature of mind it is no longer possible to seek answers outside of the self, indeed, there is no self that needs to seek. And herein of course, lies the biggest challenge that we face along any perceived journey. The fact that there is no 'i.' There is no one to seek, no where to go, no thing to do, no journey, no goals.

The Buddha was reported to have said that the hardest part of the 'journey' was the last part, the letting go completely of any sense of the 'i.' An 'i' that doesn't exist, has never existed and will never exist. We can see how all 'problems' on the world can be brought back to this attachment to the 'i.' It is also easy to see why it is so difficult to let go of any attachment to the 'i' in part because the rest of the world seems to be taking 'it's self very seriously indeed, a hard one to break free from and our 'own' conditioning that is trapped in a world of justifications.

The letting go of the 'i' could be the ultimate non attachment. While we still believe that the 'i' is who we are, we continue to believe that 'we' are on a journey. That there is some where to go, something to achieve, something that is going to make us feel valued, something that will take us to a place where we are free from the everyday worries of life. This belief is the very thing that we need to move beyond and is also the very thing that blocks us from realising that which 'we' seek is not 'out there.'

It may be that a sudden realisation that there is no 'i' could be quite traumatic as the body has a conditioned way of seeing life. Remove that conditioning and the body is easily lost in trying to anchor itself to something that makes sense. This need to understand may well pull us back into the body and the 'i', in fact, it is quite possible that we are truly living in the true nature of mind most of the time, it is only when we stop to question the manifesting reality that we step back into the 'i.'

This happens without our realising it, for if there is no subject/object, no witness to our thoughts words and actions, then there can be no comparison. If there is no one observing, no one comparing, no one questioning, then there remains the true nature of mind. It is only when we return to comparing, blaming, judging and identifying consciously with the phenomena that we return to the subject/object, witness based perceptions, back into the world of duality.

Whilst we believe there to be an 'i' on a journey then the least we can do is to prepare the mind/body for the moment the 'i' drops away. Prepare so that we are more easily able to accept the lack of the 'i' and not go into a state of shock or denial.

So, we practice non attachment to possessions. We see ourselves more as caretakers rather than owners, whilst we have something, we take care of it, but we do not get attached to the objects. Becoming attached to the physical world is a trap causing you to be more concerned with losing your possessions than simply enjoying them.

Next we practice non attachment to the emotions that arise in our awareness. We recognise that emotions are simply the chemical product of a conditioned way of thinking. The emotions are no more ours than the music coming from a radio belongs to the radio. The body, we realise, is simply a device, a magnificent device, but a device nonetheless that is interpreting what it perceives to be external signals that it picks up into chemicals. The emotions are the product of this interaction the body has with is 'external' environment.

And when we are ready we practice non attachment to the thoughts that arise. Because the thoughts are directly related to the world we manifest we realise that by continuing to identify with and thus energise old thoughts we are simply recreating the old world. When we can notice a thought and let it go, we allow a new thought to arise, practice letting that new thought go as well, until there is a stillness replacing the busy-ness.

Don't fall back into the creative 'i', simply rest in the moment and observe what arises. You might be pleasantly surprised.

A Piece to Start the Day

ARE YOU AWARE OF YOUR WORDS?

Do you ever pause to think before you speak? Are you conscious of your words? Where do your words come from?

Most words come from the conditioned mind, the part of us that we have become so accustomed to that we never bother to question it. That is, after all, who we are! Or at least, who we believe ourselves to be. "This is who I am!—I cannot change who I am"!

Well, with a belief system like that in place you are probably right, you will not be able to change who you are. If we try to understand where the words we use come from, and why, we can see how they create the world that we live in. We may think we have a choice of the words we use, but really, there is little, if any choice. We speak the words that our current level of awareness dictates.

Our words arise from a belief, or perception we have around who we think we are and our place in the world. For example, if I were to have experienced 'not being heard' as a child I would do everything I could to balance that out. Often the steps we take appear to be negative and excessive as we try to balance out our frustration at not being heard. Those steps would, for the most part, be subconscious, in that we would not be aware we were behaving in a way that may appear to others to be negative or excessive. If we are not able to see ourselves from a more objective point of view, then it is not possible that we are able to question our behaviour and the words we use. We would, quite simply, be operating in an automatic reactionary way, a way that we would not even be conscious of and therefore unable to accept any responsibility to support fundamental change.

While we remain unaware we often blame, and externalise the cause for any difficulties we may encounter, blaming others, events or places for our discomfort. The language, the words we use reflect that perception thereby adding energy to whatever it is we are co-creating.

If then our words are the product of our conditioned mind, our mind is directly responsible for creating the world in which we 'find' ourselves. Our words are the tool through which we express ourselves and our words shape the world. If we come back to the example of 'not being heard' we will either have learnt to close up, to avoid social situations or we will 'over express' ourselves.

If we have learnt 'scarcity' in our childhood we would believe there is 'not enough' in the world and our words will reflect that perception. It doesn't stop there, our words are vibrational, they send messages out to those around us and our environment in general. Those vibrations, all added up, create the world. If we are not conscious of our thoughts (why we think this or that, what we think and when we think) then our words cannot be conscious creative forces. The words will still create, but they create the opposite to what we believe we need in order to be happy, for the words are the result of a mind that is lost in a way of being that is not conscious of its actions.

Without consciousness we continue to use words without thinking first, even assuming we do think before we speak, if our minds are clouded by events from the past then the 'choices' we have as to what words to use and when to use them are limited by this conditioned state.

Whenever we speak from a place that lacks clarity, our words are, like our mind, chaotic. They create chaos, which only serves to justify a belief that we hold that the world is indeed a place that doesn't listen, or is a place of scarcity. When we get this feedback we are forced into 'doing' more to overcome the scarcity, to be heard. All this does is deepen the hole we have been digging for ourselves.

If you are uncertain whether or not your words come from a place of clarity of chaos, look around you, how is the world manifesting for you? Any problems that seem to just keep coming round again and again. How easy, how effortless is progress? Do you struggle still with certain people or situations. Do you feel as though you are heard? Do you have 'enough'?

Pause for a moment. Take a look inside, where do these words you use come from, and why those words in particular? They will be a reflection of your internal state. What is it that you feel you need to 'do' to help yourself?

We are all conditioned by our pass to some degree or other. When we can truly be free of judgement, of blame then our past ceases to control our present. When we are at peace within, the words we speak will arise from a peaceful mind. Peaceful words, words lacking in greed, fear or ignorance will create a world that is also lacking in greed, fear or ignorance.

It is not possible to imagine such a world while you are still speaking words that are fear based, greed based or from ignorance of your true nature.

You cannot imagine such a world, but you can create the conditions from which it can arise.

And This!

INSECURITY

I have noticed that, of the people I work with on a frequent basis, no matter what symptoms are manifesting, they all have their root in one fundamental issue, insecurity.

The most obvious are those with anxiety manifesting. Why would we be anxious, what is it that creates this reality in so many people? It would be easy to say that the current conditions around the world are enough to make any sensitive person anxious. These conditions may well be to blame, but they may also equally be the product of an already anxious society. Constant identification with anxiety leads to other health related issues for which we seek answers, failing to recognise the deep seated cause for those health issues.

It is not just anxiety that manifests, though that is a big one. Very often the employment that we seek out is an expression of aspects of the self that are not fully made conscious. Relationships in particular are often the result of sub conscious conditioning. Health issues that manifest later in life can often be traced back to deeply rooted, subconscious patterns that we have either inherited from our ancestral gene pool, brought 'in' as charge from other experiences or acquired along the way due, in major part, to our early childhood conditioning.

We cannot blame anyone for this 'insecurity'. We learn much from our parents, our siblings, the society that we are born into and those parents, those siblings, that society, all learnt from their parents, their siblings, the society into which they were born. It seems that very few people actually stop and question the world/reality into which they are born. Instead the same conditioning is passed down the line, again and again and again.

We are taught, from an early age, at least most of us are, that the world is not a safe place to be. We must learn how to survive, at home, at school, at work, in relationship. These lessons are not overt, they are subtle, hinted at, played out by the behaviour of those around us who have already learnt these subliminal lessons. We simply follow directives that have been laid down over centuries, if not millennia, adding our own energy to the belief that we have to strive to do something in order to create a safe environment.

We often fail to realise that much of what we do, how we respond/react, how we feel, what we see has its roots in insecurity. A lot of people seem to be suffering from depression. It is common for us to externalise our problems, and seek answers outside of the self, thinking that another can make us happy, feel safe and secure. We seek approval from the world but seem unable to give it to ourselves. This continual belief that we can only find that which we seek outside of the self.

Depression may arise as a result of our apparent needs being constantly undermined but we are not 'depressed' as such, depression arises because of a conditioned mind that has as its base, insecurity. The difficulty is compounded when, because of that same conditioning, we believe ourselves to be depressed.

| And This! |

Our world is a manifestation of our thoughts. Our thoughts are a product of conditioning which includes past charge that we carry with us and conditions imposed upon us by family and society.

We spend most, if not all in some cases, of our lives looking for that security but by externalising our search we simply guarantee that there is no end to the search. We don't even realise that the search is due to deep rooted insecurity. It doesn't matter who we believe ourselves to be, how wealthy—how poor, how powerful—how weak, we are all born into the same world, apparently, and we all struggle with the same issues.

Until we can learn to fully accept and embrace all aspects of ourselves we will continue to create the same old same old. When we can truly accept ourselves then those parts that created problems just fall away. Try it for yourself.

Something to Think About!

BEYOND INSECURITY

Last month I wrote about 'insecurity' and how it may well be the root cause for all issues we, and the world, face today. To look beyond insecurity, and no doubt there is something beyond insecurity, we must first move beyond the limitations that this 'insecurity' has imposed upon us.

Is it really necessary though, that we keep looking for any fundamental cause for the state we find ourselves in now? Even assuming we could find the fundamental issue, what good would it do us while we are still caught in the old patterns, the conditioning that arose out of insecurity. None at all, because the conditioning itself demands that we either come to terms with it or try to change our lives, again, from within the conditioning that created the perceived need for change in the first place.

Perhaps there is a shortcut to moving beyond our conditioning. If we were to ask who is it who feels insecure? Who is it who identifies with insecurity? Who is it that continues to suffer the effects of insecurity? We might, just might, be able to step out of the old model. For it is only the continued identification with this old model that sustains it. We should be aware by now that where we put our energy, our attention, creates the world we live in. Yet while we insist on continuing to energise conflict we continue to live in a conflicted world.

To begin understanding this elusive 'who' we need to practice non judgement. All the time we judge a feeling, a thought, others, a situation or ourselves we are perpetuating the illusory state based upon insecurity. While we judge, and energise, we remain caught trying to find a way out, a release, yet it should be obvious by now that there is no way out of this illusion, at least not from within the mind-set that created it.

Common feedback to this suggestion is 'too hard' 'I cannot do that'. Listen to yourself? Who is finding this idea challenging? The 'who' who is lost in the drama of course. Yet it is not necessary that we release all judgement in one moment, although this happens more often than we credit ourselves. The difficulty is seeing a mountain, an obstacle, so great that we are discouraged before we even begin the journey.

Even this self defeatist attitude is a product of insecurity. Accept the mountain, accept the idea that this is difficult, accept the thought you cannot do this, accept the thought that this is too hard. As you accept each thought, each feeling that arises, without judging those thoughts or feelings, what are you left with? More thoughts and feelings, naturally. Thoughts and feelings continue to arise whilst the consciousness remains polarised. Judgement guarantees ongoing polarisation. So whilst the consciousness from which all thoughts and feelings arise is conflicted, in a judgmental condition, conflict will continue to arise giving cause for action, further judgment. And so it goes.

By noticing a defeatist attitude and naming it but then moving on, releasing any attachment or judgement we return to a more balanced, harmonious state. With practice this becomes easier to notice and let go.

Acceptance then is the key, not returning to a murky past to try to discover why you have a murky past, simple acceptance. On a moment by moment basis. Not difficult at all. Each moment that you are conscious of thoughts and feelings is a moment of choice, to move beyond the old conditioning, or to energise the past. A past that has given you many experiences but does not allow the creation of a new reality.

As you practice non judgment, as you allow, as you accept it becomes increasingly obvious that the 'who' you were looking for doesn't exist. The 'who' is a construct of the searching mind. After all, someone has to be searching! Don't they! But with continued acceptance the need to search fades into irrelevance. When there is nothing to look for and no 'searcher' there is no 'who', there is no one holding onto a past built on insecurity. There is no one, nor any thing to clear, it is what it is.

Ponder This

Have you ever wondered how you can change the world you live in?

For years now, at workshops, I have been quoting this piece from the book, *Dreaming While Awake*, by Arnold Mindell, PhD:

> The other possibility is that we move out of time and space and let go of our identity. We become lucid about our sentient experience and, even before it manifest positive or negative figures, we become edge less. Even before we can talk about a tension, we change and let go of our hold on time and go with the flow. Such moments require a lot of awareness, personal courage and flexibility.

This state or edgelessness is one of the many goals of the practitioner of 'Clearing.' We, in the 'clearing community' may use different language, but the end result is the same. We can also see one of the goals for the practitioner to be similar to the Buddhist practice of Tonglen where the master takes on the pain and suffering of those round and transmutes it through the power of the compassionate heart.

What does this mean for the person practicing 'clearing'?

Imagine, for a moment that who we believe ourselves to be is nothing more than a collection of points of view that we hold about ourselves and the world around us, for simplicity we can call this collection the personality.

Ponder This

When we begin the practice of 'clearing' we begin to release judgement, blame and attachment to various points of view. The attachment to the identity of the personality becomes more fluid, we see how our attachments have created particular responses, which in turn have created the world we live in. Slowly, as we continue the practice, our world changes because we are no longer energising old, accepted, ways of being. There are many patterns we hold that seem to be buried deep within us, aspects of what Jung referred to as our shadow. This idea that we have a 'shadow' becomes meaningless as we develop our ability to embrace these aspects of our self through a growing sense of safety that non attachment allows.

These are the 'personal' benefits, the freedom from the past allowing our system to relax, to heal itself of all sorts of trauma, physical, emotional or psychological that we have previously taken personally. The 'clearer' will also notice the effect their own growing peace and clarity has on those around them.

If we return to Mindell's quote, "…even before it manifests positive or negative figures…" surely this is the essence of changing the manifesting reality that we believe ourselves to exist within.

For example: If you still harbour anger or fear in your sub conscious, you are going to meet anger and fear along the road. (Constantine Cavafy, *Ithaca*). If you have these aspects deep inside you and you walk into a room where others hold the same conditions and you have not yet recognised them for what they are, you are likely to externalise, to blame those around you for your current state.

But ponder this, if you have embraced the anger or the fear, completely, without reservation, then, before you even enter the room where the potential for conflict exists, conflict which would have previously triggered off in you a reaction of blame and judgement, the energy of potential conflict would have collapsed.

This serves at least two purposes, one, if you enter an environment where you experience anything other than loving kindness, you know you still have work to do. Two, if you have accepted all fear, all anger, then you heart will allow all conflict to collapse before you even become aware of the existence of anger and fear. And this is what Mindell means, it is the essence of Tonglen, it is the heart of the 'clearing.' If you collapse the cause of conflict before it can arise you will step into a very different reality, you may not realise you are living in a different manifestation because for you to realise that there would have to be subject/object and you would again be in a judgmental state.

We do not have to 'show up' to make a difference, we simply have to learn to love ourselves without reservation. This simple, yet difficult, achievement has no boundaries, no limits. There is nothing that will not be affected by the power of your compassionate heart. Just know that while you still judge there is room for more compassion. We can see the opposite of compassion all around us and we may wonder how we can make a difference while so many people appear to be feeding old fears.

Remember, it takes a lot of energy to sustain old patterns, it takes no energy at all to be compassion.

And This!

SIMPLICITY VERSUS COMPLEXITY

Clearing is simplicity personified, yet we struggle with the simplicity because of the complexity we have built in our attempts to understand the simplicity. Crazy, eh!

We are so conditioned to 'do a lot in order to achieve a lot' we completely miss the point. Remember, "Do a lot, achieve a little—do little, achieve a lot, do nothing, achieve everything".

Yet we stubbornly refuse to see the truth in this simple statement. The conditioned reality, that we continue to energise, is so strong that we believe by doing nothing the 'others' will win. Many societies have so conditioned their populations that any time away from the work environment is so limited there is no time to reflect, to truly relax and look around at what is really going on. We see time away from work as some sort of reward for good behaviour yet we know we are going to have to return to 'work' because our lifestyles have guaranteed we need to 'work' to sustain them. And so we believe.

And this is all 'true' as far as it goes, as far as we are prepared to believe it to be true and continue to subscribe to this belief. This is, after all, the world we live in.

Many people simply do not get the time to reflect, they are into survival big time, that is their reality. Many people who have the time are not interested in reflection unless it benefits them in some way.

We are continually trying to make the world a better place; create a better future for ourselves or our family; save this; save that. No matter what you try and do it is fundamentally doomed to failure, simply because the energy that you are putting into the conflict is supporting the illusory nature of the world that you have come to accept as reality. There are no answers that are going to solve the 'problems of the world' down that path although the illusion leads you to believe that you can make a difference.

Sure it is a fascinating ride, so much to learn and understand, but don't for one moment believe that it is going to make any fundamental difference to the manifesting reality.

There are several ways to view this message. We can deny it. Tear it apart. Believe it but feel powerless to 'do' anything about it Continue to try to change the system from within the system. Try for another revolution and fight the system. We can try to change ourselves so that the manifesting reality changes. Or we can simply accept this is how things are.

I suspect that the last 'answer' is the way to go. For, if we are truly lost within a complex illusion, then anything we try will originate from within the limitations of that illusion and thus doomed to failure. If we try to change ourselves we will be coming from a place that is telling us we are faulty, at fault. This is simply a product of the illusion, it is not real at all, yet our conditioning either lays the blame for anything perceived as 'wrong' often at the feet of others, the next step being to blame the self.

Acceptance, why should we accept the manifesting reality. Because accepting requires a total lack of judgement.

When we do not judge we are not coming from a polarised state, when we are not polarised we are not energising the manifesting reality. When we do not energise it, it collapses. Out of the ashes of the past a truly new future can unfold. A new illusion? Of course, how could it be anything else, but, an illusion that sets the mind and heart free to explore the multiple illusions which then become available to us. Illusions that are not based on greed, fear or ignorance and of course, need to be released as they arise!

A quote from a Rinpoche:

> Since all things are naked, clear and free from obscuration, there is nothing to attain or realise.
>
> The everyday practice is simply to develop a complete acceptance and openness to all situations and emotions.
>
> And to all people—experiencing everything totally without reservations and blockages, so that one never withdraws or centralises into oneself.

Remember: Do *NOT* Believe A Word Anyone Tells You. No one really knows what is going on, and even if they did they are either not going to tell you, or you are not going to believe them if they did.

Musings

LOVING KINDNESS IN THE BUDDHIST TRADITION 'METTA' IN WESTERN SPEAK 'CLEARING'

In the Theravadin Buddhist tradition, this practice begins with the meditator cultivating benevolence towards themselves, then one's loved ones, friends, teachers, strangers, enemies, and finally towards all sentient beings. In the Tibetan Buddhist tradition, this practice is associated with Tonglen whereby one breathes out ('sends') happiness and breathes in ('receives') suffering.

I suspect that the only path out of the current heavily polarised dilemma the manifesting world faces at the moment is the practice of 'Metta' or loving kindness.

No matter what situation we observe, it is our own personal judgement that dictates whether or not that situation develops into conflict or collapses. There is a danger in watching televised accounts/perceptions of what is going on in the world, of listening to the news, or reading newspapers. We don't even have to believe what we see, the words and images are still very powerful and have a significant impact upon us. If we take for one moment seriously that which we are exposed to, even on social media, then we are still lost in the polarised world. To imagine that any information is an accurate representation of what is going on is a mistake.

| Musings |

'Clearing' is, essentially, developing our own practice of loving kindness. Through noticing our thoughts and feelings and giving them less energy, judging them less and less we are cultivating benevolence towards ourselves. As our heart opens more and more, with less and less fear we begin to feel more peace within ourselves. There is less room for anxiety if there is no fear, and fear cannot exist (for more than 90 seconds!) in a compassionate heart.

As the heart opens so the body is allowed to heal itself. Once started and practiced often this has a domino effect, upon ourselves and all around us. This cascade of change that started as a moment in time when we noticed and did not judge that which we noticed, when we failed to take whatever it was personally, ripples throughout our awareness and spills over into the world around us.

Hard to see or understand while we are still lost in the duality that appears to be the status quo, but, as we practice and as those around us notice change, then we are encouraged to practice some more. The more we are able to embrace all aspects of the self, without judgment or attachment, the more the heart opens.

Then, as though effortlessly, the loving kindness that we are becoming expands to our loved ones, friends, teachers, strangers even our enemies. This is not something we think about, not something we practice, it is just the result of who we are. The inner peace that arises as a result of the practice simply allows all that is around to release old conditioned stress and patterns and return to a balanced, loving state.

Clearing = Metta = Tonglen = Loving Kindness

Not the easiest state to discover, let alone remain within. There always seems to be something on your path that calls you back into the past, a past that only arose because of the polarised mind.

For me, the practice is to observe the unfolding drama, but not to take sides, not to judge and certainly not to take it all personally. To notice where I still have preferences, judgments about right and wrong, good and bad, and then to remember the teachings. "Since everything is a product of one's own mind, empty of meaning, like a magicians illusion, having nothing to do with good or bad, right or wrong, one may well burst out in laughter."

Change, true change, can only come about, according to my current beliefs, through each and every person practicing 'Metta.' Many may not even be able to acknowledge this but there can be no blame when there is so much polarised charge holding the collective. For blame to arise there must be a lack of loving kindness, yet, with each person who begins to walk the path, no matter where they start or which road they take, the collective is impacted in such a way that, without confrontation, without anyone being 'right' (or 'wrong') that which has not been built on love collapses.

If you fail to see the value and the impact such a state of being can have upon you, your family, friends, neighbours, colleagues, the earth itself, then you have simply bought into the idea that change comes about through opposition and so it goes.

Ponder This

COMPLICITY

THIS IS GOING TO BE A HARD ONE FOR SOME BECAUSE acceptance is often a big challenge for most people. There are levels of course, degrees to which we can accept some things and not others. Those 'levels' reflect more of our own subconscious than we may be willing to agree with.

On some level I believe we are all complicit in all that appears to happen to us. Not easy to see how this can be so when individuals are confronted with events seemingly outside of their control: disease; war; famine to name just a few.

No one can affect you unless you allow it! Fact or fiction?

Why would anyone 'choose' to experience being a refugee? Or any casualty of war? To suffer disease or sickness?

I suspect we don't choose, we have lost the ability to choose by the decisions, or lack of decisions we made in the past and we are now very much 'victims' to circumstance. How far back do we need to go when we did have a 'free' choice? Was there ever a point when we got to truly choose? The simple fact of our being born into human form in this day and age is in itself enough to guarantee certain conditioning.

We may think we make choices now, to a degree perhaps we do. But all choices made now arise from within a framework, a very limited paradigm, that is a product of our past, not necessarily our personal past, but the collective past.

This ongoing state of limited choice is perpetuated by the constant externalising of the cause of all our ills. While we continue to personalise with all experiences we support the current 'reality' that we find ourselves in.

And this is where we are all complicit in whatever happens to us. We may attract abusive situations but only if on some level we are willing or allow ourselves to be abused. No one, I would imagine, would choose to be abused. But the choice is no longer ours to make, we are driven by the subconscious conditioning now so deep and strong that we are unable to recognise this.

Failing to recognise the responsibility we have in the unfolding drama we tend to blame others. 'They' are doing this to me; 'They' should know better; 'They' are responsible for this problem, and so it goes. While we are unable to see that our own subconscious conditioning has allowed the 'situation' to develop we will continue to blame. While we blame we seek answers, some resolution which we can never find all the time we are driven by the past.

If we are not truly 'clear' within ourselves then we should not expect others to be clear. Although others may be 'clear,' relatively speaking, if we are still viewing the world through the filter system of our own judgemental past we will not see clarity, simply a reflection of our own value system. This perception leads us deeper down the rabbit hole as we try to 'work things out' as they present to us. We employ various methods that we have learnt and come to believe in. Yet those methods were invariably taught to us by others equally lost down the rabbit hole, themselves trying to discover a 'way out.'

Common perception, supported by the mass media today, is that we are unsafe. Believing in this lie we are offered various ways to create safety or simply to create the illusion of safety. All of the ways offered require us to 'do' something further increasing any polarised charge we may hold, often on a subconscious level. In order for this lack of safety to be maintained, we need something/someone out there who is a threat. It should be completely obvious to any thinking person that this road leads to further control, more fear, more polarisation and hence, more conflict. A heavily polarised mind, lost in its own perceptions, perceptions created out of no-thing like a magicians illusion, can do nothing other than react in a very fearful and judgmental way.

We may not be able to change the collectives polarised point of view, but we can change ours.

It all starts with us. It is no good waiting for the next person in line to change the world, the choice is yours. To continue to believe in the nonsense or start the path of acceptance. By accepting what is showing up in your life, without judging it, any charge supporting the illusory nature of that reality will begin to fall away. Accept responsibility, at least until you see and accept the world for what it is.

Not easy to do while you still believe the rabbit hole reality is truly who you are. Not easy to do if you still hold onto anger, fear, judgement, grudges, anxiety, blame, all the time looking outside for the answers. Not easy until you hit the reality wall and discover for yourself that the answers are not 'out there' but in here!

And This!

A FUNDAMENTAL MISUNDERSTANDING

Most problems people face today arise from a fundamental misunderstanding of their true nature.

This 'misunderstanding' begins at birth, for we are born into a society that has already fully accepted the 'misunderstanding' as reality. It really doesn't matter which society you are born into, various habitual patterns are passed on without question. They may appear to be different yet each has this fundamental concept buried deeply within their psyche.

This 'misunderstanding' may be seen by many as a part of what being human is all about, but that statement is also a product of the 'misunderstanding.'

This misunderstanding is that we are all limited, separate, isolated individuals, as such we need to strive, work hard, do more, in order to survive in what appears, as a result of the conditioned upbringing, to be a hostile environment. This sense of 'me'–'my'–'you'–'your's simply reaffirms, on a moment by moment basis, our sense of separation.

According to Buddhist teachings, we are born anew every moment of every day, the potential, when we truly realise this, is enormous. So much 'more' than we are currently able to accept. Not 'more' in the sense of more money, more possessions, more power. Rather, more fully grounded in our true nature, which is not limited by past beliefs, not restricted in what it can achieve.

Imagine spending your life in a magnificent tower, or a dungeon, a palace, a slum. No matter in which reality you live, there are no windows in your tower, your dungeon, your palace, your slum, you are limited to what you can see, feel, touch, taste, your view of life is just a narrow picture that you may, or may not, have grown to accept. You have no first hand knowledge of the sun on your face, the wind in your hair, the smell of the sea or the pasture. You have no real concept of life, other than what is fed into your tower, your dungeon, your palace, your slum.

We have become so accustomed to our limited point of view that anyone offering an alternative must be deluded. We fail to see that it is us who are deluded, constantly, by all those around us who have brought into the limitations. We cannot wake in the morning and not be reminded of our limits, the family who—through no fault of their own—go along with the collective conditioning. Colleagues at work, friends and acquaintances, the media bombarding us 24/7 with their own agendas that support the old. Everywhere we look there is something to remind us of who we believe ourselves to be.

It is hardly surprising that we are caught in this web of deceit, when all around us, to some degree or other, support that traditional status quo. It is no less surprising that when we are offered a way out of our self perpetuated coma that we try to rationalise the way out from within the structure that we believe to be real. This is an impossible task, for the perceptions that hold us just keep coming up with more 'reasonable' solutions to our problems. We seem determined to find solutions from within the drama not realising that the drama, or the attachment to it is, in itself, the real issue.

And This!

If we are rebuilding ourselves moment by moment perhaps we should look for new bricks not keep re-using the old ones over and over again. Perhaps when we rebuild with new bricks we may begin to see new possibilities, we may even come to the realisation that we don't need any bricks at all.

'Clearing' is simply one path of many, a path that is designed to self destruct the more you walk it. As you walk this path perceptions shift, attachments fall away, addictions to the old are seen for what they are—addictions to a limited way of being and clarity arises. Pretty soon the new you that arises is no longer a product of the old you, no longer conditioned by a limited past.

The sooner the better I say.

Another Day, Another Thought

SURVIVING!

Are we surviving, managing, just coping, or truly living?

We all 'do' what we think is necessary in order for us to have a 'good life.' We are all driven, to some degree or other, whether consciously or sub-consciously, by desires and fears of which we are not even aware.

We can see, in hindsight, as we look back over our lives, that the paths we have taken were not always with complete awareness. Why do some people follow certain paths? Is there some deep programming that only opens particular doors for us? What professions do we choose? And do we really choose them or do they choose us? Where does intelligence come from? Is it intelligence that dictates out journey?

I have noticed, in my own journey and that of others I have worked with, that if we do not break the mold early on we tend to get stuck on a path that has been laid down by societies expectations, not necessarily one of our own choosing. Though the person who thought they might have the choice is but a product of their past and while that past remains a dominant part of their reality, there really is no choice.

We tend to settle into our path, often without realising it, it creeps up on us, surrounds us, envelops us until there is only the path, no options are open to us, or it appears that way, until either disaster strikes or we move beyond the power of the conditioned past. Disaster can mean major health issues that force us to re-evaluate, it can be emotional trauma, it can be that we have worked though the 'lessons' on that part of the path and are ready for a new direction or it can be that we have simply come to the end of the road.

Many people come to the end of the road without recognising the fact that they have failed to live the life they would have chosen had they 'woken' up earlier. This was, in our recent history, a very common phenomena. Societies expectations made sure everyone towed the line, paid their dues, lived the life laid out for them and never questioned the truth of that life. It still is for many people.

Many people take a path dictated by their own insecurity, the need for recognition, for money, for power, for prestige, for safety. We follow the rules, we do what we are expected to do. Now and again someone will break free from this established way of being and set out on a different journey, a journey that is more about self discovery than it is about conforming. To reach the point where we are ready to look outside of the accepted for a different way certain conditions need to be met. One or more of the following may apply. We need to have enough personal desire to experience more. We must reach a place where we feel safe enough to step off the well trodden path. We must have worked through all charge associated with the path we currently walk.

We choose employment, or employment chooses us such that our basic needs will be met. Employment is a condition of acceptance into society, or so it seems from within the broad path that we are born on. We believe we have no choice and take the necessary steps to 'fit in.'

We carve out a spot for ourselves, we often use our employment as a means of identifying ourselves within the broader collective. For some that spot is pretty permanent, meaning we will remain in that spot until we retire/die/or suffer significant trauma that prevents us from continuing. For some, the spot is but a step along a bigger path. There is no right or wrong here, no better or worse, the world is made up of such diversity, there is room for all. Yet if you continue to tread the path blindly, without reflecting upon your own deeper needs you will find, one day, that you remained a slave to conditioned society.

It can take a long time to work through all of the karma, the charge that previously dictated your path. This is not for everyone, conditions have to be just right on many levels for an individual to either stay put or move out.

Do you still have dreams? Do you still have goals yet to be attained, places to visit, things to do? This drive can be understood as karma, as charge, as desire and it will need to be exhausted before you can find true peace. You have a choice. Work through all desire, all karma and all charge, piece by piece until no charge remains. Or, simply accept everything that shows up on your path with absolute equanimity, no longer giving energy to the old, conditioned, way of being. This doesn't imply acceptance of the old path. The old path will slowly cease to exist, as you stop energising it, new opportunities, previously hidden from sight, will show up.

There is no journey that we need to go on in order to discover the self, as we develop our ability to accept, the journey will come to us, the journey will choose us as we release preferences, judgement, fear and desire. Yet still we live life, but the 'who' who is now living life will be inseparable from the life, no veil of personality getting in the way confusing things. No fear driving us, no insecurity, no part that needs completing.

This is how we change the world.

Sleep on This One

POLARISATION

I WOULD LIKE TO EXPAND ON A COUPLE OF MY RECENT POSTS to the 'Life Skills For Now' page on Facebook.

The Polarised state, the world in which most people live may well be 'responsible' for the wide range of viewpoints currently held in the world. Polarisation of consciousness arises out of judgment, which arises out of a fundamental misunderstanding we have about our 'place' in the world.

A greatly polarised collective allows for an incredibly broad range of experiences, from the sublime to the darkest of the dark. Without a strong degree of polarisation worldly experiences would cease to exist to the degree we currently experience them.

No matter which 'point of view' you hold, there will be an equal and opposite point of view. The more energy you give your point of view the more energy of 'opposition' you will have to deal with along the way.

It is difficult to know if strongly polarised thought gives rise to a lack of humanity or the absence of humanity creates polarisation in consciousness. Either way, the lack of humanity that appears to exist in this world continues to increase because many can only find good in those that agree with their heavily polarised perceptions. This apparent lack of humanity, i.e. affections for a few people who are nearest to us is, in Albert Einsteins words, a prison we have created for ourselves based upon the fundamental misapprehension that we are separated from all other sentient beings.

Another 'issue' with a heavily polarised state is the need to make decisions, choices. When we choose from a polarised state there is always a price to pay. If we are not clear when we choose then the choice itself is not clear. This leads to consequences that we have to deal with forcing us to make more choices. As we consciously reduce our own polarised judgemental state the need to choose less arises, instead of believing we are choosing, the path begins to appear to choose us.

I suspect that the busy, monkey, mind is also a product of polarised thought and points of view. This could well be the result of past conditioning, conscious, but more likely, not. As we appear to be torn between good and bad, right and wrong, there will always be decisions that need to be made. Choices about this or that, here or there, good or bad. On it goes. The mind is kept busy trying to manage the polarised state, this busy mind prevents access to a higher, more balanced awareness, that of the heart. Hard to feel what is happening in the moment if the 'mind' is caught up in the past always projecting an imagined future.

Failure to notice the 'now' not only robs us of the perfection of the moment but it prevents us from dealing effectively with whatever presents in the moment. Lots of emotions and physical feelings that arise out of our passage through time and space get stored in the body if we do not process them effectively as they show up. These emotions and physical feelings are destined to become 'real' problems later in life, which then create a state that requires we 'do' something about them.

Processing the feelings and emotions effectively is one of the many benefits of practicing 'clearing' on a daily basis.

While we have any attachment to a judgement we are in a polarised state. Whilst we identify with thought, feelings and emotions we are lost in the goldfish bowl of an acted, albeit, illusory state.

Imagine, if you were to be free of judgement, how different your world would be. Most people assume that judgement is a necessary part of the human condition but this misunderstanding only arises from within the belief that the illusion that you are responsible for creating is real. It is only real to the degree that you, and many others, give it energy. You give it energy by your polarised beliefs. People operate from the fear that if they do not take sides then the 'opposition' will win, thus maintaining the very thing that they feel is 'wrong.' Yet, as your personal judgements begin to lose energy your manifesting reality changes. You are no longer confronted by such a broad range of experiences because they are no longer a part of your world. If the product of a heavily polarised society is not energised then the polarisation, to some degree, collapses. Balance is maintained but the extremes no longer arise. This, I believe, is the middle way the Buddha referred to.

Notice where and when you judge. Breathe and smile, don't judge yourself for judging, simply acknowledge your judgement and put your attention elsewhere. Develop your practice of non-judgment by deliberately bring to mind people or situations that you have judged in the past, notice any feelings, physical or emotional, associated with the judgement and do your best to release those feelings by nor giving them anymore energy. This may take time, but that is only measured by the degree you stubbornly resist being in the moment. You may need to deliberately put your attention elsewhere in the early stages of practice. Yet, the more you practice the more you will experience the benefits of the practice.

And This!

HOW WE CAN CHANGE THE REALITY WE LIVE IN

As a result of the many years developing and practicing 'clearing' I have learnt many things. I have also 'unlearnt' many things. Ideas, beliefs, perceptions are simply nothing more than ideas, beliefs and perceptions, there is nothing real or sustainable about them other than the power we give them. They continue to manifest because of the constant input of energy we, as individuals, give them.

By continuing to give old beliefs energy we perpetuate the current reality in which we 'find' ourselves. It seems as though there is a lot of dissatisfaction with the current reality in many parts of the world, more and more people are voicing their discontent and attempting to change their reality. It also seems, to me, that most people are trying to change that reality from within the very reality they wish to change. This approach, as far as I can understand, is doomed to failure because the nature of the problems that challenge many people arise from a basic misunderstanding of the nature of reality.

While we try to change a system from within we simply give energy to that system creating more challenges along the way, which in turn create conflict and require more energy to overcome.

Perhaps this can best be illustrated from the 'clearing' perspective.

There appear to be six stages through which we pass on this 'clearing' journey. These stages only arise because of our attachment to old conditioned beliefs, they are no more 'real' than any other perceptions, they just have the appearance of reality. While we are lost in that particular illusion we feel the need to 'do' something to bring back a more balanced state for ourselves and our family.

Number One: The stage at which there does not appear the need for a journey, there is little or no understanding that we are co-creating the world we live in. Here we are lost within the bubble that has been created out of our past, where we believe what we see, hear and read. Where we struggle within our self imposed limitations trying to find ways to improve our lives. Imagine walking in to a room that holds a lot of conflict and without any awareness, reacting to that conflict, blame and judgement and identification with the conflict in full force. That approach feeds the flames of conflict, whether we want to or not our blame and judgement affects those around us adding fuel to the conflict.

Number Two: After being introduced to 'clearing' we begin to notice how our feelings shift and change in relationship to our environment and those around us. Still we externalise, we blame and judge, unconsciously giving energy to that which we oppose. Now, we walk into the same room, we notice the conflict but are still lost in the conditioned past of blame and judgement, our attachment to this way of being still, subconsciously, controls our perceptions.

Number Three: As a result of our exposure to 'clearing' (for example) we walk into that same room and recognise the feelings associated with conflict. We are able to say "this is what conflict feels like" yet there is still a part of us that is reacting, subconsciously, to the feelings that arise in our awareness. We still try to do something with the feelings, lessen them, even perhaps 'clear' them. We are still reacting to the energy of conflict, while we continue to react we continue to give energy to that which we find uncomfortable.

Number Four: With more practice we are able to walk into that same room, notice the energy of conflict, recognise it for what it is but we do not identify with the conflict. Instead we are able to accept this feeling, of conflict, embrace it without fear, without judgement, without blame. This approach literally collapses the energy of conflict in the room. We no longer identify with the symptoms of conflict yet we are still processing the information that we notice, basically we are still 'doing' something with the feelings.

Number Five: As we have developed our practice so we have changed our neurological conditioning. By failing to give energy to that which we have noticed in the past we have allowed any subconscious addictions to certain ways of thinking, feeling or being, to fall away. In return we are better able to be in the moment, responding to situations rather than reacting to them.

We begin to see the world through different eyes. This may be a gradual process or can happen quite suddenly and dramatically. Yet the more we practice the more the heart opens to allow all information it receives which in turn creates a very different reality.

Number Six: As we have changed our neurological conditioning and opened our heart, fearlessly, to embrace whatever it encounters we create a very different manifesting reality moving away from the limits of any past conditioning. Now, even before we enter the room which holds conflict, we change that reality. Our heart literally collapses the conflict even before we meet it, for if we no longer hold conflict in

| And This! |

our heart we can no longer meet it on the road. Now, walking into the room, there is no conflict, there is nothing to 'do' to change things because we have already done the work, on our selves.

This is how we can change the manifesting reality, not by fighting the status quo but by refusing to give it any energy. Polarised opposites which create conflict only arise from our giving more energy to one of the 'poles.' Yet we see people lost in the drama, fighting for this or that, when all they are really doing is acknowledging the manifesting reality as real and continuing to support it by 'taking sides.'

Learn to collapse the chaos instead of feeding it and see for yourself the changes that arise on your path.

A Piece to Start the Day

Last month I wrote about 6 levels of understanding that we can apply to the clearing work.

If you read that you will recall level five, where we are still engaged in 'doing' something about whatever shows up, remember we are mostly concerned with charge that makes us feel uncomfortable.

When we experience discomfort of any sort, and we have been practicing our 'clearing' then, on one level, we know that the feelings we experience are not ours, simply the way the body has become accustomed to 'feeling' the energy and interpreting it. This level of awareness requires us to 'do' something with the feeling. With awareness, we acknowledge the feeling (name it) accept it without blame, judgement or, most importantly, identifying with it.

When we can reduce the degree to which we identify with the feeling, whatever it may be, then we have begun the process of disengaging or breaking the addiction the body has to not only that feeling, but all feelings. This can happen because we are re-educating the body in how it relates to information that it picks up on the journey of life.

For most it takes time and practice because we are so lost in the conditioning that claims all feelings as ours. This attachment to 'body consciousness' according to Buddhist teachings needs to be released in order for us to transcend the conditioned limitations that hold us prisoner.

Since, ultimately, there is no one to release the conditions, no one to go anywhere, nothing to do, it seems as though we are caught in a paradox. No one to 'do' anything, no where to go, no goal, no journey, just the moment. For those lost in the drama that appears as reality, there is obviously someone, there is something to do, somewhere to go, a journey, a goal. With this in mind, 'clearing' provides an opportunity for those who are lost to begin to see through the veil, by taking, what appears to be, conscious action.

Remember, 'clearing' has been 'designed' to self destruct, a bridge, that once crossed, becomes irrelevant. The more we practice 'clearing' the less we need it.

Which takes us to level six. Where we have managed to release all attachment, judgement and blame around any one issue, that issue is no longer controlling our actions from the subconscious. What this means is that a particular issue around which we have no charge whatsoever ceases to show up in our lives. Before we noticed the feeling and had to 'do' something to move beyond it. Level six means that the issue no longer shows up. We only realise this in retrospect.

While there is still someone 'home' who believes that there is something to do, then this process happens piece by piece. Eventually the realisation arises, after we feel safe enough to let go of more pieces of the puzzle, that it is all the same stuff, just wrapped differently. It is all just stuff, none of which is 'ours.'

There then appears to be a period of rapid growth, a time when much of the conditioned expectations fall away, yet because of the training involved in the clearing process the shock of the transition is reduced and the mind has already begun to accept the concept of 'no-self.'

We know while we are still attached to a sense of self whenever we take a situation, person or emotion personally.

The 'clearing' provides a way to understand that and to work through such attachments in a safe and gentle way. It is only by regular, frequent practice that we can experience the many benefits of this way of being.

When level six starts showing up, or not, in your life your system starts to relax more. When your system is no longer stressed it spends less time in fight or flight, there is less vulnerability to sickness and disease, less challenging choices to make, less to worry about. Combine all of this and a different world view begins to emerge.

While you dance between levels five and six despair and frustration may arise as you are beginning to see the 'old' world through eyes that are not based in a fear based perception, another reminder to take that which you perceive personally.

When the world that you are creating is not based on fear or attachment to feelings you are actually changing the world, your world. By not trying to impress your limited desires the illusion begins to collapse. Remember, even this will pass, if you let it.

Don't get hung up on phenomena that shows up, acknowledge, accept, without blame or judgment and without identifying or attaching your self to some new vision or dream.

Breathe and smile, keep up with your practice, change your world, not based on personal likes and dislikes but learn to see it for what it is and who you are.

Something to Think About!

EVERYTHING ARISES FROM...

In the years that I have been practicing and teaching 'clearing' it has become increasingly obvious how all things arise, and why.

My own path has been one of healing. Perhaps 'healing' is the wrong word, it may be better put as my coming to understand why I have acted as I have in certain situations. In fact, why those situations arose in the first place requiring me to act as I did. Together with the understanding a freedom arises, a recognition of an underlying issue that has coloured all aspects of my life.

Everyone I work with—and I suspect everyone that I don't—suffers from their own conditioned past.

Our past is often buried so deep we can no longer recall major points along the way, we bury it partly because we were not fully conscious when the conditioning took place—we became lost in the experience—and partly because of fear, shame, a desire to feel only 'good' things, to run away from pain.

For example, if we have trouble relating to others we will attract others who also have similar troubles. The real issues start when we, as a part of our conditioning, blame the other for our discomfort. Why though would we have trouble relating to others in the first place? What happened to make this so?

If we experienced significant trauma as a child when attempting to relate to others, we would spend much of our life compensating for this experience. Effectively this means that we would be controlled by our own issues when relating to others, we would 'see' problems that others have and want to 'fix' them. We externalise our own issues, projecting them onto those around us in our attempt to heal our self. We may not realise this is what we are doing at the time for we are so lost in our own drama we cannot even begin to recognise it.

We try to keep the peace, to make everyone happy failing to see we are the ones needing to be at peace, to be happy. We find our own happiness when others are happy, for then they are no longer a threat to the peace and harmony we so desperately seek for ourselves.

Out of this apparently troubled past everything arises. The way we relate to others, and those we attract with whom to relate. The 'other' will have their own issues, and as said earlier, while each blames the other conflict is inevitable.

But beyond this immediate effect we begin to see how all of our decisions, right down to the clothes we wear, and why we wear particular styles, the jobs we are drawn to, the very thoughts that are a constant undercurrent to our existence, all arise because of trauma, or conditioning from childhood.

Our whole life is based upon a huge misconception, a misunderstanding that arose because those around us also suffered from their own conditioned past and simply passed that past onto us without any real conscious awareness. No one stopped to question just what the heck they were doing, We do the same, we pass our own lack of true awareness onto our children and complain when they act out our own dramas.

This is not meant to condemn or criticise the past but to help make us aware that one issue, one single event, that was repeated over and over in the past, may well have controlled our lives, and continues to do so to this day. We are so lost in dealing with the results of that conditioning that we spend our lives trying to make sense, to create a safe place, to manipulate, to control our environment, always looking for that peace and happiness.

As a result of this constant externalising we become more radical, polarised, easily manipulated by fears that lie beneath the surface. Following this pattern we continually fail to recognise that in order to truly find peace and happiness we must look within, to stop struggling, stop trying to control, to avoid, to dominate. We need to pause, take a breath and accept who we appear to have become and learn to stop giving energy to that which opposes our goal. Essentially, to learn to love the self and all that shows up.

Clearing, for me, has provided that safe haven, a place where I could embrace the pain and suffering without taking it personally, a place where I could learn to love the self without the need to blame others for the journey.

A place where I could see—and embrace—the truth and set myself free from a conditioned past.

And This!

I WILL BE OKAY WHEN...

MANY SUFFER FROM THE PERCEPTION THAT ONCE they have achieved a certain goal then all will be well. Marriage! Children! Perfect Job! New Car! Better relationship! More Money! Better Health! Enlightenment! New House! Greater Safety!

The list can be endless. Until that goal is reached, assuming it is ever reached things will either go as planned/expected or another goal arises because the nature of insecurity is to continually seek something outside of the self. Most likely the goal is never truly attained for reaching it may satisfy the outer longing but does nothing to satisfy the inner cry for help out of which the desire for 'more' arose.

We will, for the most part, find ourselves in a constant struggle, trying to achieve, attain, realise a particular goal. It may even be peace of mind, a content heart, something really simple which of course is not simple once you try to find it. All sorts of objections, blocks, sabotage arise along the way seemingly making our journey so difficult.

There will always be the social expectations, the pressure put upon us by those around us, who, in their turn, have had pressure put upon them. Few people stop to consider where and why we experience such pressure, for surely this pressure has not created any real peace or happiness. Often the pursuit of 'more' is just a distraction, a sense that we must have 'this' or 'that' in order to be what? Accepted? Valued? Justified?

I spoke of this in last months newsletter, the concept of polarisation. While we remain heavily polarised and locked into personal values—which ultimately mean very little—the simple fact that we are polarised is enough to keep the machine of desire moving forward. Yet very little answers the inner call for help. We may temporarily side step the issue by becoming more involved in the pursuit of whatever, but sooner or later we will come face to face with the real issue. The fact that we have been chasing empty dreams without realising the dreamer has been deluded.

Because of the nature of the mind that led to this realisation the mind is still stuck in process. It needs to find an answer to this new dilemma. So now we look for spiritual answers through the various techniques available to us. And off we go again, another path, this one has to be better than the last because it is 'spiritual.'

Pretty soon we discover that nothing has changed, we are still driven by old conditioned responses, still seeking the answer outside of the self, still creating, moment by moment, yet another reality from within which we spend time, effort/money to discover the solution, the answer. If the searching mind has not been stilled then it will look for another path, another modality to, essentially, distract you from the real solution.

The idea that there are indeed 'wounds' that need to be 'healed' is itself a big part of the problem. That there is somewhere to go, to be, to do, while driven by the restless mind is the very problem we try so hard to overcome.

But surely, the idea that there is a problem is a state of mind, a perception a belief pattern, nothing more, nothing less. The idea that we need to do this, or that, to achieve this, to own that, are all, in themselves, belief patterns. All of which arise from a restless, insecure, perception of the self.

A perception which is reinforced, on a daily basis, by those around us, by the media, both corporate and social. We cannot listen or watch media of any sort and be unaffected. In workshops we have seen how one word creates a major string of responses/reactions in the individual, imagine what whole strings of words, graphic images, sound bites, what insecurity they can, and do, create.

We can try to come to terms with or deny the pressure we are subject to on a moment by moment basis, or, we can simply stop giving energy to it. The initial idea of not energising a point of view will, at first, seem like madness, all sorts of arguments will arise to justify your point of view, all based in insecurity.

Yet, as you practice disengaging from all the noise, all the distraction, so the polarised state reduces, so the need to defend reduces, so the need to be right reduces. So all of the 'external' noise that maintained a conflicted state falls away.

This cannot make any sense whatsoever to someone lost in a polarised state. It is only by reaching the understanding that nothing that arises from conflict will produce peace can we begin to accept responsibility for our actions and begin the process of finding that peace, within.

Yet even that is a misleading statement, one that itself arises out of the misconception that there is still something to do.

Once we truly accept that which is, then all else falls away. There is no 'peeling of the onion' involved, no steps to take, nothing to do other than accept that which is. Therein lies the challenge of course, for one to accept that which is one must be without insecurity or conflict.

| And This! |

Enjoy the life you have, accept it all with equanimity, it is only the initial stages of this 'journey' that appear to be a problem. This paradox can only remain so while there appears to be subject/object, until that falls away, 'you' will still need to be somewhere, other than here, to be at peace.

Musings

FEAR

If I were to ask most people if they were afraid, in that moment, most people would say no. If I asked them again in a stressful moment, they may say yes.

Fear is something that we all live with, in fact most of our decisions, our actions and our words are fear based. This may seem ridiculous, impossible, doesn't apply to me! Yet the fact remains that insecurity is one of the most prevalent underlying conditions in humankind today.

Insecurity shows up in many diverse ways, we often fail to realise it is insecurity that is behind the manifestation or feeling. Anxiety is a huge underlying issue yet ignored for the most part, ignored until it manifests as a problem. Then of course we try to 'fix' the manifesting problem, coming from a place of insecurity there is no fix possible, we simply add chaos and confusion to the situation having failed to recognise why it, the situation, arose in the first place.

If we look, in more detail, how it is possible that most decisions and actions are based on fear/anxiety it may be easier to recognise cause and effect and 'do' something positive about it—reduce the intensity wen it does happen, even eliminate if from our future—rather than wait for the issue to manifest and then have to do something about it. Denial is a wonderful ally but it doesn't help you escape from who you are, in the bigger picture you are going to come up against all that you have avoided /denied. Best start working on it now, the sooner the better, before it manifests and forces you into another reactive situation.

It is easy to list areas in which fear/anxiety control our lives on both conscious and subconscious levels: Health! A major aspect of our lives. While our lives are controlled by a media that has its own agenda we are easily manipulated into believing that we need to 'do' this, take that, buy this, practice this, avoid that, eat this, don't eat that, get this check up, get that procedure.

If we don't do as we are told then we are told there will be terrible consequences. The amount of information currently available is enormous, much of it conflicting. Who to believe! What to do? If we had no fear or anxiety then it is quite possible that we would not be affected by external forces that are trying to move us in particular directions. Being force fed a diet that has been designed to play upon deeply rooted fears we simply give more energy, consciously or otherwise, to those fears which allow them to manifest at some point.

For many of us it is obvious that where we put our attention leads to a strengthening and eventual manifestation of that energy. Put your attention on anger, anger arises.

If you are afraid of contracting any disease, simply because the media tells you that you are in danger, a high risk case, then on a subconscious level fear has been triggered. Fear is going to be the force that allows the illness to manifest. There may not be a great deal we can 'do' about old, inherited conditions, situations that we are not aware of until they become a problem. However, the more we practice not giving energy to that which shows up the more likely we are to lead a relatively pain free life simply because we no longer give energy to every little thing that shows up in our awareness.

Are you afraid of losing something? Health. Wealth. Material Possessions. Friends. Are you afraid of heights? Of being closed in? Of spiders? Of your neighbour? Are your fears anything more than a lack of awareness of your true nature? In all the years I have been practicing and teaching 'clearing' it has become obvious that fear is the root cause for all disease, for all poverty, for all discrimination, for all chaos, for all wars. It is the one simple fact that underlies our experience.

Fear arises, basically, from a lack of awareness, the awareness of our true nature, not the conditioned awareness that is so prevalent today. This lack of awareness is not something new, though the broadening knowledge of it is relatively new. While we continue to give energy to our subconscious, conditioned mind, fear will always play a great part in shaping the world we live in. It is not possible to create a new world while the majority of those who are wanting to create a new reality are still fear based.

We need to see these fears for what they truly are, a conditioned response brought about by mass hypnosis.

Rather than face all of these fears individually, which are all imaginary anyway, we should simply address whatever shows up in our life, in our reality, in our mind and in our hearts. Recognise that for the most part these thoughts and feelings arise from subtle levels of fear and stop empowering them. Stop feeding them. Stop identifying with them. Stop being a part of the problem and become a part of the solution.

There are many who say that there is nothing wrong with the world, it is an illusion after all. But for those lost in the illusion, feeding and empowering the illusion, there is something drastically wrong. Until we can all wake up from the illusion there appears to be something to do, wrongs to right, issues to take sides over. All of which simply adds to the chaos, confusion and conflict thus perpetuating the belief in the illusion.

The practice. Notice thoughts and feelings; recognise, accept and let go of the feeling/thought before it becomes a problem. Don't wait to deal with a problem when there was no problem to begin with.

A Piece to Start the Day

PROGRAMMED LIMITATIONS

Are we nothing more than a programmed intelligence inhabiting a biological body?

We 'think' we have free will, we 'think' we are free to choose. But is that free will, or are those choices all contained within a larger construct of limitations? We call that construct humanity and believe there are certain rules that apply and that we must follow.

I have often said, in workshops, that I believe planet earth to be the psychiatric institute for the Universe. A place where all the crazies are sent until they can come to their senses. Bars are not needed on this 'prison' because we have a body, we are surrounded by repeat offenders who just confirm any mistaken belief we may have had that this is reality. We cannot escape this prison until we do indeed come to our senses, and I suspect that entails, in part, not taking ourselves so seriously.

On one hand it is quite amusing to imagine this to be the case, for even those who think they are in charge of the hospital are themselves trapped here the same as everyone else.

I am reminded of a piece from one of Ram Dass's books, *Grist for the Mill*, where he went to visit a friend in a psychiatric hospital, on one side of the table stood a man, jeans, tshirt and bandanna, thought he was Jesus Christ, or the other side of the table was a man in a white coat, thought he was a psychiatrist!

No matter 'who' you 'think' you are, while you continue to 'think' that you will maintain that 'reality'.

Yet, if we are indeed locked into a pre-programmed limited awareness, there doesn't appear to be too much real opportunity to escape. Even the idea of the need to escape, to create a new world, to manipulate our current reality into something that we may prefer could be simply a part of the greater limitations. After all, we all need hope, hope that there is an end to the madness in sight.

Most people escape into their individual lives, the lives of the families, friends work, sports, politics. This, for many is enough. This, for most, is all there is. The bigger issues, the global issues are out there but what can they, as an individual do?

I used to look at the smaller issues, then let them go to look at the bigger issues. Then became overwhelmed, there were so many! Where to begin, and if I focused on one or two, what happened to the rest? And what was being done on a fundamental level to introduce greater peace and harmony into the world. Then I looked at heavily polarised societies and I see what is being done. What appears to be happening is an increase in the polarised consciousness of groups. This leads to more conflict, not less, more control, not more freedom. Less true choices, the absence of free will.

While we continue to take sides, any sides, in any situation, any argument—we both remain a part of the bigger problem—all the time failing to see that there is a bigger problem. We are constantly distracted by an increasing polarity in the collective. We give energy to any one concept, thought, point of view, judgement and we give energy, in an indirect way, to that which we oppose.

We have got to the stage where we are fighting among ourselves, scrabbling to be heard, to be right, to be safe, to be better, to have more, all the time failing to see this behaviour is simply adding another term, or two, to our sentence in this, the psychiatric institute of the universe.

It is not easy to see through the drama, to feel compassion but not sympathy. To see that our emotions are being abused, asked to support a corrupt system, a system that is failing to take care of the people for the sake of profit and control.

Without extreme polarisation there is no means to control the collective. When we stop all this in-fighting then issues that were previously 'real' fall away. Issues only arise from a conflicted personality. No conflict within, no conflict without. No more right or wrong, no more judgement needed. Yet most people hold onto their point of view, afraid that if they were to give it up they would encourage the opposition. Yet this argument can only arise from the internal conflicted state, which is a product of a fear based, limited awareness. It is the bars on the prison, bars of our own making, that keep us locked into a cycle of conflict. It is not real!

But then, what is?

Did You Know?

ON DEATH AND DYING

The leading cause of death today is, unsurprisingly, birth. There are contributing factors that either speed up the process or slow it down. But birth is the fundamental cause.

Next on the list is greed. Greed in all its many forms is probably responsible for more premature deaths than any other factor, except maybe fear. Fear is a big killer and may even outrank greed in the race to claim as many lives as early as possible.

Birth! Well that is obvious, without a body there can be no death.

Greed! Greed arises as a result of the birth into this third dimensional world. Greed arises often because of fear.

The number of people I have worked with whose fundamental issue is fear based is enormous. Most, if not all symptoms that manifest today arise because of fear, of anxiety. This runs so deep that many people fail to recognise it, or, if they do, just accept it as a part of the price we pay to be alive in these times. We have become so used to high levels of anxiety we don't see this as something that is man made, and perpetuated by man. Something that we could step out of were we to realise its true nature.

Fear arises because of a fundamental feeling of insecurity, a result of being born and kept in ignorance.

And the third, or fourth if we take into account birth, is ignorance.

Not meant in a demeaning way, but if we fail to educate our children, and remember, we were children once, in a way that is free of fear, free of greed, then we are just perpetuating the cycle. If we educate our kids to focus on the 'I' not the 'we,' we keep separation alive and well, while at the same time reducing our own experiences to those that fall under the general heading 'greed and fear.'

If we maintain an attitude of us and them, we support a polarised society. A polarised society remains ignorant of even remotely understanding the true nature of who we are. Time spent in defending the body/society against an imaginary enemy—the product of greed fear and ignorance—is time devoted to a self imprisoning illusion. While you may enjoy your illusion, as long as you recognise it for an illusion little harm can arise.

When you take the illusion seriously/personally you are supporting a state of separation, or polarisation that makes it even harder to see through and awaken.

A Catch 22 really. To see through the illusion we shouldn't take ourselves too seriously, the illusion however doesn't allow us to be objective.

Is there a fundamental issue leading to a premature death? Is the time and nature of our death predetermined? Is it karmic? Or is it a lottery? Is there anyone who is able to choose how they live their life? We may believe that we have choices, but when examined closely we can see that there is in fact very little choice. We may not be born into greed, fear or ignorance, but it doesn't take long for society to impose greed, fear and ignorance upon us. How can our parents educate us in the true nature of the self when they—in their time—accepted the nonsense passed down to them. They just perpetuate the nonsense without questioning, on a fundamental level, what they have been taught, by their parents!

The Buddha was reported to have said, "Once you begin the journey—of self discovery—you will reach an enlightened state in three lifetimes." Which presupposes that there is some continuation of consciousness after death. It also implies that there is someone who becomes enlightened. I suspect that this part is true only while there is some attachment to the personality/body/mind/emotions. The realisation that there was no one to become enlightened arises when the individual no longer identifies with the body and associated thoughts/emotions.

If this is the case, then who was it who began the journey in the first place? Confusing no.

Imagine a world without greed, a world without fear, a world without ignorance.

Just remember that you won't be able to create a world without greed, fear or ignorance if you still carry greed, fear and ignorance within you.

Ponder This

SUPPRESSION/REPRESSION

Very often I notice people going through some equal and opposite reaction in their lives.

The first time this became obvious, many years ago, was when a friend who had been heavily involved in a hedonistic lifestyle found religion. A true Jekyll and Hyde scenario. Such a massive shift away from one lifestyle into another so opposite as to be almost unbelievable.

Many people who are forced through circumstance—early childhood, social conditioning, whatever—are unable to express themselves in a positive way. This suppression leads to anti-social behaviour which leads to more repression which leads to more extreme anti-social behaviour. Most people fail to realise the extent of the suppression because it was applied from an early age and very gradually, primarily because freedom from repression was never experienced to begin with. So, nothing to compare our lives to.

We seem to get forced into situations that continue to keep us unaware of the extent of our suppression. We never question this because we have nothing to compare it to, we just go on believing this is our life and we must live it as best we can. This continued denial of self expression leads us deeper into the drama we believe is our lives, it also adds charge to the imbalance that has been created and continues to give energy to all of the suppressed aspects of our being. It is not hard to see the difficulties that will arise as a result of this severe internal polarisation.

While we remain unconscious of this build up we remain victims to all those aspects that are not being expressed in an open conscious way. The more we repress these aspects the more our behaviour becomes unreasonable, reactive, aggressive. This of course leads to those around us responding/reacting in their own oppressed ways adding fuel to the fire of conflict. We are judged by those around us as something that doesn't measure up to their expectations, even though their expectations are once again, products of their own suppressed past. We may be criminalised by society as we act out our own confused imbalance, judged by those who have yet to accept and move through their own buried past.

These are extreme examples of the suppressed nature that has never been allowed to be brought into the light of day, there are many more less obvious.

Most people appear to continue to act out the denied aspects of the self, where one has found compatibility these aspects seem to be kept hidden, under control, we remain unaware of the tempest within because we believe we are safe. Relationships often serve to maintain the illusion of safety meaning that we never have to face our own pain. We continue to seek shelter from the storm in the familiar failing to see that the familiar is simply a product of our expectations. These in turn are a product of the combination of the accepted and denied parts of the self. Often the suppressed aspects maintain the relationships. We come to believe that the uncomfortable parts of any relationship are a natural part of life and we do our best to live within the confines of such relationships.

When these relationships begin to breakdown because they are no longer sustainable we scramble, looking for a replacement, another relationship that offers us the same sense of security we had before. The same level of comfort that our repressed self is 'used' to.

When this fails to work—when we are forced to confront our distorted requirements—we face what has been called the dark night of the soul. A place that we cannot run away from any longer, we can no longer remain hidden in a false sense of security. It appears as though our worse nightmares unfold, we find ourselves in places we have never been before, nothing is familiar, nothing is safe. There is no solid ground, no place of refuge, instead we are surrounded by those repressed aspects of the self. Aspects that we no longer knew existed. Aspects with which we have no known relationship.

To the extent these aspects have been repressed we will experience an equal and opposite reaction. The more we have either consciously or unconsciously denied parts of the self the more intense the energy of change appears. This is neither easy to recognise—remember the self has been 'comfortable' for a long time, never having to deal with this other way of seeing life—nor is it easy to work through. Like a rudderless ship in storm tossed seas we go where the suppressed energy of the past takes us.

Our introduction to this release of suppression can be overwhelming in its intensity, in part because we believed, in the past, that we were somehow in control and developed many methods which would help us maintain that illusion and survive. When that particular rug is torn from beneath us our practiced skills are no longer applicable even though we continue to try to bring them into play. Nothing works anymore, we have been cast adrift into an unknown sea.

In reality (?) we have become so accustomed to a particular way of being, always coming from a past that in itself made no sense other than the reality we gave it, that we are unable to accept change.

No matter where we believe ourselves to be on this 'journey' acceptance is the key to the door through which we must pass if we are to move beyond a world that exists in perpetual conflict.

A Piece to Finish the Day

THE NEED TO PROTECT!

IT SEEMS UNUSUAL FOR CHILDREN TO GROW UP THESE DAYS without acquiring some level of anxiety. Often, even with the best of intentions, parents pass on old conditioned ways of being and thinking to their children without questioning their own beliefs. Because our parents failed to question their own fundamental beliefs, these get passed on and are the basis for certain anxieties.

Whether, as a child, our experiences are truly causing deep anxiety or not, if the child is in anyway uncomfortable, or not feeling safe, then it will develop methods to create a personally safe environment. What may be meaningless to an adult can have a major impact upon the mind of the child. This can mean a closing down of the heart, split personalities, even depression. Anything in fact which prevents them from feeling insecure.

These 'skills' that are learned at a very early age without the benefit of a rational mind get buried deep within the child and tend to influence all thoughts and all behaviour patterns subsequently. The child sets itself up with tools to help survive what it once considered a hostile environment. These 'coping mechanisms' create all sorts of problems in the life of the child, a life which is then spent as a victim to unseen, unremembered events, all the time trying to manage to deal with the repercussions of a trauma, real or imagined, from the past.

Imagine then, building your house on perceived insecurity, how on earth do you expect to be happy, healthy, to live a fulfilling life if you have no personal power, or what personal power you believe you have is simply an illusion based upon a belief that has no real foundation in today's world.

So we hide behind walls, walls where the heart is closed, afraid to open because of possibly, remembered pain. Where we hide under the blanket of depression, if we are depressed then we are not feeling, if we are not feeling then we are safe. Really? I doubt most people who experience depression follow this line of thought because they are so far down the rabbit hole they don't know which way is up anymore.

Now imagine this need to hide ourselves away to feel safe expanding out to all those we love, all those we work with, all those we are acquainted with, and then imagine it expanding out some more to include pretty much everyone on the planet. Is it any wonder that we have co-created a reality where we have less and less personal power, where we are simply parts of a money making machine, money which we don't get to see or use.

In spite of what we might hope for, wish for, want above everything else, until we shake ourselves free from the fear, which, for the most part is totally illusory anyway. Our fears are imaginary, based upon an event(s) in the past no longer relevant to today. Until we can move out from beneath the cloud of depression, until we can recognise anxiety for what it is—a weapon of mass hallucination—we are destined to continue to co-create a world that arises from a common misunderstanding. This misunderstanding has led to fear, to anxiety, all of which we are 'treated' for with 'modern' medicines. Yet are we cured of these fears, these anxieties, or are we simply becoming oblivious to all of the pain and suffering of our own creation. While we fail to recognise this, we continue to create more chaos, more confusion, more fear. And so it goes.

Simply wanting a new reality is not enough, just praying for a better way is not going to work. Thinking that you can dream a new dream is nonsense. Most of the 'stuff' we follow today is a distraction. There are countless ways we can distract ourselves from the fundamental cause for all conflict.

Until we can understand why we feel fear and find a way to move through it, anxiety will continue to undermine all efforts that seek change. While we are still lost in the greed, fear and ignorance of the collective any attempts at change arise from the common misunderstanding. There are no answers to be found down that path, no solutions, just more of the same.

I still believe that acceptance of what is is the beginning of the path towards true change. Acknowledge. Accept. No judgement. No blame. No identification with phenomena. This will, though challenging to do at first, set you free from your old perceptions. Acceptance will open the door to new possibilities. Instead of trying to fix a system that has been designed to take all of your energy and give nothing back, fix yourself. Learn to love unconditionally, all aspects of yourself by using who and what shows up in your life as the mirror to discover those parts that could use a little extra loving.

You want change! Then start with yourself. There is nothing more important in this life than to learn to love the self completely.

Continue to live your life but remember, it is but a shadow of your potential.

And This!

THE DIFFICULTY AVOIDING ILLNESS

You may have often wondered, when disease or sickness show up in your life, 'Why me?', 'Why them?' There are often no easy, or obvious answers. Yet often the cause may be hidden within certain beliefs that we, or the 'sick' person have held for many years.

Lifestyle plays a part of course, the food we eat, how we live our lives, are we physically active? Do we smoke? Drink to excess? Take any medication? Are we happy? Are we fearful? No matter what reasons or justification we identify with they are just manifestations of a deeply held conditioning.

The reasons for any behavioural patterns are not easy to recognise or accept. It is hard for someone lost in a diseased state to accept any responsibility for their condition. The inability to accept responsibility is often the result of a conditioned way of seeing ourselves.

This 'conditioned' way has led us to externalising our problems and blaming those around us, this way of being has been a part of our lives for so long and is, in a very real sense, a fundamental reason we get sick. While we remain in an internal state of blame and judgement, the conflict that arises because of this state creates problems both outside of the self and within the self.

Looking outside is one of the most dis-empowering processes imaginable because every time we believe we need someone or something to 'fix' us we are affirming, on a cellular level, that we are incapable of 'fixing' ourselves. This may well be a truth for the person who is so far down the rabbit hole they don't know which way is up anymore. Having spent a lifetime giving our power away, freely or otherwise, we are left powerless. The powerless are easily manipulated into believing all sorts of nonsense which only serves to further erode any personal power that may have remained.

If we continue to look outside of ourselves for answers we are simply playing a part in the same game that created our current reality. Yet for someone lost down the rabbit hole there is no other reality, no choice outside of the system/beliefs that created the imbalance so the struggle continues.

Common beliefs are that we are not good enough, or that we are plain, ugly, smart, stupid, not worthy, that we will be abandoned. These are all programs that we either inherit or pick up along the way. If we have been conditioned to think that we are not good enough then there will be a tendency to try to prove ourselves 'good enough,' which may well lead to an over compensation where we praise others too much in the unconscious hope that they will 'need' us.

If this, or any other similar pattern takes hold in our subconscious mind we will continually come from a place of lack. A great part of our mind will be consumed with the need to fill that empty space. This leads to an internal imbalance and a very polarised consciousness. The polarised consciousness gives rise to an insecure, questioning mind, do this, do that, go here, go there etc. The polarised mind is full of judgement, which is fear based even though this may not be apparent. When we give so much attention to any one emotion, whether this is done consciously, or more often than not, unconsciously, we create a significant imbalance in our cellular structure.

If the 'intelligence' of the cell is taken up with focusing on one particular chemical/emotion more than any other, then the function of the cell is impaired. If this focus continues over time then it is not surprising that we start noticing our health beginning to fail. In 'reality' our health was at risk many years ago when we failed to recognise the early signs of an internal imbalance. It is not surprising that we failed to see this as the total reality that we were born into supports that way of thinking. So no matter where we turn to look for answers, we are simply perpetuating the internal imbalance without being aware that this is what we are doing.

If we continue to live in the dream world that our subconscious has created, supported by all those around us, then, when sickness or disease arises we are stuck, seeking help from within the system that helped to create the illness.

If we begin to question that reality we may begin to look for alternative ways to deal with imbalance.

While we are still products of the conditioning our attempts to seek alternative help must remain a product of the conditioned mind. We cannot explore beyond our imagination!

It is difficult, if not impossible to just accept illness and disease, again because the ground that gave rise to the disease is a part of the problem and objectivity is not a part of that reality.

This 'drama' will continue to unfold all the time we energise it.

Time to make a change. If not now when?

Another Day, Another Thought

A FUNDAMENTAL MISUNDERSTANDING

I have been in the 'business' of presenting workshops and consulting both personal and space clearing for over 26 years... In all that time there is one thing that has never changed! And that is the 'story' I hear. Every issue people face, every emotion they feel, every physical problem that may be manifesting, they are all just symptoms of something that came before.

Symptoms are not the problem. Symptoms are a manifestation of the problem. People are so far down the rabbit hole there is no longer any awareness That there is a rabbit hole. This applies to everyone, not just those who show up for workshops or one on one sessions.

Everybody comes from a past, a past that has created, with their help, their manifesting reality. So, be it health issues, emotional, psychological, be they personal or planetary, internally or externally manifesting, it is all the same, a product of their past.

Many people believe that by understanding the why's, when's and what's they will somehow be free of the past, laying it to rest and moving on. This has not been my experience at all, and I don't believe that path truly helps anyone.

Think about it. Every time you recall a memory you are still seeing through the eyes and feeling through a system that has been fundamentally affected by an experience that you are now trying to understand. Already, before you start, your vision is clouded, filtering, as you do, through your conditioned mind.

And this isn't the worst of it! Every time we try to understand the cause of something, which I don't believe we can ever truly discover, we are saying to ourselves, "This is real—It happened to me, now, what can I DO about it?" We are either expressing the past or internalising it. We may come up with a story that fits our current ability to understand but the story is still contained within the conditioned mind, and therein lies the problem.

Every time we buy into the belief that there is something to be done it gives rise to a change in the chemicals in the body (emotional or physical symptoms) we identify with those chemicals and essentially give more energy to that 'reality.'

By trying to understand, identify or work with any chemical shift that we experience, be it as an emotion or a physical feeling (other than immediate trauma to the body) we are saying to ourselves that this is a feeling that we have to 'do' something about.

By accepting the chemical shift as 'ours' we give that memory energy. The more energy we give it in our search to uncover information about original trauma the more we guarantee it is going to show up in our future. The more we continue to energise our past the more we will get caught up in trying to understand and 'do' something to alleviate any pain we continue to experience.

We are well and truly stuck on the hamster wheel, around and around we go, always looking for a solution and always failing to recognise that there is no way we will ever truly understand why because the 'reason' is beyond our current capacity to grasp. Each time we allow the mind to explore the past, we are acknowledging that the past is real. For all the time we continue to identify with the past we are caught in trying to understand and fix, manipulate, change the manifesting reality that we find ourselves in.

When we start applying the brakes to the old conditioned way of 'being' in this world it becomes increasingly obvious that at sometime in the past we suffered the effects of a fundamental misunderstanding. Everything that we now experience, everything that we think, that we feel, that we say has to be a product of that fundamental misunderstanding. Everything that arises in our world is a product of this misunderstanding. Everything!

THE MISUNDERSTANDING?

Is that you are not the chemicals that the body manufactures, you are the observer, not the emotion. Out of this simple misunderstanding all else arises. You may think you are happy or you are sad because of this identification with the chemicals, but the more you think sadness/happiness, the more you become sadness/happiness, or whatever else you happen to think you are at the time.

So you see why, no matter what you tell me, no matter what you are feeling, thinking, experiencing, it is all just symptoms that have arisen. Symptoms that arose as a result of a fundamental misunderstanding.

This is what you are feeling now. This is what you are thinking now. This is what you are saying now, This is what you are experiencing now. None of which has any truth outside of the energy you continue to give it.

Your choice.

Perpetuate the past or leave it behind!

| Another Day, Another Thought |

To 'Clear' or 'Not to Clear' that is the question. Depending upon your choice it can offer a way out of the misunderstanding into a greater reality, or perpetuate the road into a more polarised state, which brings its own problems.

Ponder This

IF PRAYERS WORK?

YOU HAVE TO WONDER, IF ALL THE PRAYERS OVER THE ages for world peace, if all those people 'sending' love to others whenever challenges arise, have made any difference at all to the state of the world.

Hard to prove or disprove of course, we cannot turn back the clock and tell everyone to stop praying and then compare the outcome to the 'reality' we find ourselves in now. I currently believe that we live in a make it up as we go along type of universe, that which we believe in and give energy to manifests.

So, this being the case, everything should be possible, right? The depths of that which we believe—that which we give energy—regulates the manifestation of those beliefs. The more people believing in a particular path, the more 'real' it appears to be. So it seems to come down to a numbers game, get the numbers, get the reality.

Surely there are enough people on this planet wanting a more peaceful reality to manifest? Yet we continue to see, if we are to believe even half the media, social and otherwise, that peace is not a significant manifestation on the planet at this time. That people get sick, hence some feeling the need to 'send' love, all conflict internal or external, in all its many forms is a major manifestation in these times.

| Ponder This |

Are those praying and sending love merely a counter balance to the chaos? Are they holding the chaos in check, slowing it down? Or making absolutely no difference at all! The 'world' seems to be going through it's stuff regardless of what many would prefer. The manifesting conditions on the planet appear to be holding all who live here in a strongly polarised state, hence the apparent need to 'pray' to 'send love' to counteract the manifesting chaos. Is this truly 'reality' that we live in or are the conditions within which we live a self perpetuated chaos that we now believe to be reality?

Hard to see the light when you are so far down the rabbit hole you have forgotten there was even a rabbit hole to begin with. So long have we existed in this state that we no longer question fundamentals, we are all, to some degree or other, caught up in a fight or flight condition, always trying to put out the fires, in damage control mode, trying to 'do' more to create a more suitable reality.

The big issue here of course is that there are a lot of people on this planet at this time, and each may have a slightly different preference for change. Everyone cannot have their own way because this would lead to more conflict as different belief patterns strive to get their own way.

I suspect that the power of any prayers or 'sending' of love is limited by the person praying or sending. Praying implies that we are asking someone/thing outside of ourself for help. Not sure what 'sending love' is all about, maybe just a phrase that has become common usage recently. No matter what we say, think or do, that saying, thinking or doing is limited by our own ability to be that which we seek.

You can't be praying for world peace, or sending love, if you go home and scream at the kids. Or take sides in any argument, or if you judge your neighbour, or if you are envious of a work mate, or if you lose yourself in anger or anxiety.

These are all symptoms of a lack of understanding of your true nature, of a polarised personality. All chaos arises out of a polarised consciousness, all personal and global conflict arises out of a polarised consciousness. If we weren't so heavily invested in polarisation there would be no need for prayers, no need to 'send' love.

It seems obvious to me that our polarised state is contributing to the manifesting reality, a manifesting reality that then appears to need something to bring it back into a more balanced state. That something may take the form of prayers, or the act of doing something—sending love? Yet if we are not representing the peace and love that we seek we are just another part of the problem that manifests. A reality within which we feel uncomfortable.

If we pray, recognise that we are praying for our selves, for until we can reduce the polarised state within which we appear to live we can never find that peace outside of the self. Recognise that whenever we feel the need to 'send love' to another, we are asking for more love in our own lives. We may feel as though we are love, but if you look around, what do you see?

The importance of loving the self, in all its many aspects, cannot be overstated. For only through practicing love of the self can we even begin to love others, only through the practice of loving the self can we begin to see a more peaceful manifestation in the world. This is not loving the self in a narcissistic way, but exploring, with an open fearless heart, all aspects of the self. The world is a mirror, reflecting back to us all those parts of the self we have yet to love. Recognising that it is all a manifestation of the self, we gradually accept more and more responsibility for the part we play in co-creating the chaos, and thus the chaos reduces. This happens effortlessly as we become less judgemental, less fearful, less attached to our own points of view.

The need to become the change is more important now that the world appears to be spinning out of control. Develop your practice, become the change, live the change to allow those around you the opportunity to change, Stop holding yourself and others prisoners to your outdated expectations.

Something to Think About!

DENIAL

HAVE YOU EVER BEEN TOLD YOU ARE IN DENIAL? WHO, IF anyone, told you you were in denial?

I find this idea of denial fascinating, for many reasons, many of which have become clearer to me only as a result of my practice of the 'clearing.' The majority of us are, almost without exception, in some degree of denial or other. While we continue to blame others, while we continue to judge others, or ourselves, while we still take personally all the feelings that arise in our awareness, we are in denial.

But denial of what? This is where my thinking has diverged from the collective beliefs around denial.

While we still identify with good and bad, right and wrong we remain at the mercy of our past conditioning. This past conditioning is self perpetuating because we are attached to our preferences, our ideas of right and wrong, good and bad. This belief, this idea is, in itself our self imposed prison. We are convinced that our perceptions regarding good and bad are 'right' and we must hold fast to these beliefs else we fall into a state of apathy and end up supporting that which we previously opposed. We truly believe that our way of thinking is important, more important than someone who holds an opposing point of view. This creates either a defensive attitude or an aggressive one, both of these are heavily polarised points of view that, in themselves, perpetuate the illusion that there is a problem.

When we are accused of being in denial this most often means that we are unable, at that moment in time, to see the shadow aspects of the self. We could be deliberately shutting something out that is close to the surface of our awareness but, again, there has to be a reason for our avoidance. For the most part we are not aware of these shadow aspects, otherwise why call them the shadow? If we are not aware of them being called out on it is hardly going to help. There is a reason we have not embraced these parts of the self, why we have spent a lifetime running away from these old thoughts and feelings.

I suspect one of the main reasons we have failed to deal with the past, thus enforcing the shadow side, is a lack of personal safety. Here of course, lies the real issue. The hamster wheel of our lives, the conundrum within which we exist. If we are not feeling safe because of memories, ours or anothers, then we are not going to be able to address these issues. Being judged for our lack of awareness often by those who lack their own awareness, is hardly a situation that is designed to make either party feel safe, thus deepening the divide between what is and what we think is.

We are always projecting our expectations onto the world around us and those in it. Our projections are the product of our own past, judgements, blames, fears, desires, all of which have only arisen because, at one point along the way, we took the thoughts and feelings personally. If we keep projecting our fears, which are still the products of a greater ignorance, onto those around us we can expect them to react, based upon their own 'ignorance' of their true nature. You can see where this leads, to more of the same, which requires us to deal with that which arises in a way that we have become accustomed to. And around and around we go.

During my work as a consultant I am often asked, "isn't that a denial of the issue" when I suggest that people notice the signs of a feeling arising, acknowledge it, accept it and let it go. People, attached to their perceptions, believe that by letting go of a thought or feeling, that they are denying the reality presented by that thought or feeling.

Now, think about this for a moment. If that which we believe we are denying arose, in the first instance, as a result of a misunderstanding, which was then taken personally, the result being a deeply held belief, what exactly are we denying?

By trying to understand, to recall, to remember, to work out when, to know why, we are simply reminding ourselves that this thought, this memory, this feeling is somehow real. As such it requires me to 'do' something about it. Now, the moment I acknowledge a thought, memory or feeling as real all I am doing is perpetuating the illusion. The more energy I give to the past, the more the past has to show up in my 'future.'

So really, are we in denial? Or is the denial the idea that all of the thoughts and feelings don't actually belong to me. They are not 'mine' have never been 'mine.' Only my attachment to the idea that my thoughts and feelings are 'mine' has led me into a deeper state of identifying with those thoughts and feelings as 'mine' so much so that I cannot conceive of a reality where I am other than my conditioned thoughts or feelings.

I cannot understand why denial of an illusion is a bad thing!

The next question that arises may be, "If the thoughts and feelings aren't mine, whose are they."

For that you will have to wait until the next newsletter.

And This!

IF IT IS NOT MINE, THEN WHOSE IS IT?

In last months newsletter I wrote about denial, and what exactly it was that we were denying, if anything! I ended that piece by saying that no matter what we may think, the feelings we experience do not actually belong to us. Our identification with feelings in the past has created a strong association with those feelings, this doesn't mean they ever belonged to us, we just assumed they did.

So, a feeling arises in the awareness/body, we are certainly noticing something, so then if it isn't mine, whose is it? Well no ones until some one takes a hold of it and claims it as theirs! This identification with phenomena is a process into which we are all indoctrinated from a very early age. Those 'doing' the indoctrination are simply following their own conditioning and passing on to you their beliefs about what is going on. No one questions the fundamental issues here, just passes on what they believe to be real.

To try to understand who, if anyone, this 'stuff' belongs to we need to take a step, or three, back from our current understandings.

Imagine that we live in a 'holoverse' a term coined in the book, *The Holographic Universe*, by Michael Talbot. A 'holoverse,' simply put, is a continual unfolding of a manifesting reality that is created by the thoughts and energies of those inhabiting the 'holoverse.' This concept has been demonstrated to me time and time again in my practice of 'clearing' where the package that we believe ourselves to be provides the input into this 'holoverse.' The input, a mix of various beliefs, both conscious and sub-conscious, is like an energy transmission. We send out signals, waves/particles based on who we believe ourselves to be.

'Shit' happens because there is still a lot of deeply held patterns, locked away in the sub-conscious making them unavailable to our conscious mind. As long as these sub-conscious thoughts, beliefs, desires, fears remain hidden we will remain a victim to them. Simply because they are not in our conscious awareness doesn't mean that they are not there, they are very much 'there.' It is just that we are very much un-aware of them. So, these transmissions, the signals that we send out are a combination of and often a product of, our subconsciously held beliefs.

If you have ever entered a room which has just witnessed intense emotional conflict, you may have noticed a feeling of discomfort, sometimes so strong you had to leave the room immediately. This 'feeling' that you have picked up certainly did not belong to you, you just walked into it. How your body responds /reacts is up to you. Up to you within certain limitations. We may like to think we have control over what we think and feel but the truth(?) is that our ability to decide is also a product of our subconscious conditioning.

The point here though is that energetic conflict between two or more people creates a third energy, the one you felt when you walked into the room. This 'third' energy is held in the space, various conditions being met, and subsequently affects all those who come close to the charge. So the principle of the holoverse is, where thoughts/feeling/words / actions are expressed into the holoverse they create the reality within which you 'find' yourself. The thoughts/feeling/words /actions are not yours, you just exist within the field of information. Your nervous system is interpreting the information which you then experience as thoughts or feelings.

As you experience thoughts and feelings your conditioned mind grasps onto those thoughts and feelings and identifies with them, thereby making them yours, at least you assume them to be yours. The more you have, in the past, identified with thoughts and feelings the more they seem to belong to you, creating a certain degree of intensity which you equate with ownership.

The alternative is that all thoughts, all feelings, exist within the holoverse (call it what you will), they exist because of the energy those inhabiting the holoverse have given them. The stronger we associate with any thought or feeling the more energy we give it the more 'real' it becomes. The stronger the charge the information held in the holoverse contains the more intense it appears, the more intense, the more likely it is that we are going to identify with it, thus perpetuating the illusion that it is real.

So, by our, and everyone else's identification with phenomena we have created, within the holoverse, a reality that is so strong we believe it to be true. The feelings that we experience belong to no one, they are just manifestations of energy equal to the energy they have been given. Not mine, not yours, not anyone's.

Not until, at least, someone, somewhere, takes them personally which then gives the impression that they 'belong' to that person.

Madness no?

Sleep on This One

HEALER HEAL THYSELF

How true, and how often misunderstood. Or, if not misunderstood, failed to be truly grasped and acted upon. We are so busy trying to fix the world, for ourself or others, looking outside all the time that we fail to see the real problem behind all of the manifesting symptoms.

We are all healers, but perhaps more so for those that are working consciously for the well-being of others, there is a need to recognise the fundamental issue involved and not get caught trying to 'fix' the symptoms.

No matter what knowledge we possess, what skills we have learnt, what experience we have gained, we cannot help others beyond the degree we have helped ourself.

We become skilled in certain arts, certain ways of being where we dedicate our lives to the support of others or our environment, but we still look outside for answers, we approach all 'problems' from the belief that the symptoms/problems are real. "In the real world...." This is often used to validate ones experiences and try to understand what to 'do' about moving beyond the pain and suffering. Yet what is this 'real world' that people refer to?

The majority of people I see, when asked what they believe the problem is, talk about the symptoms they are experiencing. Western medicine seems determined to work only with the symptoms, some other 'therapies' seek to go beyond the symptoms. Both approaches have their limitations. Obviously to treat symptoms with medications just masks the real cause and no progress in healing the fundamental issue is addressed. When a more alternative approach seeks to understand the why and when of a manifesting problem they fail to see that by acknowledging a problem, by giving energy to a problem they are empowering the problem at the same time as they dis-empower the individual.

Bottom line: we try to 'fix' things using the tools we have learnt. All the time seeking ways to develop and improve our skill set so we can 'do' more. All the time not recognising that we too are lost within a system, a structure that is responsible for the problems arising in the first place.

My experience has been that everything works, to some degree or other. Effectiveness of any process can be defined by results, results are dependant upon the belief of the individuals concerned. It is the nature of the world we live in for all things to work to some degree or other, yet the limitations within which we operate set the parameters and limits for any change.

Are we just changing situations within the system, are we just dealing with symptoms, or are we looking from outside the system? Are we applying a band aid to a problem or have we seen beyond the manifesting problem and allowed healing on a fundamental level to arise? If we still believe in the more traditional ways of dealing with problems, then chances are we are still toying with symptoms. If we have brought about the necessary changes within ourselves, healed our own pain and trauma, moved beyond our old limitations, then we may well see beyond the current conditioning.

When we are no longer confined by the old reality our abilities to be available for ourself and others increases dramatically. We no longer need to 'do' anything because the work of 'do-ing' has been completed. When we have truly healed ourselves, not just wishing, hoping or imagining we are that which we seek, then what more is there to 'do'?

And the journey to heal the healer is a total win win situation. The more you understand and let go of your attachment to the past, the more you become available to support your environment and those in that environment in a more positive, profound way, without actually 'do-ing' anything.

So, no matter what path you believe yourself to be on now it can only be enhanced by working on yourself, healing the healer, developing greater compassion and letting go of the need to 'fix' anyone or anything.

Ponder This

WHO OR WHAT IS CLEARING WHO?

A QUESTION THAT OFTEN ARISES, AT ALL 'LEVELS OF clearing, is "Who is clearing who"? Or, "Am I clearing the land or is the land clearing me"? A good question and one that is not easily answered in a word or two.

This applies to each one of us, whether we are actively involved in 'clearing' or not. We need to understand what happens, energetically, when we pass through various environments or we meet/connect with other people. The two opposite positions that most people come from are a) those of us who do not notice very much, this is not an indication that nothing is happening, it is just that we are not receptive to what is happening and b) those of us who are extremely sensitive and we notice a lot, often beyond our ability to deal with effectively.

There is a sliding scale in between these two extremes, there may be some areas, some feelings that we notice, or not, and other areas where the opposite applies. Essentially, our ability to notice is a product of our past. Our ability to change is also a product of our past. For those of us who do notice and who are practicing non attachment to that which we notice, then the question may arise, who is clearing who? Am I clearing the land or is the land clearing me?

To begin to understand this we need to go back to basics. What exactly happens when we clear another. Perhaps 'exactly' is too strong a word, there are no exacts, no definitive truths, no 'this is it' realisations in clearing. 'Clearing' is simply a word given to a process during which the practitioner develops their ability to notice without blame, judgement or identification with whatever phenomena arises in their awareness.

We all have a natural talent to clear to some degree or other. What this means is that there are aspects of the broad spectrum of feelings associated with being human that we are able to embrace effortlessly, those parts that we have truly loved within ourselves. When we meet these parts of ourself on the road we clear the other person or environmental energy without conscious participation. It just happens. It may not remain 'clear' after we pass, but for the moment of connection, the two energies become comfortable with each other.

If the person we connect with has also embraced those similar aspects of the self, then we have a rapport with that person, to the extent that the loved parts are similar. Where we diverge into our own unaccepted parts, the shadow as Jung referred to it, then the rapport is challenged or ceases. We will often fall into judgement at this stage, whether we do this consciously or not is not relevant at the moment.

If the person we meet has embraced parts of themselves that correspond to aspects that we have not, they have the potential to 'clear' us. Whether they do or not depends upon our own attachment to our way of being. Again, the clearing, if it happens at all, may not last beyond the meeting, something else has to happen to affect that.

Similarly with our environment. We may notice a strong energy in a certain environment, our body may react to that energy, whether this appears to be a positive or a negative reaction depends very much on our own judgmental points of view. Even so, some energies are hard to ignore and the body will have a unique reaction similar to that which we experience when we are clearing a person or a place.

To even begin to determine who is clearing who or what, we must understand that it is all relative to our own ability to be present, without blame, judgement or personalising with that which arises. If we have judgement then that will likely show up as resistance which in turn shows up as discomfort. If we continue to take on the discomfort it would be a sign that the other person, or the environment, has the ability to 'clear' us but we have retreated into an old pattern of identifying with the symptoms.

Ideally we would reach the stage where there is very little, or no, bodily reaction to others or the environment. This state would be an indication that we have truly 'dealt' with the information that is presenting. If we 'clear' others who may be clearer in more areas than we are, then the re-balancing that takes place is very much aligning you, the clearer, into a more balanced state.

So 'clearing' is a win-win process, no matter who or what you open yourself up to a re balancing occurs. This brings your system into a more peaceful state and a greater accord with its environment and others in that environment. Practice non judgment, no blame, non identification as much as you can through the day. Experience for yourself the benefits of this way of being, and, along the way, support others and your environment in a powerful and beneficial way.

Something to Think About!

CLEARING! A MENTAL EXERCISE?

For many who study and practice 'clearing' it is a mental exercise, an intellectual process. Yet this is only the beginning of the journey, for 'clearing' is so much more than that.

For me 'clearing' has been a path, at first I thought it was just a job, an interesting job, but still just a job. It wasn't until I was well down the path that I realised this was not a job but a way of life, a way of be-ing. It was a path that allowed me to begin the journey of unlocking my past, of seeing the past conditioning for what it was and to move through all of the associated pain, fear and suffering that past brought with it.

The reason, I suspect, that people get caught in the intellectual aspect is that it is so much easier to learn the words and actions than it is to apply them to the self. One thing I repeat in workshops is that for any change/growth to occur we must feel safe. Clearing has provided the safety I was looking for even though it may have been a hard reality to face at times, the understanding gained through the practice made it so much easier to face.

If I were to look at the bigger picture of my journey this time round, I would see that there was a void in my early childhood. There are many possible reasons for this void to exist, but the reasons are not important. It was as though I was waiting for my orders, from a very early age I waited for the postman and was disappointed when they failed to deliver. Every morning, waiting for something that I could not put a name to.

Life gets in the way of our dreams and we grow up, but the void just took a back seat, it never really went away. What did happen was that any sensitivity I may have had in early childhood was lost in the need to survive. This need to be safe caused me to shut down any sensitivity, any real way of relating to others, because it was not safe to open up.

This is common for many of us, though the symptoms may differ. It is hard to get through childhood without experiencing some sort of trauma, real or perceived. Trauma prevents us from being open to our natural sensitivity and we learn ways to cope with 'reality'. Unfortunately the 'reality' that we are trying to cope with is, in itself, a manifestation of our personal trauma. So answers are not to be found within the drama but we have no way of seeing life through anything but the filter of our own past.

As I got older, so the 'void' pushed me in certain directions, a search for the self if you will. I left my country of birth, feeling stifled there and unable to even begin the search while still surrounded by the past. Then the journey took another big step. But the step was still about looking for answers in the external world, the physical. There was nothing else to do given my past, given the past that most of us carry with us. We don't even realise that safety is the thing we are looking for.

Without safety 'clearing' is certainly an intellectual exercise. Yet the more we practice the more the need for safety becomes obvious. Slowly we begin to see, through the practice, that all we notice doesn't actually belong to us, it is simply information passing by. This allows a sense of safety. When we reach a certain point in the journey where we are truly beginning to feel safe then the next stage of the road unfolds. The journey into the heart. Life doesn't have to unfold for us in this way, we are all, to some degree, unique beings, this was my path not yours.

First there was the physical exploration of the world, then the 'spiritual' journey, and lastly, to date, the journey into the heart. This was, by far, the hardest part for me. A journey where we face all aspects of our life, the others in our life, situations that show up, as simply reflections of our self. This is hard because there can be no blame, no judgement, and certainly no more taking these aspects of the self so seriously. The perceived lack of safety is a mechanism we employ to prevent us from facing our own shadow.

Blaming the outside world, the people who show up in that world is simply another excuse to avoid the real issue, and that is, this is me, it is all me.

The next step may be even more challenging than the journey into the heart. It is the letting go of the self, the moving beyond the limitations the past has created. Perhaps if we were to realise this last part first there would be no need for a journey at all, but where's the fun in that! It is only insecurity that prevents us from letting go and accepting all that shows up with equanimity. It is the insecurity that hangs onto the mental constructs, the intellectual understanding, until we are feeling safe, we can never really understand what 'clearing' is all about.

And This!

CHANGE/IMPERMANENCE!

IT SEEMS TO ME THAT ONE OF THE FUNDAMENTAL PATTERNS we fail to notice, which gives rise to a lot of unnecessary suffering, is 'change' or recognising the impermanence of all things.

We base our life on things remaining the same, or at least within boundaries that we set, patterns within which we feel safe and comfortable. The attachment to how things were, or how we wanted/expected them to be fails to see that nothing really stays the same. We try to impose our will upon the environment and others so that we continue to feel safe and validated.

Most people are aware that the cells in the body are continually renewing, I heard once that the lungs take 7 years before all cells are new. What I find fascinating is the possibility that the cells of the body are continually renewing, yet sometimes old conditioned patterns (of ill-health for example) re occur in spite of the bodies ability to self renew.

We have seen this in blood samples we have observed using 'Dark Field Microscopy' the 'fact' that the body is indeed renewing itself but in a chaotic manner. Something/someone, is interfering with the process, maintaining a state of ill health, of imbalance while the potential for greater health, balance lies waiting patiently in the background.

| And This! |

Not so hard to understand why this state of imbalance is allowed to happen. If we can be objective when we look at various communities around the world, no matter how large or small, we can see how communities shape people. This happens with or without the awareness of the individuals. For the most part we find ourselves in resonance with our community, either that or we have to leave 'not fitting' in is a popular reason for leaving. I have witnessed various micro communities within larger communities that, for instance, take their local sporting team very seriously, if you were not a follower of sports, or heaven forbid, supported a different team, you would find no place within such a small community. If you were neutral in your favouritism, it would not take long for you to be as fanatical as the rest of your community.

To varying degrees we are all shaped by the community within which we live. If you live in a wealthy suburb, a poor suburb, a religious, sports oriented, alcohol or drug affected environment, these are going to influence your world view and therefore your view of your place in society.

It is hard to fight such a persuasive system, not recognising how it is influencing you. You live in a country with a unique language! You learn the language, you identify with the local people. Your parents and friends all go to the same religious gatherings? You follow. We identify so much with a small, unique part of the whole, we hold onto that identity, it defines who we are, yet we rarely, if ever, question the part we are playing. By our attachment to this group we hold ourselves a prisoner to the past, to the collective expectations, hopes and desires, fears and anxieties. It is hardly surprising we resist change and suffer the consequences. Everyone around us does the same.

For many it is only by removing ourselves from the known and accepted that we can begin to see how we are

And This!

shaped and manipulated by our environment. How the collective beliefs keep us limited and bound to repeat the same patterns over and over again.

We have two kookaburras on the veranda right now. They are very territorial and keep attacking their reflection in the large glass windows. They seem to be unable to learn despite bashing into the window 20 times a day. One does it, the other follows, same as humankind. Perhaps if one stopped the other would also stop, but while they are following old conditioning nothing changes.

The illusion that the world wanders in needs new role models if it is to change in any fundamentally meaningful way, without it, they will continue their lemming like march over the cliff without ever realising they had a choice! I guess without any awareness that such a basic change is possible, people will remain submerged in their identities, all the time trying to bring about change from within the limited collective perceptions.

One has to wonder what is required for people to live their own life, free from the many minor habits they pick up from those around them, to live lives no longer dependant upon the collective to make up their minds!

Did You Know?

TRUE OR FALSE

IN THE INCREASINGLY POLARISED TIMES WE FIND OURSELVES in it pays to sort fact from fiction, illusion from that which is 'real.'

From what I can see, most people are very much lost in the current illusion, an illusion that uses fear to control the populace. They accept the illusion, feel bound to follow the ever limiting rules and regulations as though they were, in any sense of the word 'real.'

And because people continue to fall back on their old, accepted ways of being, those illusions are kept alive.

People may have been introduced to clearing and leave a workshop thinking they understand, rarely do they truly understand, people take what they are capable of taking, adapt the information to fit their accepted belief patterns and simply carry on.

For many 'game changers' it is more about adjusting, manipulating, modifying the current illusion than it is stepping outside of that illusion, we are easily led, not necessarily by our dreams but by our own deeply held insecurities. They may not be seen as insecurities, but most symptoms that arise, arise because of a fundamental insecurity.

Those insecurities exist within the illusion and are perpetuated by our addictions. When we take a look at the world though any form of media we are fed back the perceptions of those who are themselves deeply lost in the illusion, this adds weight to the idea that the illusion is the reality we currently find ourselves within. Hardly surprising that the collective continue to struggle within the illusion of greed, fear and ignorance when everyone around them seems to be similarly lost.

If we look at the Taoist concept of Yin and Yang, an eternal balance of opposites which give rise to the world we live in, then, no matter how polarised the 'world' becomes, there is always balance. Not seen from an individual, personality attached point of view, but from a more objective perspective. What we see is an ever expanding polarisation, growing more and more each day.

Yet balance is maintained, for as anyone takes one side to a point of view is given energy, it grows, so it creates and even greater polarity. Yet balance doesn't have to consist of such extremes, certainly such extremes provoke equal and opposite reactions out of which many people step up and out of their previously established comfort zone. Yet are theses extremes real? Or are they simply products of charge? Are they necessary? And if not, is there anything that can be done to reduce collective pain and suffering brought about because of such extreme polarisation? And if it is but an illusion, is anything needed to be 'done'?

From a personal point of view, anything that reduces polarisation leads to a more peaceful, balanced internal condition. A more peaceful, balanced internal condition, naturally, effortlessly gives rise to a more peaceful, balanced external environment which in turn, allows healing on many levels, which then allows a quite unique perspective beyond this particular illusion. Impossible to truly comprehend while one remains a victim to their past.

| Did You Know? |

You can continue to live within the illusion or you can take steps to see beyond the illusion. There is no moment you can 'choose' to do either, the choices have already been made, whether you are able to practice acceptance of that which is, or you continue to try to impose your will on that which presents, you have little freedom of choice. Any choice you may believe you have exists within very narrow limitations.

If you are able, practice acceptance of that which is. The going may get tough as the polarities continue to expand but it is possibly the best way through challenging times. Depending upon your developed abilities, practice gets easier, more natural, more effortless. Instead of adding your weight to one or other of the extremes, learn to embrace both polarities and collapse them in your heart.

I believe this path leads to what the Buddha referred to as the 'middle way.' Neither this nor that, right or wrong, better or worse. Seen through the eyes of someone caught in a heavily polarised society this concept is ludicrous, for in their eyes there is always right and wrong, good and bad, better or worse. It is the sustained belief in these opposites which keep them alive.

Take what little choice you have and allow all to collapse into you heart, and see for yourself what a difference that can make.

A Piece to Finish the Day

INTEGRATING THE SHADOW

Jung's words on this subject are interesting, and for many are just words, an unknown ideal to work towards. "One does not become enlightened by imagining figures of light but by making the darkness conscious."

Yet they are so much more than words, their true meaning can only be recognised by when you have truly embraced your shadow. Before that, they are just words! We may imagine we understand, we may want to be in that place. We may think we are there, but in 'reality' this is all wishful thinking.

For many the idea of the shadow is beyond their comprehension. So lost down the rabbit hole are they, there is no longer an up or a down. People struggle within the reality that they, in part, have been responsible for creating. We try to fix things, change things, manipulate things, destroy things, run away from things. All the time in a reactive state—not realising we are simply reacting to our own subconscious conditioning. This is one of the most amazing little hamster wheels imaginable. The failure to recognise we are on a self perpetuating hamster wheel.

We are driven by our past, failing to see that the past is another product of an earlier misunderstanding, never questioning why we seem to be where we are or why!

A Piece to Finish the Day

Whether we are in the middle of personal drama or what appears to be communal or even global conflict, the more we identify with the conflict the more fuel we add to the fire. Hard to take a step back when the worlds seems to be going mad and see the manifesting reality is both created and perpetuated by our continuing to give energy to such polarisation that gave rise to any current conflict.

Hard to recognise that our personal, manifesting reality is simply a product of our own mind. While we fail to see the part the shadow is creating then we will continue to struggle within this self made drama. Even more interesting is that once we have truly faced the 'shadow' we understand that it is not 'ours' it never was 'ours' but the inability to embrace what we perceive to be the dark side, our fears, doubts and negativity, gave rise to the belief that it was 'ours.' See how cute this hamster wheel is? Whichever way we turn, there is the hamster wheel.

I think therefore I am! Right! and by my thinking it becomes so. Yet I try to understand my true nature while running as fast as I can in the hamster wheel, madness no?

I suspect I came to the current understanding assisted by my continued practice of 'clearing.' Without recognising what I was actually 'doing' the shadow was embraced. As I continued to 'clear' others I was, in fact embracing the shadow side, little by little, facing my 'own' shadow and through unconditional acceptance so any power this 'shadow' had over me was reduced. Until, one day, there was no shadow, just recognition and acceptance.

The road gets less 'rocky' the more we clear, judgments fall away, the 'future' arises effortlessly, for without judgement—no longer identifying with the shadow—there can be no good or bad, right or wrong, think about that for a moment! If it is not within us, it cannot be on the outside either. For those of you who maintain the argument that there is evil in this world, take a look at yourself!

To arrive at the place of non judgement we may have to pass through the dark night of the soul, a place where our own hidden fears live, but by practicing 'clearing' the dark night is slowly understood and embraced, until, one day, it ceases to be. This dark night may last a while, in fact it will last as long as you resist, in this instance, the 'choice' is yours. This dark night can certainly be uncomfortable, how uncomfortable depends on how long you have been running away from it. And, how much you continue to identify with it.

Again, the choice, to some degree, is yours!

About the Author

Author, teacher, and 'energy' worker **Eric Dowsett** has been sharing his process of change for over 25 years. During this time he has come to see in greater detail how and why we live the lives we do, and how, through applying his simple process of 'clearing,' change can arise from deep within us.

Eric has written four other books, *The Moment That Matters*, *Loving Who Shows Up*, *First Aid: A Guide to Greater Health and Happiness*, and most recently, *Collapsing the Wave*, a must read for those serious about bringing change into society.

Learn more about Eric and clearing at:
www.ericdowsett.com

www.ingramcontent.com/pod-product-compliance
Lightning Source LLC
Chambersburg PA
CBHW050849160426
43194CB00011B/2088